FOR

ONLY

FOR GIRLS ONLY

EVERYTHING GREAT ABOUT BEING A GIRL

LAURA DOWER

ILLUSTRATED BY

HEADCASE DESIGN

FEIWEL and FRIENDS
NEW YORK

for Olivia

A FEIWEL AND FRIENDS BOOK
An Imprint of Macmillan

Design by Headcase Design

Library of Congress Cataloging-in-Publication Data Available

ISBN-13: 978-0-312-38205-6
ISBN-10: 0-312-38205-7

Feiwel and Friends logo designed by Filomena Tuosto

First Edition: May 2008

10 9 8 7 6 5 4 3 2 1

www.feiwelandfriends.com

ACKNOWLEDGMENTS

To Liz Szabla, Allison Remcheck, Jessica Tedder, Dave Barrett, Rich Deas, and all the friends at Feiwel and Friends, but especially, Jean Feiwel, who always believes in me, even when I stumble; to the mega-talented design team at Headcase Design; to everyone who brainstormed with me while writing this book, but especially, the amazing Wohls; to the Bronxville Five writing group: Madisen, Margot, Perry, Madeline, and Lauren (you grrrrls were my inspiration!); to the original "girl" in my life, Mom, who always told me I was smart and pretty, even when I felt the opposite; to any girl with whom I've ever shared a deep secret or stayed up all night, especially Liisa and Melanie; to my non-girl contingent at home: Rich, Myles, and Nate the Great; to Ro Stimo, my über-agent (among other things); and to Ms. Karen Fein, my sounding board and beacon, who proved her true girl power by having baby Noel in the middle of this project.

CONTENTS

CONTENTS

A FEW WORDS ABOUT
BEING A GIRL

Sugar and spice and everything nice.
That's what little girls are made of.

WAIT A MINUTE. IS THAT REALLY WHAT girls are? Last time I checked in the mirror, I was made of a lot more than sugar or spice.

This nursery rhyme was penned in the early nineteenth century, but it lingers. When I was small, my mom told it to me. Back then, I didn't mind being classified as "everything nice." After all, being made of "nice" was way better than being made of "snips and snails and puppy dog tails," from the boy version of the rhyme.

In elementary school, I decided that I was going to read every book in the library. My friend John did, too. And I won this battle of the fourth-grade sexes, claiming a small victory as the "smart" girl in class. But still, I suffered a little bit from a girl identity crisis. I wasn't just nice or smart or good at softball or piano. Who was I?

When the song "Girls Just Want to Have Fun" came out in seventh grade, I gladly traded my "super-sweet" and "super-smart" and "super-sporty" girl-dentities for something a little more fun and, at the time, cool. My favorite lyric in that song was, "I wanna be the one to walk in the sun." I wanted to be in the spotlight, just like that. Although I like reading serious books, talking about serious feelings, and getting serious about anything, I know I'm also a girl who wants to have fun—and lots of it. I'm guessing you do, too. Go ahead, admit it. I won't tell anyone.

The fact is that girls like us defy expectation and explanation. We can be a kickin', kung-fu mama and a pretty princess all at the same time. A girl can chart her destiny, ace that soccer penalty kick, get an **A** on the science quiz, and plan the best sleepover all in the same day. She can sleep late and daydream about getting a makeover, or she can grow up to be the next conductor of an orchestra or president of the United States. Or she can do it all. Girls really do rule, just not necessarily by following the rules.

A quick note on the book's title: *For Girls Only*. That doesn't mean boys can't read it. They just might not get it. But that's okay. Because, girls, we're just here to have fun. And we don't need boys for that.

Your amigo / friend / buddy / pal / BFF / comrade
in arms (the hugging kind),
—Laura Dower
xox

YOU GO,

FASHION HALL

3500–2600 B.C.
Ancient Sumerians, Babylonians, and Assyrians don calf-length sheepskin skirts and shawls over one shoulder. A fashion statement is born.

3000–1000 B.C.
Because the dyeing process is slow to arrive in ancient Egypt, most Egyptians wear white. But they decorate themselves with brightly colored, jeweled collars, otherwise known as ancient bling.

500–1 B.C.
Greeks and Romans wear variations on the tunic including chlamys, chitons, peplos, and togas, all belted fabric of different lengths.

Centuries later, college kids will throw "toga parties" at their Greek fraternities.

1–900
What's that smell? Outer clothing in the Middle Ages is rarely laundered, but some say its super-strong smoke scent (from cooking or tanning) was as good as perfume or deodorant.

950–1100
Although Vikings sewed modest tunics, aprons, and cloaks for practical wear, their wardrobes are anything but ordinary. Vikings bring fine silks, linens, and wools back to Scandinavia from their trades (and raids!) in the Mediterranean and Asia.

1100–1200
The emperor's court in China's Sung Dynasty forces young women to bind their feet with bands of silk or cotton. These bandages are wrapped and tightened every few days for years, until the girls' feet are three or four *inches* long! Some say that the story of Cinderella (and Prince Charming's search for the fair maiden with the smallest foot) actually evolved from this painful, crippling ritual.

1100–1300
During the Crusades, rich Europeans begin to wear more silks, satins, damasks, brocades, and velvets in bright colors. With the invention of the spinning

GIRL! OF FAME

Our closets are crammed with last year's hot looks and this year's cool looks. No matter where we go or what we do, someone will be watching us and our clothes. Personally, I've never really cared what anyone thinks of my fashion choices, whether it be my clogs or too-faded jeans, or the funny-looking, homemade holiday sweater my aunt gave me about ten years ago. But it does make me wonder what counts as "style" through the ages. Here are some hits and misses from ancient tunics to really big hair:

wheel and the loom, clothes become more ornate. Thankfully, it will be many, many years before tacky sequins hit the scene.

1400–1500
Show off your swag! European women wear the fabric-heavy houppelande gown with sleeves that reach the floor. Also all the rage in your medieval town: mantles (cloaks), templets (hair coils), headdresses, and turbans.

1500–1600
From corsets to farthingales (otherwise known as hoop skirts), English women get pinched, poked, and prodded for the ideal Elizabethan look. Best fashion statement of the

bunch: ruffs, those honeycomb neckpieces you see in art and movies about Shakespeare.

1600–1700
Real stars of the Baroque period? Curls, curls, curls. Everyone's got long, poofy hair, including the men. Bring on the stylists!

1700–1800
Order in the court? Women wear more elaborate gowns, puffed-up petticoats, and oversized wigs like Marie Antoinette. However, as the century goes on, hoop skirts and high heels morph into narrow skirts and flat shoes. Why the switch? The French Revolution and the American Revolution are partly respon-

sible. Popular fashion is not all about the rich anymore; it's about all the people.

1800–1840
Average women in the early part of the century really go for the layered look. A typical outfit: a chemise (slip), corset, more than one petticoat, underwear (also known as drawers), matching skirt and bodice, stockings, shoes, gloves, bonnet, and shawl. And you think it takes you a long time to get dressed in the morning!

1846
Sew Important Moment: Isaac Singer patents the first-ever sewing machine, which allows mass production of clothing.

1850–1900

In the middle of all the bones and ruffles, a practical, American fashion takes hold. Levi Strauss introduces the first pairs of riveted jeans, and a Wild West style is born. Cartoonist Charles Dana Gibson popularizes the "Gibson Girl," showing a woman who is free to dress in comfortable skirts and tailored jackets. With the invention of the bicycle in 1878, women's sweeping skirts are replaced by bicycle bloomers.

1910s

Fashion kicks into gear mid-decade with World War I, the women's suffrage movement, and the Great Influenza Epidemic of 1918. But get this: Even the strong-willed suffragettes are slaves to fashion. Some wear pencil skirts that are often so tight and restrictive that women can hardly walk in them.

1920s

Prohibition, jazz, and mass media bring a new look and a "Roaring Twenties" voice to fashion. Now women aren't afraid to drink, curse, wear short skirts and flapper dresses, and roll down their stockings to show some knee.

1930s

After the huge Wall Street crash of 1929, fashion falls in line with the Great Depression. More women sew at home and patch old clothes instead of purchasing new ones. One exception: fur. Sable, mink, chinchilla, and silver fox are in demand.

1940s

World War II ushers in the 1940s and Rosie the Riveter's working-class look is considered chic. Although artificial silk had come to the U.S. in 1910 and was named rayon in the 1920s, it isn't until the 1940s when pantyhose production really ramps up. While men are off fighting the war, women back in the U.S. hold down the home and jobs in comfortable, casual clothes. The most outrageous wartime fashion statement? Designer gas masks made to match elaborate eveningwear.

1950s

Television moves fashion into a new zone because now everyone wants to look—and be—like the families they see on TV. Top looks: conservative skirts, sweaters, pumps, and the grey flannel suit. Teens, however, get a little more adventurous. Called "bobbysoxers," they wear Converse sneakers, saddle shoes, ponytails, Levi's, penny loafers, and poodle skirts. And between Elvis Presley's blue suede shoes and beatnik culture, the times are a-changin'. . . .

1960s

Baby-doll minis! Bellbottoms! The Beatles! And don't forget Barbie! Hippies and surfers set the biggest trends this decade. Like, wow, dude.

1970s

"The uglier the better," is the best way to describe this lost decade of fashion. Polyester pants, wide ties, thick platform shoes, sherbet-colored chiffon dresses, Wonder Woman boots with short shorts, and of course, punk. Okay, you can stop laughing. I was there in my too-short plaid pants, blue Winnie the Pooh sweater, and red parka with the fake white fur collar . . . and it wasn't pretty.

1980s

Fashion takes the 1980s by storm . . . a cyclone, in fact! Working women wear men's styles, from suit jackets to trousers to big shirts. If clothing doesn't have shoulder pads or leg warmers, it isn't any good. The biggest trend of all, however, is hair. From moussed-up to mullets, it's all a big tease.

1990–2000

The end of the century is marked by a sort of "anti-fashion" movement. Music dictates a lot of the trends. Grunge means dark colors and flannel shirts and an angsty, "I haven't bathed in a really long time" look. The style shifts to hip-hop with its modern bling. Skater style gets big, too. A look we'd like to forget: sagging, or wearing your pants about five sizes too big, so your underwear shows.

BEAUTY MARKS

A N IMPORTANT THING TO REMEM-ber when talking about style and fashion: One culture's ugly is another's beautiful. You may look at some of the examples here and think, "Ewww, that is soooo freaky!" However, whether women wore incredibly tall wigs or flattened their heads, they thought that particular practice made them lovel*ier*, not uglier.

For years, women in Chad, Africa, have had their earlobes and lips stretched by metal rings as the ultimate statement of beauty. Today, women in Western countries inject their lips with collagen and Botox. Are these two actions really all that different? Irish novelist Margaret Wolfe Hungerford once said, "Beauty is in the eye of the beholder." For sure.

In ancient Egypt, women wore headdresses that looked purely ornamental, but were not. They were actually "unguent [pronounced 'unjent'] cones," a combination of animal fat and wax mixed together with spices and fragrant oils. After being worn all day, a cone would gradually melt and the odors would cloak the wearer with a strong scent.

In the first century, Roman women boiled walnuts and leeks together and applied the gooey mixture to their hair to make it dark and shiny. In the fourteenth century, women boiled lizards in olive oil to produce their sleek conditioner. Today, people wash their hair with everything from avocados to beer to mayonnaise.

In the Middle Ages, European women carried long, forklike back-scratchers to reach their heads beneath fancy hairdos. What were they scratching? Lice and fleas. Women started shaving their legs and armpits in this era, too, but it wasn't for beauty purposes. It discouraged the bugs from sticking around.

After 1760, the higher the hairdo got, the better it looked. Women piled on horsehair, natural hair, and wooden padded frames to create a tower of hairdo—sometimes their 'dos would be as high as thirty inches! This was, of course, a huge hindrance for women getting through doorways and into carriages. In 1776, the roof of St. Paul's Cathedral in London was raised primarily to make room for women's wigs, which kept catching on fire when they bumped up against the chandeliers!

During the nineteenth century, women used heavy makeup and beauty patches of velvet or silk to cover smallpox scars and large, black skin spots. Sometimes, the spots were "designer," shaped like stars, moons, or hearts. The placement of the patches was significant, too. A patch on your right cheek meant you were married, but a patch near the squint of your eye meant you were having an affair. How scandalous!

In the late eighteenth century, Napoleon's wife, Empress Josephine, thought her hands were so unattractive that she had gloves made to cover her hands and arms up past the elbow. Voila! The opera-length glove was born.

Corsets have been around for thousands of years. Popular legend says that most nineteenth century Victorian women, hoping to have the perfect seventeen-inch waist, squeezed into corsets a few sizes too small and ended up fainting because they cut off their circulation. Although it's true that corsets were hugely popular, none could instantly reduce a waistline to such teeny proportions. It took many years of corseting to train the waist to be smaller and corsets came in a range of sizes all the way up to size forty-two.

In the 1920s, women wore a flapper style of dress. But to make the dress look straight and clean, they also wore a flattener bra. Yeowch! Today, designers promote the opposite kind of undergarment. Women don items like the Wonderbra to lift and enhance their chests. Go figure!

GOT LIPSTICK?

THANKS TO INCREDIBLY WELL-preserved ancient Egyptian tombs, we have untouched evidence of makeup dating as far back as 10,000 B.C. Egyptians wore heavy eye shadow and kohl (black) eyeliner, lip ointments, and henna (reddish-brown) nail stain. They also traced lines of blue paint and liquid gold around their faces and other body parts.

Roman women loved makeup, too. The Roman philosopher Plautus wrote, "A woman without paint is like food without salt." Women applied pastes (made from things like lentils, honey, wheat, eggs, and other ingredients) to make their skin look as pale as possible. Consumption (or, "sickly") was the "in" look. And the paler a woman was, the wealthier she appeared to be. While poorer women worked outdoors under a hot sun, wealthy women had lives of leisure away from the burning rays.

In the nineteenth century, Victorian women carried on the pale tradition at great risk to their own health. Homemade cosmetics included dangerous compounds like arsenic, lead, or mercury. There were many wild ways that women achieved their whiter shade of pale.

• Staying indoors with blackened curtains and no contact with the sun
• Painting their face with paints and white powder
• "Bleeding" themselves with leeches
• Drinking vinegar and avoiding fresh air

• Applying urine to fade freckles
• Painting the veins on their faces to make their skin appear translucent
• Washing the eyes with lemon and orange juice, or rinsing the eyes with belladonna, a dangerous juice from the poisonous nightshade plant—all to make their eyes appear brighter against their pale skin

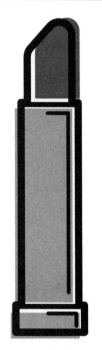

By the turn of the twentieth century, attitudes about makeup shifted. Women bit their lips or pinched their cheeks to get more color, rather than applying makeup! Between World War I and World War II, there were many developments in the field of cosmetics. Women like Helena Rubenstein, Elizabeth Arden, and Coco Chanel produced an array of lipsticks, blushers, shadows, cleansers, nourishing creams, tonics, lotions, and other makeup and skincare products.

In the 1950s, color movies influenced the makeup industry. A face appearing on a huge movie screen showed every blemish and wrinkle. How to fix that? Makeup artist Max Factor created "pancake" makeup, a foundation that made all skin look smooth and flawless.

Today, although arsenic drinks, giant wigs, and white-powdered skin are mostly long gone, they've been replaced by a whole new lineup of beauty must-gets: fat-reducing creams, hair extensions, and self-tanner in about fifty different shades. Beauty is big business that keeps on getting bigger.

BRACE YOURSELF

CHANCES ARE YOU MAY HAVE TO get braces—if you haven't gotten them already. A lot of times, our teeth just don't grow in straight. But braces don't have to be scary or painful. I won't go so far as to say, "Braces are the most amazing things EVER!" because then you know I would be lying through my . . . er . . . teeth. But braces have come a long way from the clunky, metal-mouth contraptions of long ago. These days, they're less noticeable, they're available in an assortment of cool colors, and they're doing something fabulous for your smile and your health.

A FEW BRACING FACTS:
• Braces don't hurt—except when they are first fitted and sometimes when they are tightened. Oh, and if you get socked in the face.

• Braces do not usually change the way you talk. You should have the same ability to speak, sing, yell at the cat, and make fun of your little brother.

• Braces are now made with wires from a space-age material that straightens teeth faster and easier than ever before. And (bonus!) they come with rubber bands in colors you love. Pink and green look great together. Or try black and orange for Halloween.

• Braces that come apart in your mouth are not dangerous. This means: If you swallow a piece of your braces by accident, it shouldn't hurt you. You will, however, need to rush to the orthodontist to have it replaced. Braces stay on for an average of two years—if you take care of them.

• Braces last longer if you don't eat gum or gooey candy. And no popcorn! Stuff that sticks in your braces will give you nasty cavities.

• Don't do karate or play contact sports without wearing a mouth guard.

• Today's braces will not pick up radio signals. Years ago, when AM radio was big, people said they could hear radio signals on their fillings. But there have been no recent reports of *American Top 40* coming in loud and clear on braces. Sorry.

• Braces do not have to be clunky or boring. Some designer styles come in gold and sapphire, or bright purple, neon green, pink, or black—with or without sparkles! No one will ever call *you* Metal Mouth or Train Tracks!

• Braces will not embarrass you . . . if you don't let them. So smile, proudly—at school, at your next soccer game, *and* at the school dance. Chances are that your school crush is already wearing braces, too.

• If you have braces and you kiss someone wearing braces, it's unlikely you'll get stuck together. But if, by chance, you do—relax! The meeting of the metal won't last forever.

HAIR

DOS AND DON'TS:

GOING TO THE SALON

We've all lived through the hair horror stories. You go to the hairdresser with hair down your back . . . and leave with a bowl cut. Help! Fear not. There are simple things you can do to make sure you get the look you want. Remember these next time you head into the salon.

1. Your stylist is not psychic. He or she cannot read your mind or tell you what you want. Feeling pressured to make a decision? Maybe you shouldn't get a cut right away. Make an appointment for a consultation first. Talk it out.

2. Show up on time for your appointment. This is one of those Grandma rules. When you show up on time for anything, you're less stressed out and that makes all the difference. Plus, it gives you more time to read those back issues of *Us* and *People* at the salon.

3. Bring a photograph. Having trouble explaining the haircut you want? Try showing your stylist a picture. Maybe it's a photo of the cut you got last time, or maybe it's a photo of your favorite Hollywood star walking down the red carpet. Visual aids are always a good thing.

4. Haircuts aren't always that dramatic. The best kind of cut will make the most of your natural texture and length, but it probably won't change your face or your life. Don't expect too much, unless you're cutting off five feet of long hair in exchange for a pixie cut. As if.

5. You don't have to be all that dramatic, either. Stay cool and calm during your hair salon visit. And be realistic. If you have straight, thin hair, and you want a shimmering, curly 'do, you need to rethink your expectations.

6. Let the stylist do his/her job. Step outside of the box. Just because your hair has been parted in the middle since you were in second grade doesn't mean your hair stylist shouldn't part it on the side.

7. No matter how attached you are to your hair, it's just hair. It will grow back. And it will still be as beautiful as ever. I promise.

8. Visit the salon solo . . . but meet up with your pals afterwards. Let your BFFs see your new 'do when it's all perfect and blow-dried by the professional. That way you can show off and get all the oohs and aaahs you deserve.

Mohawk

Princess Leia

Mullet

Feather-Back

Crimp

Bouffant

Shag

Ringlets

BAD HAIR DAY

HOW TO

FRENCH BRAID

HEADS UP! THERE ARE A FEW important things you need to know about French braiding before you begin.

The key to a perfect French braid is practice, practice, and patience. You can practice while watching TV, listening to music, or in the backseat of the car.

Try French braiding your best buddy's hair first, so you get the hang of all the steps—and practice your hand position.

Don't be afraid to start over.

1. Take a section of hair at the top of your head, on your crown or behind your bangs. Divide the section into three even pieces, separating and holding them between your fingers. This will start off your French braid.

2. Cross the right-hand strand over the middle strand. Now hold all three strands in your left hand.

3. Take a new strand of hair with your right hand and add it to the right strand.

4. Cross the left strand over the middle strand. Now hold all three strands in your right hand.

5. Take a new strand of hair with your left hand and add it to the left strand.

6. Cross the right-hand strand over the middle strand. Now hold all three strands in your left hand.

7. Take a new strand of hair with your right hand and add it to the right strand.

8. Cross the left strand over the middle strand. Now hold all three strands in your right hand.

9. Take a new strand of hair with your left hand and add it to the left strand.

10. Continue to add strands and switch hands, braiding as far down as you can. Remember to keep the braid as tight as possible as you go. Be sure to gather up all the loose hair.

11. When you've braided as far as you can reach, shift the braid to one hand and gently pull it to the side, over your shoulder. Continue braiding at the side of your head. It might feel strange at first, since you are now braiding in the opposite direction. But continue braiding until there is no more hair.

12. Done braiding? Tie it off. Now take a look in the mirror. Congratulations! Sometimes there may be a "lump" of hair at the top of your head where you started the French braid. This is easily smoothed down. Remember: Don't get upset if the braid gets messed up. You can start all over again!

YOUR OWN HAIR

Step 1

Step 2

Step 3

Step 4

Step 5

Step 6

Step 7

Step 8

Step 9

Step 10

Step 11

Step 12

CRAZY
COSMETICS!
Absolutely True!

- Chili Pepper Face Wash—hot stuff!
- Cheetos-flavored lip balm—the cheese taste stays with you forevah!
- A chocolate bar that doubles as acne scrub—huh?
- Bubble bath that smells like vanilla pound cake. (Okay, wait . . . maybe that one's not so bad. . . .)

"I REALLY DO LOVE MY _____."

THE NEXT TIME YOU ROLL OUT OF BED and wander into the bathroom, plant your bare feet firmly on the floor in front of the mirror. Now take inventory. Give yourself a morning pep talk. Not to get all touchy-feely on you, but positive affirmations—especially ones said out loud in front of an enormous mirror under fluorescent bathroom lights at the crack of dawn—really DO work.

Sample, starter affirmation (does any of this sound familiar?):

"I know that my tummy isn't perfect, and my toes are too long, and I really need a haircut . . . BUT . . . I really do love my nose. And I love my toes. And I love my hair . . . and my elbows . . . and my eyes . . . and the way I look at the world . . . and . . . well, golly gee, I love being me."

Take a few deep breaths. Say it all over again. Of course, the list can go on and on if you want it to. There's a lot to love about you!

IF THE SHOE FITS . . .
RANDOM FACTS ABOUT FOOTWEAR

OLDEST SHOES? Evidence of Native American shoes found in Missouri dates back to 8000 B.C. When archaeologists uncovered the "Ice Man" frozen in the Alps since 3300 B.C., he was wearing shoes made from bearskin and woven plant fibers. Now those guys had sole!

STRAIGHT SHOE FACTS? As late as 1850, most many shoes were still made on straight lasts. (A last is the oblong block the shoemaker uses to measure, make, and mend shoes.) Why is this so weird? It means no one had left or right shoes until the late 1800s. During the American Civil War (1861–1865), shoes were mass-produced, and a more detailed left and right shoe-sizing system was invented. Each soldier was given a shoe size along with his name tag.

POINTIEST SHOES EVER? First place: The Gothic fifteenth-century garment called a houppelande ended in leather shoes with extremely pointed toes that needed wooden clogs (aka patterns) to support them. Second place: Stilettos. Third place: All shoes belonging to Santa's elves and court jesters.

SMELLIEST SHOE FACT? New Yorker Herbert Lapidus invented the odor-eater insole in the early 1970s, because he claimed his wife had super-smelly feet.

SHOE FACT THAT SOUNDS LIKE AN EPISODE OF *BATTLESTAR GALACTICA*? The manufacturing process of vulcanization, discovered and patented by Charles Goodyear (the tire guy), uses heat to meld rubber to cloth or other rubber components for a sturdier, more permanently bonded shoe.

BEST SHOE NAME EVER? The word "sneaker" was coined by Henry Nelson McKinney, an advertising agent. He said the rubber sole made the shoe quiet when you walked, as if you were "sneaking" around.

HOW MUCH BEAUTY SLEEP DO YOU NEED?

DOCTORS RECOMMEND THAT YOU GET AT LEAST eight hours of sleep per night. The perfect night's sleep is one that leaves you alert and active the following day. But everyone has different sleep requirements. Even animals! What amount is right for you?

ANIMAL	APPROXIMATE TOTAL SLEEP TIME PER DAY
Python	18 hrs
Tiger	16 hrs
Dog	13 hrs
Cat	12 hrs
Chimpanzee	10 hrs
Sheep	4 hrs
African elephant	3 hrs
Giraffe	2 hrs
Shark	0 hrs*

* This is actually a trick answer! The truth is that scientists don't really know how sharks sleep, or if they sleep. Since sharks must maintain a forward motion to keep their gills moving, rest probably isn't the first thing on their minds. Only time—and research—will tell.

Contrary to some beliefs, sleep is NOT a time for the body or brain to shut down and stop. Although the metabolic rate slows down some, the body is still busy. During sleep, your brain's delta waves actually increase dramatically! Your endocrine system (which releases hormones that help us grow) is also very active during sleep. That explains why sometimes kids wake up with literal "growing pains" in their legs during the night.

OFF TO
Dreamland

Having trouble falling asleep? These may be the culprit:

- Watching TV or playing video games too closely to bedtime
- Too much (or too little) light
- Cold or heat
- Too much noise
- Soda with caffeine, or chocolate
- Sirens
- Loud music
- Other noises: your hamster on its wheel, a drippy faucet, the radiator

Next time you get ready for bed, try these simple steps to guarantee happy sleep:

- Try to go to bed at the same time every night.
- Keep your bedroom cool, dark, and quiet.
- Don't eat a big meal before bedtime.
- Run and play for at least three hours every day.
- Take a warm shower or listen to quiet music.
  Source: sleepfoundation.org

DREAM TRIVIA

- Ancient Egyptians thought that the gods sent dreams as signs of luck or danger.
- Ancient Greeks decided that it was not the gods, but *people*, who created their own dreams.
- Around a third of dreams take place in houses, and a fourth in trains, buses, boats, cars, or other vehicles.
- Nearly 40% of dreams are about strangers.
- Sometimes people remember their dreams in black and white, even though everyone dreams in color.
- Robert Louis Stevenson wrote his book, *The Strange Case of Dr. Jekyll and Mr. Hyde*, according to nightmares that he had about the future.

WHAT YOUR DREAMS

AIRPLANE—a means of escape for your troubles

APPLE—immortality and love

BABY—something new has begun

BEE—you're too busy jumping from one thing to another

BIRDS—freedom

BOOK—wisdom and information; if the book is hidden, you're seeking something you cannot find

BUTTERFLY—transformation

CHAIR—if you're sitting down, you're repressing something

CLOUDS—you face the unknown and the unknowable

CROSS—you need to make a choice

DANCING—you are moving from one phase of your life to another

DOGS—one dog shows you the right way to do something, a pack of dogs means your situation is out of control

DOOR—there is an opportunity ahead

DROWNING—you are unable to deal with your emotions

FAMOUS PEOPLE—you are connecting with whatever traits and qualities that person has: good looks, fame, wealth, intelligence, etc.

FEATHER—truth

FIRE—you believe in passion and the burning away of bad things

FLYING—you are not stuck; you will find a solution

FOREST—the unknown (offering some shelter and protection)

MEAN

You wake up in a bundle of blankets, your hair is a tangle, and all you can think about is the giant airplane that crash-landed in your bedroom while you were sitting on a chair under a rainbow. Wait a minute. That didn't really happen, did it? But it seemed so real, especially the part about the tidal wave, the volcano, and the birds! That's how dreams work. They throw us vibrant, meaningful symbols and ask us: So, what do you think it all means? Here are some dreamy definitions.

GARDEN—safety and peace is coming your way

HAIR—you are strong; however, loose hair means freedom, while bound hair means loss of power

HATS—you need to share your opinions

HEART—you are holding on to a secret

HORSE—represents the human body; so if a horse is injured in your dream, it could mean that you'll get sick

INSECTS—you are suffering from anxiety

JEWELS OR TREASURE—you are on a spiritual quest

MAP—you are afraid to take risks

MIRROR—your true self

OCEAN—the unknown (offering uncertainty and no limits)

PATH THAT LEADS NOWHERE—you took a wrong turn

RAINBOW—a promise

SNOW—you have feelings that you're keeping to yourself

STAIRS—going up represents growth; going down represents your inner feelings

SWIMMING—you're navigating the unconscious; if you struggle against waves or a sea monster, you're afraid of something

TEETH—losing teeth means that you are growing wiser, although it also could mean that you also may lose power or get injured

TREE—a symbol of growth and branching out

VOLCANO—a great change is about to happen

WINDOW—you can see yourself clearly

GAMES GI

RLS PLAY

GET A GROUP OF GIRLS TOGETHER and you can be assured of a few things.

Gossip. Everyone usually likes to talk about everyone else. Hopefully, all things that are said are nice. Yes, that's a hint.

Makeovers. Everyone enjoys testing out new 'dos and makeup on each other, which is cool as long as no one gets too carried away with the purple glitter eye shadow.

Games. But not just any kind of games. Sure, we like the ordinary playground games like tag and hide-and-seek. And we love board games like Battleship and Monopoly as much as the next kid. But there is an entirely separate category of *girl* games. And we like these best.

MASH

THE GOAL OF THIS GAME IS TO discover who you will marry, where you will live, and some other important details about your future.

Write MASH across the top of a piece of paper. This stands for Mansion, Apartment, Shack, House.

Then write down the names of four boys you like. They do not have to be people in your class at school. You can put down some cute movie star's name if you want. After all, who knows what could happen in ten years?

The short lists of four continue on the page. Write down four places where you would like to go on your honeymoon, four cities where you would like to live, four jobs you would like to have, four pets you would like to own, and four cars you would like to drive.

Now, take a pen and close your eyes. Somewhere on the bottom of the page, begin to draw a spiral. Stop after a few seconds. Now mark each line in the spiral. Count those marks. What number is it? That will be the number to reveal your ultimate MASH results.

Say that the number you got is seven. Now, starting with the M in MASH at the top of the page, count out that number through each item. Each time you get to seven, cross off the item, skipping over the items you've already crossed off. When you get down to one in each group of four, you have the truth about where you'll live, who you'll marry, and so on. But make sure you really like all of your choices before you start to eliminate. One time, I wrote down the North Pole as a place where I wanted to live. And that's what came up!*

Make a MASH notebook. Get your BFFs together and decorate a notebook that you can pass around the group. Inside, keep track of your latest MASH charts. Or make up MASH charts for your friends with people and places they don't expect! Try MASH categories like POP STAR MASH (only famous singers), HOLLYWOOD MASH (only famous actors), or SPORTS MASH (famous sports hunks).

*How to make it interesting: Have your BFF pick one item for each list that's something *horrible*. Have her add in "garbage dump" for a honeymoon destination or put down the boy you like the *least*, and see if his name pops up at the end. It's good for a laugh!

LOVE AND MARRIAGE

♥ ♥ ♥ ♥ ♥ ♥ ♥ ♥ ♥ ♥ ♥ ♥ ♥ ♥ ♥ ♥ ♥

LOOKING FOR LOVE? Look no further than the letters of your own name. Grab a piece of paper and a pen and check the odds of marrying your crush.

Write down your first and last names.

Under your name, write down the first and last names of your friend/crush/person you think you might like.

Do you have any of the same letters in your first name and his last name? Cross those out.

Do you have any of the same letters in his first name and your last name? Cross those out.

Now start to cross off each letter remaining in your name. As you cross off each one, say another word in this sequence: Love, Hate, Friendship, Marriage, Love, Hate . . . and so on. Whatever you say on the last letter of your name says how you really (truly, madly, deeply!) feel about him.

Do the same thing with his name, repeating the same sequence. This tells you how *he* really feels about *you*.

AN APPLE A DAY

DID YOU KNOW THAT YOU CAN FIGURE OUT the name of the person you love with any ordinary apple? Get to the green market and find a firm apple with a strong stem.

Take the stem and twist it in circles while reciting the alphabet. When the stem pops off, the letter you say is the first initial of the FIRST name of the person you will love forever.

Now take the stem and poke it into the apple repeatedly while reciting the alphabet once again. When the stem pokes through into the apple flesh, you have the first initial of the LAST name of the person you will love forever.

Eat the apple.

BY THE NUMBERS

THIS ISN'T REALLY A GAME, but it works a lot like MASH and Love and Marriage. It's adapted from a chain letter that I've gotten in my e-mail at least a bazillion times. Have someone read the instructions to you as you write down what is needed. Then you can read it and ask your friends to do the same.

- On a blank sheet of paper, write the numbers from 1 to 11 down the page.
- Beside the numbers 1 and 2, write down any other numbers you want (your age, your house number, your lucky number). One number per line, please.
- Beside the numbers 3 and 7, write down the names of two members of the opposite sex.
- Beside the numbers 4, 5, and 6, write down the names of family members or friends.
- Beside the remaining numbers, 8, 9, 10, and 11, write down the titles of four songs you like. (Or the first four songs that pop into your head.) When you've finished, here's what your answers tell you:

- The number of friends who are thinking about you right now is what you wrote on line 2.
- The person on line 3 is the person you secretly love.
- The person you like but can't seem to connect with is on line 7.
- The person on line 4 is the one you care about the most.
- The person on line 5 is the one who knows you best.
- The person on line 6 is your lucky star—and the person who always gives you the best advice.

- The song on line 8 goes with the person on line 3.
- The song on line 9 goes with the person on line 7.
- The song on line 10 is the song that best describes your state of mind.
- The song on line 11 is the song that best describes the way you feel about life.
- Finally, the number on line 1 is your lucky number. Keep that in mind if you're ever playing a game of chance—or helping Dad choose numbers for Lotto.

TRUTH OR DARE

YOU NEED A LARGE GROUP OF FRIENDS to play this game. The bigger the group, the more fun the game can get. Sit in a circle. One person volunteers to go first. That person turns to anyone else in the circle and asks, "Truth or dare?" Someone chooses TRUTH to answer a question, or DARE to take a dare. I always opted for dare, fearing mortal embarrassment if I had to face my friends' questions. The goofiest thing I ever had to do on a dare: Yell something dumb out of my friend's apartment window.

Here are some TRUTHS and DARES to get you started.

TRUTH

- What is your biggest secret?
- Have you ever gotten homesick?
- What do you like the least/most about ___ (someone's name here)?
- What is the most embarrassing thing you've ever done?
- What is the silliest thing you've ever said?
- If you could be anyone for a day, who would it be and why?
- What is the worst nickname you ever got?
- Who has the best outfit in the room?
- Who in the room is most likely to succeed and why?
- Who in the room has the best 'do?
- What did you dream about last night?
- If you had two wishes, what would they be?
- What is the strangest thing about you?

DARE

- Recite the alphabet backwards.
- Do a cartwheel. (see page 105)
- Put an ice cube down your T-shirt until it melts.
- Bark like a dog.
- Hop around the room on one foot.
- Lick your knee.
- Kiss your own foot.
- Make a toilet paper turban and wear it.
- Snort like a pig.
- Do a robot dance.
- Sing a silly song.
- Eat a packet of ketchup.
- Blow in someone's ear.
- Kiss your stuffed animal.
- Put on lipstick without looking in the mirror.
- Suck your thumb and cry like a baby.
- Make the weirdest face ever.
- Do the hula dance.

Make sure that all truths and dares are done with the spirit of good fun. Playing this game should never be about exposing, embarrassing, or hurting someone else.

MOST POPULAR CLASSIC BOARD GAMES

Battleship • Chess and Checkers • Chinese Checkers • Clue • Dominoes • The Game of Life • Mancala • Monopoly • Scrabble • Sorry! • Yahtzee

Ranked and rated by boardgameratings.com © 2007

WHAT IS MANCALA?

Mancala is a group of "count and capture" board games from Africa and Asia. In the U.S., the Mancala game played most often is called Kalah. On a Kalah game board, you have twelve small pits in two rows of six, two larger pits (called houses) at either end, and thirty-six beans/seeds (known as counters). Your goal is to get or "sow" the beans/seeds to either end of the board with a series of smart moves. Fun fact: The word *mancala* comes from the Arabic word *naqala* meaning "to move."

RIDDLE ME THIS

CLASSIC AMERICAN FOLKLORE celebrates the days when kids sat around making cornhusk dolls and telling riddles by the fire. And yes, those days really did exist, long before Xbox, the Internet, and digital cable TV. Here's a notion: The next time you're sitting around the cafeteria table picking at your fish sticks that look like cardboard, test out one of these riddles on your friends. Can you stump anyone? (Answers can be found at the bottom of the page.)

Humpty Dumpty sat on a wall
Humpty Dumpty had a great fall.
All the king's horses and all the king's men
Couldn't put Humpty together again.
Riddle 1: Who's Humpty?

As I was going to St. Ives,
I met a man with seven wives.
Each wife had seven sacks.
Each sack had seven cats.
Each cat had seven kits.
Kits, cats, sacks, and wives,
How many were going to St. Ives?
Riddle 2: How many were going to St. Ives?

Big as a barn,
Light as a feather,
And sixty horses can't pull it.
Riddle 3: What is it?

FIVE QUICK RIDDLES

1. What has legs but can't walk?
2. What has teeth but can't eat?
3. Four fingers and a thumb, but flesh and bone, it has none.
4. As long as I eat, I live, but when I drink, I die.
5. What goes up and down and around the house and then sits in a corner?

ANSWERS TO RIDDLE ME THIS: 1. Humpty Dumpty is an egg. 2. Only one person (the narrator) was going to St. Ives. The others were traveling in the opposite direction. 3. The mysterious thing is the shadow of the barn.
ANSWERS TO QUICK RIDDLES: 1. Chair, table, or desk. 2. Comb or saw. 3. Glove. 4. A fire. 5. A broom.

Pssst!

SECRET MESSAGE RHYMES

S OMETIMES RHYMES AREN'T AS SIMPLE as they seem. The nursery rhyme "Sing a Song of Sixpence" was supposedly a coded message used to recruit crew members for the notorious Blackbeard's pirate ship expeditions. There is no one true version of the rhyme, but many of the lines have secret meanings that are decoded here.

LINE	SECRET MEANING
Sing a song of sixpence	Sixpence would be the payment per day. That was good money in the 1700s.
A pocket full of rye	A pocket is a leather bag and rye is liquor (which pirates loved).
Four and twenty blackbirds	Blackbeard's crew dressed all in black.
Baked in a pie	Concealing something in a pie was a common way to hide a surprise.
When the pie was opened, the birds began to sing	In this case, the surprise is a pirate crew and their "singing" is the great noise made while attacking!
Was that not a tasty dish	The dish, in this case, is the ship and booty that have just been seized.
To set before the king	And the king is actually Blackbeard, king of the pirates.
The king was in his counting house/Counting out his money	This is Blackbeard counting his loot.
The queen was in the parlor/Eating bread and honey	The queen is actually Blackbeard's ship, the *Queen Anne's Revenge.*
The maid was in the garden	The garden is the area of sea where the crew would scout for other ships to attack.
Hanging out the clothes	Clothes refers to the sails they hoist on their own vessels.
When down came a blackbird and snapped off her nose!	Beware! Blackbeard will strike again!

WITH A CALCULATOR AND A LITTLE IMAGINATION, you can turn numbers into words! The next time you're goofing around with multiplication and division, flip your calculator upside down and see if you can spell a real word. I've included a clever calculator dictionary as your guide and some riddles. Watch out! The fun really adds up.

be	38	go	06	obese	35380
bee	338	gobble	378806	oblige	361780
beg	638	goes	5306	oboe	3080
beige	36138	gosh	4506	oil	710
bell	7738	he	34	ooze	3200
bib	818	heel	7334	see	335
big	618	hello	07734	seize	32135
bill	7718	high	4614	sell	7735
bless	55378	hill	7714	she	345
bliss	55178	his	514	shell	77345
blob	8078	hiss	5514	shoe	3045
bog	608	hobbies	5318804	siege	36315
boggle	376608	hoe	304	sigh	4615
boil	7108	hog	604	sill	7715
boss	5508	hole	3704	silo	0715
bosses	535508	hose	3504	size	3215
eel	733	igloo	00761	sizzle	372215
egg	663	ill	771	sleigh	461375
eggshell	77345663	is	51	slob	8075
else	3573	leg	637	so	05
geese	35336	less	5537	sob	805
giggle	376616	lie	317	soil	7105
gill	7716	log	607	sole	3705
glee	3376	loose	35007	solo	0705
globe	38076	lose	3507	zoo	002
gloss	55076	loss	5507		

Don't forget most words can be made plural simply by starting with a 5, which turns into an S at the end of the word. My stepmother always loved this game, because it could spell her name, Lois (5107)! Can you spell your name?

Try and solve these fun riddles. Then make up new ones on your own.

Riddle: My mother always says I'm a . . .
Answer: Multiply 5 by 12. Add 236. Multiply by 6. Add 8,000. Subtract 1,701.

Riddle: Something gooey this way comes. What am I?
Answer: Multiply 4 by 1,000. Add 39. Multiply the total by 2.

Riddle: Reading all the words in all those book reports will _____ your teacher's mind.
Answer: 217,001 words minus 400 words plus 160,007 words.

ANSWERS: 1. 8075 or SLOB. 2. 8078 or BLOB. 3. 376608 or BOGGLE.

MATH
ROCKS!

PICTURE THIS. YOU WALK INTO math class. Your teacher asks everyone to take their seats and then she announces that there will be a pop quiz. Your palms begin to feel sweaty. But then what do you do? Shake off the nerves and wing it? Keel over and pass out? Or do you raise your arms into the air and shout, "Bring it on!"

Whenever it came to math in school, I always felt like I was winging it. Just the thought of geometry gave me little hives. Okay, maybe I'm exaggerating a little, but I didn't have anyone telling me how much math mattered in real life.

The absolute truth is . . . math is power. It's logic, it's number theory, it's chemistry, it's physics, it's the way everything adds up and fits together. And it's fun.

Some simple things you could never do if you didn't know math:

Figure out how much those super-cool $75 platform shoes will cost with the mall's 30% tween discount. ($52.50)

Make the best chocolate chip cookie recipe ever—even though it comes from your European grandmother's cookbook. Convert her liter measurements to cups. Just check out the easy online metric calculator at www.worldwidemetric.com.

Divide one eight-slice pizza into dinner for fourteen. (Just cut each slice into two slices. You'll have two extra slices for the hungriest. You can also have the pizza parlor leave the pie unsliced and then carve up fourteen slices at home using a ruler. Note: Option 1 is easier.)

Know what Mom means exactly when she says she'll take your $10 allowance and give you a 10% increase each year for the next five years. (That'll be $14.64 a week in five years!)

Count the number of cute guys at the school dance. Then add up your chances for getting a dance with the one you really like—ha, ha! Get it?

Did you know that women have been mathematicians since at least the fourth century? Hypatia, an ancient Egyptian, was the first woman mathematician that we know about. She lived from 370–415 A.D.

MATH PHOBIC NO MORE!

Eliminate math nerves (otherwise known as a paralyzing fear of geometry, algebra, and all things mathematic). Get help with your homework and learn a few tricks about doing math from these useful Web sites:

www.mathgoodies.com • www.webmath.com
www.gomath.com • www.algebrahelp.com

I DOKU, YOU DOKU, SU DOKU!

THE LATEST PUZZLE CRAZE is just right for math wannabes. Sudoku (*soo-doh-koo*) is a logic puzzle that originated with Leonhard Euler, a Swiss mathematician who made "Latin Squares" puzzles in the eighteenth century. During the late 1980s, a Japanese puzzlemaker revamped the Latin Squares and started a new trend: Sudoku. In Japanese, *su* means a number, and *doku* roughly translates as "singular" or "unique." The game really skyrocketed in popularity in the 2000s in England. Now, it's something of a puzzle phenomenon. In 2005, some folks in Bristol, England, decided to make the largest-ever Sudoku game. Carved into the side of a hill, the huge puzzle measured more than 240 feet square with 15-foot-high numbers.

SONGS FROM THE MATH VAULT

- *Rikki Don't Lose That Number* (Steely Dan)
- *867-5309/Jenny* (Tommy Tutone)
- *99 Luftballons* (Nena)
- *One* (Three Dog Night)
- *Tea for Two* (Vincent Youmans and Irving Caesar)
- *Knock Three Times* (Tony Orlando and Dawn)
- *Add It Up* (Violent Femmes)
- *30,000 Pounds of Bananas* (Harry Chapin)
- *Love Potion #9* (The Clovers)
- *. . . Baby, One More Time* (Britney Spears)
- *Positively 4th Street* (Bob Dylan)
- *When I'm Sixty-Four* (The Beatles)
- *Edge of Seventeen* (Stevie Nicks)

A LITTLE FRIENDLY ADVICE

ONE OF THE THINGS THAT WILL make you successful with math is not being afraid to admit when you don't know something. It's okay to ask questions. It's okay if you don't understand everything (or anything) at first. It's okay to make mistakes and then go back and see where it all went wrong. The more you ask questions, the more you will learn. Plus, other kids in class, like shy friends or the new kid, will be happier when you ask. The truth is, everyone is wondering the same thing.

You know how sometimes a friend says, "Just deal with it!!!!" when something has gone wrong? Math is one of those things that shows you how to recognize, how to deal with, and how to solve all kinds of problems. It provides us with key reasoning skills that will prove useful now and in the future.

JUMP ROPE
GAMES

JUMP ROPING STARTED THOUSANDS of years ago as a game for boys to show off jumping skills like crossovers and double jumps. It was girls, however, who raised the stakes. As families migrated from farm towns to cities, girls started doing their own brand of jump roping on smoothly paved sidewalks and playgrounds—adding tricky moves and the nifty rhymes that we love so much.

1-2-3 JUMP ALONE!

These are rope tricks you can do alone. Helpful hint: Before you try it with the rope, try it without, just so you're sure-footed.

SINGLE BOUNCE or DOUBLE BOUNCE: Jump once or twice before the rope rotates all the way around.

SWING TIME: Swing the rope to your left side. As you switch, spread your hands apart and jump. As the rope comes over, swing it to your right side. On the next turn, spread your hands apart and jump.

SKIER: Jump from side to side as you jump, just like you're on a real ski slope.

STRADDLE: Do a little midair split as you jump, but bring your legs back together as you hit the ground again.

HEEL EXCHANGE: As you jump, put one foot forward and touch your heel. Then switch feet.

WOUNDED DUCK: Jump into the air with toes pointed out. Jump again with them pointed inward.

DOUBLE UNDER: Jump up and try to spin the rope around twice before your feet touch the ground again.

PUSH-UP: On the first spin, jump up and then stretch out, facedown. Put your hands and feet into the push-up position. After a few moments, do the push-up and pull the rope around your feet. Repeat.

LEG CROSS: First, jump a single bounce. Then, pull your right leg up and jump over the rope with your left leg, while putting your right arm under your right knee. Now pull your arm out from under your leg and do a side swing.

4-5-6 JUMP TOGETHER!

Two players hold opposite ends of a long rope and turn it, while a third player jumps. The people doing the turning are called "enders." Everyone counts the jumps. A missed jump means the jumper must switch with one of the enders. Some of the tricks you can try:

Double hops or alternating feet (add in claps and twists—anything to move your body around in an interesting way while you jump).

Bounce a ball at the same time as jumping (called "Rock the Boat").

Drop an object and pick it up again—before the rope gets you!

DOUBLE DUTCH

Two enders hold the ends of two ropes. The ropes are turned toward each other so that as one rope is up, the other is touching the ground. It is easier to move into the ropes at an angle, standing with one shoulder next to an ender with the opposite foot slightly forward. Watch the "front door" rope, but be prepared to jump the "back door" rope as you move in.

JUMP ROPE LINGO

Grinding coffee	Porridge	Cut the cheese
Swish-swosh	Wind the clock	Scissors
Baby in the cradle	Split the pie	Lift and lay
Low water	Sweep the floor	Up the ladder
Run through the moon	Baking bread	Hopsies
Blindsies	Feet together and apart	Yokey
Hot peas	Double-French	

The best jump rope games are played with nonsense rhymes. Most have funny words, sounds, and body and hand actions. Although some of these scream nineteenth century more than twenty-first, they are all about one thing that doesn't change with time: having fun.

Grandma Moses sick in bed
Called the doctor and the doctor said,
"Grandma Moses, you ain't sick,
All you need is a licorice stick."

Ouch! Touch your side, stomach, and head as you sing these lines.
I gotta pain in my side, Oh! Ah!
I gotta pain in my stomach, Oh! Ah!
I gotta pain in my head 'cause my baby said,
"Roll-a-roll-a-peep!
Roll-a-roll-a-peep!
Bump-te-wa-wa, Bump-te-wa-wa,
Roll-a-roll-a-peep!"

As you sing the rhyme, clap, snap your fingers, and smack your thighs.
Downtown baby on a roller coaster,
Sweet, sweet baby on a roller coaster,
Shimmy shimmy co-co-pop
Shimmy shimmy POP!
Shimmy shimmy co-co-pop
Shimmy shimmy POP!

Acka, backa, soda cracker,
Acka, backa, boo,
Acka, backa, soda cracker,
Out goes you!

Ice cream, soda, Delaware punch,
Tell me the initials of your honeybunch.
A, B, C, D . . .

Take note! Keep jumping until you trip or get tangled in the jump rope. Whatever letter stops you in your tracks . . . that's the first letter of your sweetheart's first name. Jump again until you trip again. That's the first letter of his last name!

ROPE
RHYMES

Spell cat. C-A-T.
Spell rat. R-A-T.
Now it's time for exercise:
Hands up, hands down,
Turn around, touch the ground.
Now it's time for Arithmetic:
8 plus 8 is 16, 10 plus 10 is 20.
Now it's time for History:
George Washington never told a lie.
He ran around the corner and stole a cherry pie.
How many did he steal?
He stole 1, 2, 3, 4 . . .

Down in the valley
Where the green grass grows,
There sat [YOUR NAME]
Sweet as a rose.
She sang, she sang,
She sang so sweet.
Along came [YOUR CRUSH]
And kissed her cheek.
How many kisses did he give?
One, two, three, four, five . . .

Test your "High Waters" (that's what the motions in this rhyme are called). Have the enders spin the rope a little bit higher (without touching the ground) each time the word "floor" is said.

Fudge, fudge, tell the judge,
Mama's got a newborn baby.
It isn't a girl and it isn't a boy,
It's just a fair young lady.
Wrap it up in tissue paper
Send it up an elevator.
First floor, miss.
Second floor, miss.
Third floor, miss.
Fourth floor, miss.
Fifth floor, miss.
Sixth floor, baby's floor.
All out!

GENEALOGY MADE SIMPLE (SORT OF)

THERE'S NO CLIMB MORE THRILLING than scaling your own family tree. Is anyone in your family a genealogy buff? Do you know what your great-great-grandfather did? It's time to find out. On the 46-47 is a sample family tree. Can you collect information and create one of your own—complete with roots and branches? Where do you begin? Ask questions! Your parents are a good start, but you can ask your grandmother and grandfather, too, and any other relatives, including aunts, uncles, and cousins. Are you lucky enough to know your great-grandparents? Talk to them about the past and see how far back they can remember. All this information will be the branches of your tree.

What kinds of information do you need to gather? The most important pieces of information are full names, dates of birth, dates of death (if the person has died), and other simple facts. Who did that person marry? How many children did she/he have? What was that person's occupation? Do any photos of that person exist? If photos do exist, you need to make copies. Keep originals in a safe place.

If you aren't having such good luck gathering facts, or you just want to know more, there are lots of other places to look. It's probably the coolest treasure hunt you'll ever do!

- ☑ Check your house for old photographs with writing on the back.
- ☑ Find old notebooks and scrapbooks.
- ☑ Look for old Bibles (long ago, people wrote details of family records in the Bible).
- ☑ Look for letters or diaries with valuable family information.
- ☑ Check the public library for newspaper birth announcements or obituaries (death notices).
- ☑ Visit the county clerk's office (if family members lived in your town) for deeds, notices, and other records, too.
- ☑ Check out www.familysearch.com. The Mormons maintain the best genealogy records for public use. See what you find in their database.

WHEW! WHO'S WHO?

- your mom or dad's mom and dad = **your grandparents**
- your grandparent's mom and dad = **your great-grandparents**
- your great-grandparent's mom and dad = **your second great-grandparents**
- your brother or sister's child = **your niece or nephew**
- your parent's brother or sister = **your uncle or aunt**
- your grandparent's brother or sister = **your great-uncle or great-aunt**
- your uncle or aunt's child = **your first cousin**
- your first cousin's child = **your first cousin once-removed**
- your second cousin's child = **your second cousin once-removed**
- your first cousin's grandchild = **your first cousin twice-removed**

HOW TO

CREATE YOUR

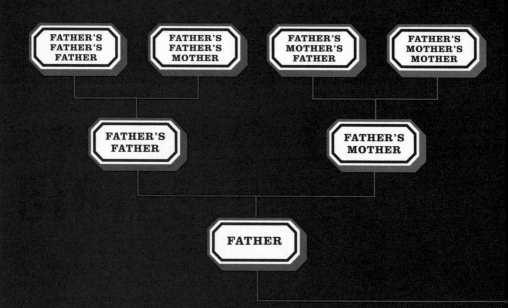

FATHER'S FATHER'S FATHER

FATHER'S FATHER'S MOTHER

FATHER'S MOTHER'S FATHER

FATHER'S MOTHER'S MOTHER

FATHER'S FATHER

FATHER'S MOTHER

FATHER

BROTHER

BEFORE YOU START TO fill it in, take a look at the way the tree works. You are the base of the tree and all the branches and leaves going upward show the many members of your family. Directly above you are your parents. And directly above them are their parents. Got it?

As you add people's names, try to include personal notes and details wherever possible. For example, under Aunt Margie Wilmer, if she had a funny nickname, write that down. Did Aunt Margie like to sew? Write it down. Keep track of everything! The fun of genealogy is all about the details. Someday, when you get really good at sewing, you could trace it back to Margie. How cool is that?

The format for the squares, beginning with you and your own parents:

- Your name
- Born when and where
- Also known as (nickname)
- Place where you live
- Job

TAKE NOTE!

All items on your family tree that appear on the same line

FAMILY TREE

```
MOTHER'S          MOTHER'S          MOTHER'S          MOTHER'S
FATHER'S          FATHER'S          MOTHER'S          MOTHER'S
FATHER            MOTHER            FATHER            MOTHER

        MOTHER'S                        MOTHER'S
        FATHER                          MOTHER

                         MOTHER

married

YOU              SISTER
```

or level, are considered members of the same generation.

If someone is still alive, just leave the date of death blank.

Use abbreviations to make things easier to read. B = Born; D = Died; M = Married; and P = Place.

If you're adopted, fill in the names of your adoptive mother and father, and so on. And if you happen to know or have a relationship with your birth mother and father, find a place on the tree for their names, too.

If you have a stepparent, make sure to add in stepparent names, stepsiblings, and other important people from your family.

Family trees don't just have to feature facts. Turn your tree into a family memory forest. If genealogy is all about your roots, that includes culture, upbringing, traditions, and more. So dig down deep! Take notes about your experiences, memories, and life lessons learned from various family members.

AUTOGRAPH-O-RAMA

IN A WORLD OF BLOGS AND MySpace pages, some old-fashioned traditions like writing letters (on paper! oh my!) are getting lost. But autographs—in little books, in yearbooks, and even on casts—still survive. Usually, the greetings go something like this:

2 Good 2 Be 4 Gotten! C U Next Yr! xox Susi! And of course there's the beloved, "Roses are red, violets are blue. . . ."

Many years ago, when the fine art of autographing was in full bloom, rhymes were a way to be clever and witty—and make up a ditty. Some classic examples:

It tickles me and makes me laugh
To think you want my autograph.

Remember Grant. Remember Lee.
To heck with them. Remember me.

Your future lies before you like the freshly fallen snow
Be careful where you walk, for every step will show.

Every time it rains I think of you:
Drip, drip, drip.

God made the rivers, God made the lakes.
God made you. We all make mistakes!

Your album is a golden spot
In which to write Forget Me Not.

If U B U and I B I
It's EZ to C the reason Y
I like U and U like I.

Maybe next time you sign a yearbook or write a message on the belly of a stuffed Build-A-Bear, you can surprise everyone with an alternate greeting from another era. If you're looking for even more autograph ideas, check out the list of "yours till the . . ." sign-offs on page 147.

NAME GAME

WHEN I WAS IN FIFTH GRADE, I had autograph books, for sure. But I also kept a separate, tiny notebook of names. I considered myself a genuine collector. If I heard a weird name, I wrote it down (over and over again!). For example, if I liked someone named John Smith*, my notebook page would look a little something like this:

Laura Smith   MRS. JOHN Smith!   Laura + John
Laura & John Smith   Mrs. Dower-Smith   ♡♡♡
Mrs. Laura Smith   Ms. Laura Dower-Smith   LD + JS

And so on. Sometimes I'd doodle about 100 possible child names, too, also with the last name Smith. This could go on for hours. You know what I'm talking about. I read somewhere that author J. K. Rowling kept a name notebook, too—and look where it got her!

The truth is, names are incredibly revealing, and playing any kind of name game says a lot about who we are. I always loved names like Hamlet and Ophelia and so many others from William Shakespeare's plays (see below). I also love names from different places around the world. Do you see *your name* anywhere on the next pages?

You may think about using some of these names for

    a) your very, very far-off-in-the-future offspring

    b) your top-secret alias

    c) the next character in your creative writing assignment

* Actual names of my die-hard childhood crushes have been changed to protect the embarrassed; namely, me!

TO BE OR NOT TO BE . . . A NAME FROM SHAKESPEARE

• Aemilia	• Cordelia	• Hamlet	• Nathaniel	• Rosalind
• Angus	• Cymbeline	• Hermione	• Nerissa	• Stephano
• Antipholus	• Desdemona	• Hortensius	• Ophelia	• Timon
• Balthazar	• Dogberry	• Juliet	• Orsino	• Toby
• Bardolph	• Elbow	• Laertes	• Othello	• Tybalt
• Benedick	• Fabian	• Leontes	• Perdita	• Ursula
• Bianca	• Ferdinand	• Lysander	• Pistol	• Valentine
• Caliban	• Florizel	• Malvolio	• Portia	• Viola
• Cassio	• Goneril	• Miranda	• Roderigo	

AROUND THE WORLD IN 110 NAMES

Here are some of the twenty-first century's top names from across the globe. Is your name here? Do you know what your name means?

ARABIC NAMES, 2006

RANK	GIRL NAME	MEANING	BOY NAME	MEANING
1	A'idah	Reward	A'waan	Helper
2	Afra	White	Xavier	Bright
3	Bilqis	Queen of Sheba	Aadam	Earth
4	Ra'eesa	Leader	Amjad	Rewarding
5	A'ishah	Lively	Ayman	Lucky

ENGLAND & WALES, 2006

RANK	GIRL NAME	MEANING	BOY NAME	MEANING
1	Olivia	Olive tree	Jack	God is gracious
2	Grace	Good will, agreeable	Mohammed	Praiseworthy
3	Jessica	God sees	Thomas	Twin
4	Ruby	Red	Joshua	God is salvation
5	Emily	Rival	Oliver	Olive tree

FRANCE, 2006

RANK	GIRL NAME	MEANING	BOY NAME	MEANING
1	Emma	Entire, whole	Enzo	Crowned with laurels
2	Lea	Weary	Mathis	Gift of God
3	Manon	Beloved	Lucas	Light
4	Clara	Bright	Hugo	Heart and mind
5	Chloe	Blooming	Matheo	Gift of God

GERMANY, 2006

RANK	GIRL NAME	MEANING	BOY NAME	MEANING
1	Anna	Favor, grace	Lucas	Light
2	Leoni	Lion	Leon	Lion
3	Lea	Weary	Luca	Light
4	Lena	Short for Helena, Magdalena, etc.	Tim	God's honor
5	Hannah	Gracious, merciful	Paul	Small

ICELAND, 2004

RANK	GIRL NAME	MEANING	BOY NAME	MEANING
1	Guðrún	God	Jón	God is gracious
2	Anna	Favor, grace	Sigurður	Protector in a battle
3	Sigríður	Beautiful victory	Guðmundur	Hand of God
4	Kristin	Follower of Christ	Gunnar	Warrior
5	Margret	Pearl	Olafur	Ancestor

ISRAEL, 2005

RANK	GIRL NAME	MEANING	BOY NAME	MEANING
1	Noa	Movement	Uri	My light, flame
2	Shira	Poetry	Noam	Pleasantness
3	Agam	To be sad	Itai	Friendly
4	Maya	Water	Ido	To be mighty
5	Tamar	Palm tree	David	Beloved

JAPAN, 2005

RANK	GIRL NAME	MEANING*	BOY NAME	MEANING*
1	Hina	Sunlight & greens	Yuuki	Gentleness & hope
2	Yui	Superiority & clothing	Haruto	Sunlight & to soar
3	Miyu	Beautiful superiority	Souta	Smoothly & big
4	Haruka	Distant, spring flower	Yuuto	Gentleness & to soar
5	Sakura	Cherry blossom	Haruki	Clear up life

* Japanese names are typically a combination of two symbols with distinct meanings

SPAIN, 2005

RANK	GIRL NAME	MEANING	BOY NAME	MEANING
1	Lucia	Light	Alejandro	Protector
2	Maria	Beloved	Daniel	God is my judge
3	Paula	Little	Pablo	Humble
4	Laura	Crowned with laurels	David	Beloved
5	Marta	Lady	Adrian	From Hadria

SWEDEN, 2006

RANK	GIRL NAME	MEANING	BOY NAME	MEANING
1	Emma	Entire, whole	Lucas	Light
2	Maja	Mother	Oscar	Spear of the gods
3	Agnes	Chaste, holy	William	Strong-willed warrior
4	Julia	Youth	Elias	Lord is my God
5	Alva	Elf	Filip	Horse lover

UNITED STATES (TOP NAMES OVERALL), 2006

RANK	GIRL NAME	MEANING	BOY NAME	MEANING
1	Emily	Rival	Jacob	Supplanter or literally, "holder of the heel"
2	Emma	Entire, whole	Michael	Who is the God
3	Madison	Son of Matthew/Maud	Joshua	God is salvation
4	Isabella	God is my oath	Ethan	Solid, enduring
5	Ava	Like a bird	Matthew	Gift of God

UNITED STATES (TOP HISPANIC NAMES), 2005

RANK	GIRL NAME	MEANING	BOY NAME	MEANING
1	Maria	Star of the sea	José	Of God
2	Sofia	Wisdom	Angel	Messenger
3	Isabel	God's promise	Juan	God is gracious
4	Adriana	From Hadria	Diego	He who succeeds
5	Daniela	God is my judge	Carlos	Free man

For more information on these and other names, including your own, you can surf some great sites on the Internet: www.20000-names.com, www.babynames.com, www.behindthenames.com

(ALSO KNOWN AS)

S OMETIMES PEOPLE ALTER THEIR NAMES for movie, modeling, or musical stardom. When they do this, they adopt a false name or a pseudonym. Stars have even been known to make up additional pseudonyms, when checking into hotel rooms to protect their identities! Here's a short list of famous gals and the names they were really born with:

Jennifer Aniston	Jennifer Anastassakis
Carmen Electra	Tara Patrick
Gloria Estefan	Gloria Maria Milagrosa Fajardo Garcia
Jodie Foster	Alicia Christian Foster
Whoopi Goldberg	Caryn Johnson
Audrey Hepburn	Edda van Heemstra Hepburn-Ruston
Billie Holiday	Eleanora Fagan
Diane Keaton	Diane Hall
Tea Leoni	Elizabeth Tea Pantleoni
Courtney Love	Courtney Michelle Harrison
Andie MacDowell	Rosalie Anderson MacDowell
Elle MacPherson	Eleanor Gow
Madonna	Madonna Louise Ciccone
Joni Mitchell	Roberta Joan Anderson
Marilyn Monroe	Norma Jeane Mortenson
Demi Moore	Demetria Guynes
Julianne Moore	Julie Anne Smith
Natalie Portman	Natalie Hershlag
Meg Ryan	Margaret Mary Emily Anne Hyra
Winona Ryder	Winona Horowitz
Meryl Streep	Mary Louise Streep
Donna Summer	LaDonna Gaines
Tina Turner	Anna Mae Bullock
Shania Twain	Eilleen Regina Edwards
Reese Witherspoon	Laura Jeanne Reese Witherspoon

MATCH THAT PRINCESS!

YOU CAN'T HAVE A BOOK ABOUT GIRLS without mentioning princesses, can you? Some are made up from books or movies. Others are found in real life. But all seem to have one thing in common: a range of power, strength, wit, smarts, and beauty. Can you match each princess with her description?

Princess Caraboo 1

Pocahontas 2

Diana, Princess of Wales 3

Princess Diana of the Amazon 4

Ariel 5

Aurora 6

Belle 7

Cinderella 8

Jasmine 9

Mulan 10

Snow White 11

Princess Leia Organa 12

Princess Zelda 13

Princess of Genovia 14

Princess Buttercup 15

Princess Fiona 16

a Chinese princess who fought the Huns

b Her beautiful voice is stolen by Ursula, the sea witch

c Indian chief Powhatan's daughter, whose name means "playful girl"

d Hates Prince Humperdinck in *The Princess Bride*

e She tames the Beast

f Princess of video game fame

g She wore the glass slipper

h Nineteenth-century maid pretending to be from the exotic land of Javasu

i Also known as Sleeping Beauty

j Falls for Aladdin

k She's from outer space

l Main character in Meg Cabot's *The Princess Diaries*

m Also known as Wonder Woman

n She lived with seven dwarfs

o Married Prince Charles of England

p Moves to the swamp with Shrek

Answers: 1h, 2c, 3o, 4m, 5b, 6i, 7e, 8g, 9j, 10a, 11n, 12k, 13f, 14l, 15d, 16p

BIRTHSTONES

What would a princess be without the jewel in her crown? Each of us has at least one birthstone that relates to the month of our birth. What does yours say about you?

JANUARY
GARNET

The word *garnet* comes from the Latin word *granatum*, which means seed. This stone looks a lot like a deep, red pomegranate seed. Way back in 3100 B.C., Egyptians used garnets in their jewelry. It stood for eternal friendship, trust, and strength.

FEBRUARY
AMETHYST

Amethyst is a light purple quartz stone that is supposed to protect you from poison. Ancient Greeks and Romans thought the stone would keep the wearer clearheaded. Put an amethyst under your pillow to bring about pleasant dreams.

MARCH
AQUAMARINE

The name for this gemstone comes from the Latin words *aqua*, meaning water, and *marina*, meaning the sea. Its beautiful pale, blue-green color is supposed to keep the wearer cool and calm. Ancient people thought it protected sailors from harm.

APRIL
DIAMOND

Diamonds stand for inspiration. They may appear colorless, but they actually come in a rainbow of hues including yellow, red, pink, blue, and green. Here's the rule: The deeper the color of the diamond, the higher its value. Diamonds are a typical stone found in engagement rings and in tiaras, and they are the hardest gemstone in existence. A diamond can cut right through a piece of glass!

MAY
EMERALD

Derived from the Latin word *smaragdus*, an emerald is a green stone that comes from the mineral beryl. The stone, mined in Egypt as early as 330 B.C., was the sacred stone of the goddess Venus. It has been known for centuries as a symbol of rebirth, and the person who wears it will have good fortune.

JUNE
PEARL OR
MOONSTONE

Pearls, the only stones made inside a living creature (the oyster), have been treasured for centuries. The 1500s were known as the Pearl Age. Moonstones have a floating play of color and light inside the stone (called *adularescence*), but they stand for confidence. The Roman natural historian Pliny named the stone for the changing cycles of the moon.

JULY
RUBY

Rubies are supposed to bring health, wisdom, wealth, and success in love to whoever wears them. The deep, red color of the gem is most important to its value. It is the second-hardest stone after the diamond. What are

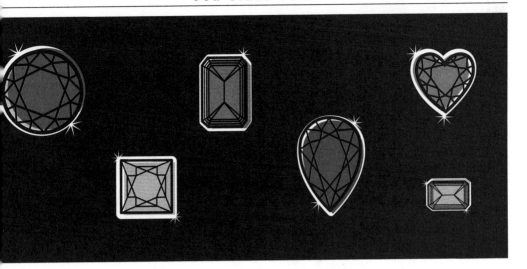

some the most famous rubies ever worn? That has to be Dorothy's ruby slippers in *The Wizard of Oz*!

AUGUST
PERIDOT OR SARDONYX

Got nightmares? Peridot is supposed to protect you! This gemstone (ranging in colors from olive to lime green) comes from volcanoes. Legend says the stone is actually the tears of Pele, the goddess of fire and volcanoes. Sardonyx, with its alternating layers of reddish brown and white banding, was carried into battle by ancient Greeks and Romans. They engraved the stone with images of Mars, the god of war, and Hercules, known for his supernatural strength.

SEPTEMBER
SAPPHIRE

According to folklore, sapphire will protect you and your loved ones from jealousy. To medieval people, the stone represented the skies and heaven. Fun fact: Although it is the most common color, not all sapphires are blue. There are red, pink, and green sapphires, too.

OCTOBER
TOURMALINE OR OPAL

Tourmaline comes in different color combinations like watermelon tourmaline that has green, pink, and white color bands sliced to look just like the fruit! The word *opal* comes from the Greek *opallos*, meaning "to see a change (of color)." Centuries ago, a kind of crystal gel flowed into gaps in sedimentary layers of earth. With time, heat, and shifts in the ground, the gel hardened into the iridescent opal stones we see today.

NOVEMBER
TOPAZ OR CITRINE

For thousands of years, all yellow gems in antiquity were called topaz, but this isn't entirely right. For one thing, not all topaz is yellow. Imperial topaz, named after the Russian czars of the 1800s, comes in brilliant orange and pink. Also, some yellow stones are actually quartz. Citrine (aka "healing quartz") will give you health and positive energy.

DECEMBER
TURQUOISE OR ZIRCON

Although turquoise comes from the French for "Turkish stone" and is one of the oldest gemstones—dating back to the thirteenth century—we probably know it best from the jewelry of the American Southwest. Zircon comes from the Arabic words *zar* and *gun*, meaning gold and color, although the red variety of the stone is the most prized color. A colorless zircon stone called *cubic zirconia* is used to imitate diamonds.

DEADLIEST DIAMOND EVER!

THERE ARE MANY legends (some fact, most rumor) about one of the most famous gemstones in the history of the world, known to us now as the Hope Diamond. The big question on everyone's mind is: can one stone curse more then 10 generations of people who came into contact with it? Or is all this one gem of a tall tale?

OWNER #1:

A statue of the Hindu goddess Sita. Her curse? Having a beautiful, enormous blue diamond stolen from her forehead.

OWNER #2:

Jean Baptiste Tavernier, a French jeweler traveling in India, lifted the 112 ³⁄₁₆ carat blue diamond and pocketed it. His curse? Some stories say he was eaten by wolves and died shortly after selling the stone.

OWNER #3:

Louis XIV, the Sun King, who bought the large, blue diamond and had it re-cut in 1673 to enhance its brilliance. At a new 67 ⅛ carats, he named it the "Blue Diamond of the Crown" and wore it on a long ribbon around his neck. He was the first of many generations of French Kings (Louis XIV, Louis XV, and Louis XVI) to own the stone. His curse? He lost all of his teeth and then died a slow, painful death from gangrene.

OWNERS #4:

Louis XV was only five years of age when he came into power. The stone wasn't a major player in his reign. His curse? Out of his ten children only two were boys and only one of those survived. The remaining son would be Louis XVI.

OWNER #5:

In the 18th century, Louis XVI became king of France with Marie Antoinette as his queen, the diamond came back! The curse? While the diamond was in their possession, king and queen met cruel fate . . . at the guillotine. They were both beheaded during the French Revolution. Then the blue diamond disappeared.

OWNER #6:

King George IV of England, whose jeweler recut it again to mask its identity. It now weighed approximately 44 carats. His curse? Massive debt. After his death, the diamond was sold to pay off his creditors.

OWNER #7:

Henry Philip Hope, banking heir and collector of fine art and gems got the famed blue diamond. It was then nick-

named The Hope Diamond. His curse? Irresponsible descendants (see Owner #8).

OWNER #8:

After the eldest Hope's son, Henry Thomas Hope, inherited the stone, it passed through the hands of a few other Hope family members, before landing in the jewel box of grandson Francis Hope. His curse? A serious gambling and high spending problem. The jewel was sold again.

OWNER #9:

Evalyn Walsh McLean came into the stone via Pierre Cartier, a jeweler in the U.S. A very rich woman, McLean fiercely believed that objects usually considered bad luck turned into good luck for her. So she wore the famed Hope Diamond all the time. She didn't even take off the necklace for an operation on her throat! Unfortunately, she

was to have the worst luck of all. Her first born son, Vinson, died in a car crash when he was only nine. Her daughter committed suicide at age twenty-five. And her husband was declared insane and confined to a mental institution! After so many years, the curse was alive and well— and the name Hope Diamond probably should have been changed to Hopeless.

OWNER #10:

Harry Winston, a jeweler, got the stone and immediately donated the Hope Diamond to the Smithsonian Institution in Washington, D.C. It became the focal point of a newly established National Gem and Mineral Collection in the National Museum of Natural History. You can still see it today . . . if you dare to see the cursed jewel up close and personal!

MOOD RINGS

A MOOD RING ON YOUR finger can say a lot about how you're feeling and what's humming inside your head. Here's how it works: The stone set in a mood ring is actually a hollow glass shell with liquid crystals inside that change and twist as temperatures change. For example, if your finger is hot, a mood ring may change to red, purple, or green. Without heat, the ring may stay a cold, black color. The fun part: Every color is associated with a particular "mood" or trait. And the ring won't lie (at least it usually works for me!).

RED = Excited, Feeling Adventurous

ORANGE = Big Ideas, Daring

GREEN = Hopeful, Not Stressed

YELLOW = Imaginative, Wondering

LIGHT BLUE = Calm, Relaxed, Lovable

DARK BLUE = In Love, Very Happy

PINK = Afraid, Lots of Questions

PURPLE = Not Sure How You're Feeling

BLACK = Tense, Nervous

WHITE = Frustrated, Bored

LIGHT BROWN = Restless, Waiting for Something

FORTUNE-T

T HERE ARE SO MANY WAYS TO READ and tell fortunes. Some people use Magic 8-Balls, although I always seem to get the same, lame answer whenever I use mine: *Reply hazy, try again.* The twenty standard Magic 8-Ball responses are:

As I see it, yes
Ask again later
Better not tell you now
Cannot predict now
Concentrate and ask again
Don't count on it
It is certain
It is decidedly so
Most likely
My reply is no
My sources say no
Outlook good
Outlook not so good
Reply hazy, try again
Signs point to yes
Very doubtful
Without a doubt
Yes
Yes–definitely
You may rely on it

But isn't there something more that fate has to tell me? There are fancier—and more tried and true—ways to explore your fate. Take your pick.

CRYSTAL BALL

What it is: A glass orb with special power, usually made from rock crystal.

What it does: Lets you "see" the future, literally. This is called "scrying."

How to use: Rub your hands over it, say a few incantations (spells), and focus your gaze on the ball.

The inside scoop: Celtic priests called Druids began using crystals to divine the future in the fifteenth century. (Fun fact: Druids were also the guys who supposedly built that mysterious landmark in England called Stonehenge, way before they used crys-

ELLING 101

tal balls). Other common crystal users from medieval times: gypsies, psychics, and wizards.

Extra credit: Best movies with crystal ball scenes: *Big, Fantasia, Harry Potter and the Sorcerer's Stone, Sleeping Beauty,* and *Snow White and the Seven Dwarfs.*

TEA LEAVES

What they are: You can "read" tea leaves as they settle on the bottom of your teacup.

What they do: Predict your future.

How to use: Make a piping hot cup of loose tea in a white cup. Wait until the leaves sink, then drink the liquid. "Read" the leaves that have settled on the bottom. You need to be familiar with all the possible symbols and their interpretations. Even more than that, you need to be able to distinguish and identify one clump from another. That's the real trick. An easy "clump" detecting chart is shown below.

The inside scoop: In *Harry Potter and the Prisoner of Azkaban,* Hermione is upset by Professor Trelawney's predictions from a cup of tea leaves. What appears? A wicked dog called the Grim. Its appearance is an omen that Harry will die.

WHAT YOUR CLUMPS MEAN

Arrow . . . you're getting some big news
Bell . . . someone is giving you good news
Boat . . . a friend is coming to visit
Bridge . . . you're going on a journey
Butterfly . . . happiness is on the way
Circles . . . you will be getting money
Crescent moon . . . good fortune
Forked line . . . you need to make a decision
Heart . . . Love is coming your way
Squares . . . you will get comfort and peace
Star . . . excellent luck
Triangles . . . one point up = good luck, but one point down = bad luck
Volcano . . . you're going to be so mad
Wavy lines . . . you will suffer a loss
Zebra . . . you'll be traveling far and wide*

*I'm sorry, but if you can see a zebra in a clump of tea, you are a total genius.

RUNES

What they are: Viking alphabet used for writing and magic. But they aren't your usual ABCs. Instead, the Runic alphabet is called FUTHARK after its first six letters/sounds

(see the chart below).

What they do: Rune masters are specially trained to bring runes into play for divination and sorcery. A Viking poet once said, "Let no man carve runes to cast a spell, save first he learns to

Rune Symbol	Rune Name	Meaning	Sound
ᚠ	Fehu	Money, new start	F
ᚢ	Uruz	Strength, health	U
ᚦ	Thorn	Force	TH
ᚨ	Ansuz	Intellect	A
ᚱ	Raidho	Power, control	R
ᚲ	Kenaz	Artistic ability	K
ᚷ	Gebo	Generosity, honor	G
ᚹ	Wunjo	Joy, luck, prosperity	W
ᚺ	Hagalaz	Harmony	H
ᚾ	Nauthiz	Necessity	N
ᛁ	Isa	Unity, self-control	I
ᛃ	Jera	Peace	J
ᛈ	Pertho	Good omen	P
ᛇ	Eiwhaz	Protection	E
ᛉ	Algiz	Awareness	Z
ᛋ	Sowelu	Hope, success	S
ᛏ	Tiwaz	Truth, victory	T
ᛒ	Berkano	Birth, freedom	B
ᛖ	Ehwaz	Trust	E
ᛗ	Mannaz	Humanity	M
ᛚ	Lagiz	Flow, growth	L
ᛜ	Inguz	Resting	ING
ᛟ	Odala	Home	O
ᛞ	Dagaz	Happiness	D

read them well." Each of the twenty-four runes has a special meaning based on a) what is inscribed on the rune, and b) the rune material (ceramic, stone, wood/bark, or even metal). Viking warriors would sometimes carve runic inscriptions on their swords to protect them.

How to use: Cast runes on the ground and then read them from left to right to tell someone's fortune. But you might want to get one of those rune masters to help you!

The inside scoop: Check out a book of Norse mythology and read the story of Odin, who was speared to a tree for nine windy nights while he learned the mysteries of the runes—and then passed those mysteries onto his people.

TAROT CARDS

What they are: A tarot deck consists of seventy-eight cards. There are the twenty-two Major Arcana cards (Arcana means "life secrets"). The Major Arcana cards include the Fool, the Wheel of Fortune, and the Magician. There are also fifty-six Minor Arcana cards. The Minor Arcana are like a modern card deck with four suits. But the suits here are not clubs, hearts, spades, and diamonds. The tarot suits are cups, wands, swords, and pentacles.

What they do: Tarot tells you what's going on in your life right now.

How to use: The cards tell stories based on their placement in the spread. A person who wants his or her cards read (called a "seeker") must focus on an important question. Sometimes, the reader will let a seeker shuffle or cut the deck so the cards can "get" the question firsthand.

The inside scoop: Tarot symbols are thought to have originated in ancient China, India, or Egypt, but there is little evidence of the formal use of tarot cards before the eighteenth century. Two cool (and random) superstitions about tarot: 1) You should let someone else buy your first deck of cards; and 2) If you keep a deck, you should wrap it in silk and store it safely in a little box.

Extra credit: Don't get tarot mixed up with taro root, a potatolike starchy food found in West Africa, Hawaii, and the Polynesian Islands.

Lay it out there: One of the most common tarot card layouts is called the Celtic Cross. See the diagram below.

To read the cards, you must interpret them in order based on the face value of the card. Each card has its own story.

Card 1: This card represents the seeker's overall personality. It is sometimes called the Significator card.

Card 2: This card shows the most important things that influence the seeker. That's why it's placed over the first card in the layout.

Card 3: This card shows the things the seeker is striving for. That's why it is placed above the other cards in the layout.

Card 4: This card represents the foundation of the seeker's question and/or background. That's why it is placed beneath the other cards in the layout.

Card 5: This card shows the things that have already happened.

Card 6: This card shows what lies ahead.

Card 7: This card represents the seeker's disposition or attitude about things.

Card 8: This card represents the seeker's influence on others.

Card 9: This card represents hopes and fears.

Card 10: This card is the overall outcome of the reading.

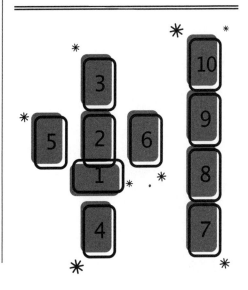

WOW! WOW! OUIJA BOARD!

THE OUIJA BOARD GOT ITS NAME FROM the combination of the French and German words for "yes," *oui* and *ja*.

Popular use of Ouija (pronounced "weejee") boards started with the American Spiritualism movement in the mid-nineteenth century. Peo-

Fig. 1 The Ouija has a flat surface printed with letters, numbers, and other symbols that are meant to reveal secret messages from the spirit world.

Fig. 2 The sun means "yes," or conditions favorable.

Fig. 3 The moon with the single star means "no," or conditions unfavorable.

Fig. 4 GOODBYE on the board means stop your session. No one is listening.

Fig. 5 The people in the lower corners don't mean much of anything and are just part of the design.

Fig. 6 A planchette is a little triangular piece that moves around the board. The word planchette is French for "little plank." You and everyone else who is playing press gently with your fingertips on this piece to see where it goes.

Fig. 7 Wherever the planchette moves (and stops), that reveals a particular letter or number. The same process is repeated again and again until the letters and numbers spell out a message.

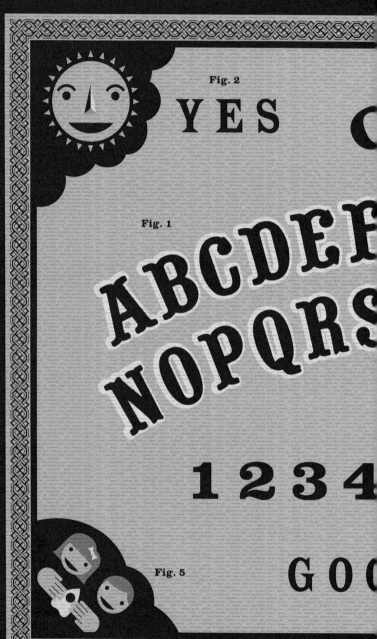

Fig. 2

Fig. 1

YES

ABCDEF
NOPQRS

1 2 3 4

G O O

Fig. 5

ple liked to divine (or tell) the future using different techniques. Some would swing a pendulum over a plate with letters around the edge, and wherever the pendulum swung spelled out a message.

One of the coolest rumored Ouija board encounters comes from the White House! During sleepovers with her friends, President Jimmy Carter's daughter, Amy, reportedly used a Ouija board to contact the spirit of Abraham Lincoln, who is believed to haunt the Lincoln Bedroom.

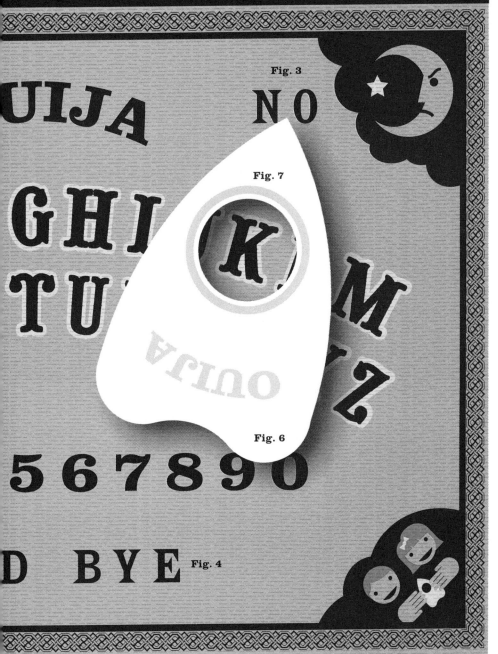

Fig. 3

Fig. 7

Fig. 6

Fig. 4

HOW TO TELL
A GREAT GHOST STORY

1. Turn out the lights. Darkness is the most important tool you have to get everyone's imagination churning.

2. Hold a flashlight up to your face while you tell the story. For a real air of mystery, like a creepy spotlight, hold it above your head. For an air of terror, so your face looks weird and distorted, hold it under your chin.

3. As you speak, use your best voice distortions like the cackle, the whisper, and the rasp. Speak in a soft voice whenever possible. That way, everyone has to pay extra close attention to your words—and it increases the chance that they'll be caught off guard with a scare tactic.

4. Build tension from the start. Open your story with a happy, ordinary setting like your own town or school. Remember that you want to start slow and build suspense, keeping everyone on the edge of their seats. Tell the story of how you and your friends are just hanging out when . . . [insert cliff-hanger here!]

5. Plan your chilling cliff-hangers in advance. Samples:
   • . . . they hear a strange noise (you make a noise).
   • . . . someone screams (you scream).
   • . . . the lights go out (you turn off your flashlight).

6. Become a master of cool sound effects. A good "WHAM!" in the middle of a calm storytelling moment really makes people jump. Some sounds you can make with your body; others may need to be prerecorded. See the list on the next page.

You're setting the scene for a pretty fearful experience, but one thing you don't have to worry about with your best pals is PARTHENOPHOBIA. That's the fear of *girls*!

7. Introduce your scariest character and describe that person in detail. Include every oozing wart, the bad breath, deep rattling voice, and whatever else makes him or her scary.

8. Build one cliff-hanger upon another, building to key moments in your story.

9. Alternate plan: Start your story, but instead of doing all the work yourself, get *everyone* involved. Everyone adds a detail as you go around the circle. Many imaginations are better than just one. Or you could get an accomplice to help tell your story. That person could flicker a light or slam a door while you're speaking.

10. Whether you tell the story alone or as a group, remember your key goal is to scare. Think about the plots and characters in TV, movies, and books that have given you goose bumps before now. Some spine-tingling stuff:

• Heavy rain
• Screeching bats
• Rattling chains
• Howling wolves
• Squirmy worms
• Sharp, gnashing teeth
• Angry aliens
• Mad scientists
• Thunder and lightning
• Squeaking doors

THE MOST HAUNTED HOUSE EVER!

BELIEVE IT OR NOT, ONE of the most haunted places in the U.S. is the White House! There have been more than eight ghosts seen there over the years, including Abigail Adams doing her laundry in the East Room, Dolley Madison watching over the Rose Garden, President Andrew Johnson pacing and laughing in the Rose Room, and President William Henry Harrison hunting through boxes in the attic. Of course, Harrison *was* the first president to die in office, so his ghostly presence makes sense.

But the biggest apparition seen at Pennsylvania Avenue has to be Abe Lincoln. He's been spotted by numerous heads of state and visitors to the White House over the years, looking concerned as he stared through the Oval Office windows, knocking on guest bedroom doors, or taking off his boots before going to bed. President John F. Kennedy's butler said that Lincoln appeared often and was always polite. He'd tap you on the shoulder or cough slightly so you would notice his presence.

SOME ADVICE FROM

(WHO HAPPENS TO BE A GUY, BUT WE WON'

Mark Twain (also known as Samuel Langhorne Clemens) was clever, funny, and above all else, he knew how to tell a terrific story. His nineteenth-century book *The Adventures of Huckleberry Finn* has been called The Great American Novel. Here is some advice from this expert about how to put the s-s-scare in your story. Twain often wrote stories using a dialect like the people in his small town in Missouri.

"I do not claim that I can tell a story as it ought to be told. I only claim to know how a story ought to be told, for I have been almost daily in the company of the most expert storytellers for years. . . .

"The pause is an exceedingly important feature in any kind of story, and a frequently recurring feature, too. It is a dainty thing, and delicate, and also uncertain and treacherous; for it must be exactly the right length—no more and no less—or it fails of its purpose and makes trouble. If the pause is too short the impressive point is passed, and the audience have had time to divine that a surprise is intended—and then you can't surprise them, of course. . . .

"I used to tell a . . . ghost story that had a pause in front of the snapper* on the end, and that pause was the most important thing in the whole story. If I got it the right length precisely, I could spring the finishing ejaculation with effect enough to make some impressionable girl deliver a startled little yelp and jump out of her seat—and that was what I was after. This story was called *The Golden Arm*, and was told in this fashion. You can practice with it yourself—and mind you look out for the pause and get it right."

THE GOLDEN ARM

ONCE 'PON A TIME dey wuz a monsus mean man, en he live 'way out in de prairie all 'lone by hisself, 'cep'n he had a wife. En bimeby she died, en he tuck en toted her way out dah in de prairie en buried her. Well, she had a golden arm—all solid gold, fum de shoulder down. He wuz pow'ful mean—pow'ful; en dat night he couldn't sleep, caze he want dat golden arm so bad.

When it come midnight he couldn't stan' it no mo'; so he git up, he did, en tuck his lantern en shoved out thoo de storm en dug her up en got de golden arm; en he bent his head down 'gin de win', en plowed en plowed en plowed thoo de snow. Den all on a sudden he stop (make a considerable pause here, and look startled, and take a listening attitude) en say: "My lan', what's dat!"

En he listen—en listen—en de win' say (set your teeth together and imitate the wailing and wheezing singsong of the wind), "Bzzz-z-zzz"—en den, way back yonder what de grave is, he hear a voice!—he hear a voice all mix' up in de win'—can't hardly tell 'em 'part—"Bzzz-zzz—W-h-o—g-o-t—m-y—g-o-l-d-e-n—arm?—zzz—zzz—W-h-o g-o-t m-y g-o-l-d-e-n arm?" (You must begin to shiver violently now.)

En he begin to shiver en shake, en say, "Oh, my! Oh,

*Pssst! A "snapper" is like a punch line or an "a-ha!" moment in the story.

AN EXPERT

(HOLD THAT AGAINST HIM)

my lan'!" en de win' blow de lantern out, en de snow en sleet blow in his face en mos' choke him, en he start a-plowin' knee-deep toward home mos' dead, he so sk'y-erd—en pooty soon he hear de voice agin, en (pause) it 'us comin' after him! "Bzzz—zzz—zzz—W-h-o—g-o-t—m-y g-o-l-d-e-n—arm?"

When he git to de pasture he hear it agin—closter now, en a-comin'!—a-comin' back dah in de dark en de storm—(repeat the wind and the voice). When he git to de house he rush up-stairs en jump in de bed en kiver up, head and years, en lay dah shiverin' en shakin'—en den way out dah he hear it agin!—en a-comin'! En bime-by he hear (pause—awed, lis-tening attitude)—pat—pat—pat—hit's a-comin' up-stairs! Den he hear de latch, en he know it's in de room!

Den pooty soon he know it's a-stannin' by de bed! (Pause.) Den—he know it's a-bendin' down over him—en he cain't skasely git his breath! Den—den—he seem to feel someth'n c-o-l-d, right down 'most agin his head!

(Pause.)

Den de voice say, right at his year—"W-h-o—g-o-t—m-y—g-o-l-d-e-n arm?" (You must wail it out very plain-tively and accusingly; then you stare steadily and impressively into the face of the farthest-gone auditor—a girl, preferably—and let that awe-inspiring pause begin to build itself in the deep hush. When it has reached exactly the right length, jump sud-denly at that girl and yell, "You've got it!" If you've got the pause right, she'll fetch a dear little yelp and spring right out of her shoes. But you must get the pause right; and you will find it the most troublesome and aggravating and uncertain thing you ever undertook.)

By the way, Mark Twain says in a few places here that the goal is to frighten the girl in the group. As if we're all chickens? Puh-lease! That is sooooo nineteenth century.

Main text excerpted from *How to Tell a Story* (1897) by Mark Twain

LIGHT AS A FEATHER, STIFF AS A BOARD

SLEEPOVER PARTY alert! You must try this at your next get-together. A little mood lighting and music will help set the stage. Your goal: levitation. Yes, you can lift your friend into the air with little more than your fingertips.

The most common ver-sion of this "trick" requires at least five people. One person (let's call him or her THE BODY) lies relaxed on the floor with eyes closed. The other four participants surround THE BODY, one on each side, one at the head, and one at the feet. Each of the participants places two fingers of each hand beneath THE BODY. With eyes closed, they begin to chant, "Light as a feather . . . stiff as a board . . ." over and over. With just the slightest effort, the participants should be able to raise THE BODY off the floor. Whoa! Talk about gravity-defying! Is something supernatural helping you?

SOUND EFFECTS EVERYONE CAN MAKE

- **RAIN** Shake rice in a pan or spray water into a bucket.
- **RAINSTORM** You need a larger group for this one to work best. Have a few people rub their palms together softly so it sounds like rain; then someone starts to snap, and then another person stomps her feet. With all the noises working together, it simulates the sounds of a real storm.
- **TRAIN** Put a handful of paper clips into a metal box or coffee tin and shake. It sounds like the chug-a-chug on the train track.
- **FIRE** Crumple cellophane or plastic to imitate the sound of crackling flames.
- **PLANE** Whistle high, and then get softer as if the plane sound gets lower.
- **MOTOR** Stick cardboard pieces between your bike spokes and spin the wheel. Or, turn on a blender.
- **WIND** Blow air into a microphone. This works well if you blow into a mic on a stereo or even on one of those cheap, plastic microphones you can get at the dollar store.
- **GALLOPING HORSE** Slap your hands on your thighs, one at a time.
- **PUNCH** Actually punch one fist into your palm.
- **THUD** Pound your fist into a cushy pillow.
- **FOOTSTEPS** Make actual footsteps with a shoe that has a hard heel (or any hard object) on a hard floor.
- **SWAMP MUSIC** In a high and then a low voice, say over and over again, "knee-deep, knee-deep, ribbit, ribbit, knee-deep . . ."
- **EXPLOSION** Blow up a plastic bag and then pop it.
- **SHIP'S HORN OR ELEPHANT** You need: a cardboard paper towel roll, a manila folder, masking tape, and a big breath. Wrap the folder around one end of the tube so it looks like a funnel and tape it in place. Blow through the opposite end.

6 WAYS TO BE A LUCKY DUCK

FRENCH DICTATOR NAPOLEON BONAPARTE did not look for courageous generals or brilliant generals. Instead he said "give me *lucky* generals." But how does a person get to be lucky?

1. Take risks. Trust your gut feelings and go for it. On a test, if you think you know the answer, write it down. Try not to second-guess yourself.
2. Expect the best. My old philosophy was to expect the worst. This way, I figured I could never be disappointed. Ha! Fat chance! What kind of backwards thinking was that? Now I expect better than the best.
3. Share. You can't let in luck if you're keeping all your toys and good ideas to yourself. There is an old saying that when one door closes, another one opens. The more doors and windows that you open, the more great stuff will come flying through.
4. Know what to say. When something lucky comes your way, be gracious. Sample: "Aw, shucks, I can't believe the sweepstakes committee came to my house with balloons and cameras and a check for ten million dollars! Fancy that!"
5. Know when to zip your lip. Listening is one of the most important life skills you can possess. If you listen real close, you'll hear luck coming.
6. Never take off your lucky purple socks. Ever.

LADY ✤ LUCK

WHENEVER SOMETHING GOOD would happen, my grandmother would say, "Lady luck must be smiling on me today." Do you think such a lady exists? The following cases seem to prove she's out there somewhere.

THE CASE OF THE SEVEN LIGHTNING STRIKES

Roy Sullivan was hit seven times by lightning and lived to tell the tale. He was even nicknamed the "Human Lightning Rod," with the scars to prove it.

- 1942: A lightning bolt struck him in a leg, and he lost a nail on his big toe.
- 1969: The second bolt hit him in his truck when he was driving on a mountain road, knocking him unconscious and burning his eyebrows.
- 1970: The third strike, in his front yard, burned his left shoulder.
- 1972: The fourth strike set his hair on fire. After that, Roy got a little worried. He carried a pitcher of water with him at all times.
- 1973: Propelled from his car by lightning.
- 1974: The sixth bolt struck Roy in a campground. He attempted to outrun a cloud he thought was following him and injured his ankle.
- 1977: After a direct hit while fishing, Roy was hospitalized for burns in his chest and stomach. As far as we know, it was his last encounter with lightning. He died in 1983.

THE CASE OF THE DOUBLE LOTTO WINNERS

Who says you can't beat the odds? Eugene Angelo Sr., 81, and his wife Adeline, 74, won the lottery in 1996 ($2.5 million) and then again in 2007 ($5 million), just a month shy of their fiftieth wedding anniversary. A New York State lottery spokesman said that the chances of winning the lottery once are 22 million to 1, so the odds of doing it twice are "galactically astronomical." The Angelos are "living proof that lightning, or in this case, random luck, can strike twice."

THE CASE OF THE MISSING RING AND THE JUNK MAIL CLUE

In Northport, NY, a man found a wedding ring in a floorboard in his home. He used the inscription in the band (Kitty to Johnny—3/31/51) to track down the ring's owner. First, he asked neighbors and used the Internet to try to find the family who had once lived in his home. But no luck. Then he phoned previous owners. No luck. Then, out of the blue, he got a piece of junk mail addressed to a Kitty Zenkus. Fireworks went off. Had he found his missing owner—fifty years later? With some detective work he located 74-year-old Catherine Zenkus, aka Kitty. Tearfully, Kitty explained that finding the ring was like getting a piece of her husband back, since he'd been dead for some eighteen years.

THE CASE OF THE BARGAIN HUNTER AND THE OLD PICTURE

Imagine buying an ugly, framed piece of art at a yard sale for a mere $4.00—and then later discovering it was worth millions. That's exactly what happened to a financial analyst in 1996. He bought an old piece of art because he liked the frame. But as he removed the muddy, worthless painting, he realized that the frame was a hunk of junk, too! And then he found something stuck inside the frame—a document hidden between the canvas and its backing. The man opened the paper and read, "In Congress, July 4, 1776 . . ." He gasped. Could it be true? An expert later confirmed the page's identity: This was one of only 500 copies of the original Declaration of Independence. Eventually, the financial analyst sold that $4.00 paper at auction for $2.42 million!

ARE YOU SUPER

SUPERST

SUPERSTITIOUS FOLKS ARE EVERYWHERE, not stepping on sidewalk cracks and totally avoiding ladders. Alas, I'm a member of that superstitious crowd. I still have one pair of ripped jeans that I keep in the bottom drawer because I aced a test once while wearing them and now I'm too afraid to toss 'em. Oh, and I cross my fingers a lot. That's a habit I picked up back in first grade.

So what's *your* superstition?

One of the coolest books on the topic of superstition is called *Cross Your Fingers, Spit in Your Hat: Superstitions and Other Beliefs* by Alvin Schwartz. I read it for the first time when I was nine. Check it out.

A TITANIC COINCIDENCE

MOST PEOPLE KNOW THAT THE *TITANIC* CRASHED into an iceberg and sank on her maiden voyage. Over 1,500 people died on that tragic April 15, 1912. But did you know that fourteen years *before that happened*, Morgan Robertson published a novella named *Futility* featuring a large ship that crashed into an iceberg on its maiden voyage? The name of Robertson's fictional ship? The *Titan!*

Another titanic coincidence involves the screening of a movie aboard the real *Titanic*. The night of the disaster, there was a screening of a little-known movie by a director named D.W. Griffith, who would later go on to make numerous acclaimed films. His movie was *The Poseidon Adventure*, about a group of six passengers and crew members who struggle to stay alive after the ocean liner in which they're traveling is capsized by a tidal wave. Some say that because *Titanic* passengers were enjoying the film so much, they didn't notice the shudder of the iceberg impact and didn't realize their own ship was sinking fast.

ITIOUS?

SUPERSTITIONS FOR BAD LUCK

- Friday the 13th
- Walking under a ladder
- Black cats
- Spilling salt on the dinner table
- A bat flying into the house
- An owl hooting three times
- A five-leaf clover
- Breaking a glass while proposing a toast
- Putting a shirt on inside out
- Putting a hat on a bed
- Breaking a mirror
- Opening an umbrella indoors
- Stepping on cracks in the sidewalk
- An itch inside your nose
- Crossed knives on the dinner table
- Mending a garment while wearing it
- Fastening a button into the wrong buttonhole
- Leaving new shoes on a table

SUPERSTITIONS FOR GOOD LUCK

- Crossed fingers (and toes)
- Knocking on wood
- Saying "God bless you" when someone sneezes
- A robin flying into the house
- Sneezing three times before breakfast
- Meeting three sheep
- Looking at the new moon over your right shoulder
- Finding a four-leaf clover
- Putting a dress on inside out
- Hearing crickets singing
- Cutting your hair during a storm
- Picking up a pencil in the street
- Walking in the rain
- A ladybug on you
- See a penny, pick it up, and all day long you'll have good luck.

ACHOO!

SOME GOOD LUCK superstitions have been around for centuries—and longer. At the time of the Great Plague in medieval Europe, if someone sneezed, you knew that he or she was sick and probably had the plague. The Pope passed a law that required everyone to "bless" a sneezer. That's how "Bless you!" got popular.

LUCKY CHARMS

10 OBJECTS YOU MIGHT WANT TO PUT IN YOUR BACKPACK BEFORE THAT BIG TEST

- Rabbit's foot
- Keys on a silver ring
- Peanut (or, if you're allergic, acorns)
- Horseshoe
- Dice
- Spinning top
- Feather
- Ankh (Egyptian symbol for life)
- Copper penny (try to get one of the "wheat" pennies minted before 1958)
- Wishbone (dried out)

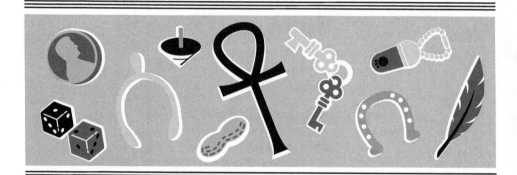

MAKE A WISH

MOST OF US MAKE WISHES ON OUR birthday cakes or when we see the first star in the night sky. But there are oodles of other ways to get your wishes to come true.

When you and your friend say the same thing at the same time, hook pinkies and silently make a wish. When you let go, it will come true.

If a ladybug lands on you, wait for it to spread its wings and just as it flies away . . . make a wish.

If you see more than three birds on a telephone wire, make a wish before they fly away.

If you see a duck, make a "quack" noise.

Does the duck talk back? If it does, your wish will come true.

Blow a dandelion so the seeds scatter. Your wish will come true if they all blow off at the same time.

Stick a watermelon seed to your forehead. If it sticks when you make a wish, your wish will come true. If it falls off, just try again!

Don't be afraid of black cats, especially ones with green eyes. Pet one ten times and make a wish.

Can you peel an apple all in one peel? If you can, your wish will come true.

Find a penny heads up and make a wish on it.

When you get a new pair of shoes, make a wish. When the shoes get too small, the wish will come true.

WORK A PAPER FORTUNE-TELLER

MAKE IT:

Start with a standard sheet of paper. Make it square by folding one corner over to the edge and cutting off the extra flap. (Fig. 1)

Unfold it and you have a square. Fold it the other way and crease again. (Fig. 2)

Unfold so you are back to the square. (Fig. 3)

Next, fold each corner point into the center of the creases. (Fig. 4)

| Fig. 1 | Fig. 2 | Fig. 3 | Fig. 4 |

With all four corners folded it should look like this. (Fig. 5)

Next, flip it over and fold all four corner points into the center again. (Fig 6)

With all of the corners folded in it will look like this. (Fig. 7)

| Fig. 5 | Fig. 6 | Fig. 7 | Fig. 8 |

Write the numbers 1 through 8 on each of the triangles. (Fig 8)

Lift up the flaps and write fortunes under here. Check the list on page 74 for ideas.

Flip it over and color or write the name of a different color on each flap.

Flip it back over and stick your two thumbs and two forefingers into each of the four flap pockets. Fingertips should press center creases so that all four flaps meet at a point in the center.

PLAY IT:

Have a player choose one of the top four squares. For example, he or she might choose RED.

Spell the color the person chose while you open and close the Fortune-Teller once for each letter in the color they selected. Open and close up and down and side to side. R-E-D.

Let the person select one of the four visible numbers on the inside. Seven.

Open and close as before as you count to the number. When you've stopped counting, look inside and let the player choose a number again.

Open and close the right number of times, then choose once more. Open the panel under the number and read the fortune under the panel. Play again and again.

CHANGE IT:

Instead of colors on the top squares, write down the name of something else, like animals, weather, planets, or TV characters!

FEELING FORTUNE-ATE

WRITE THESE MESSAGES ON the paper fortune-teller, or on slips of paper, for fortune cookies (see recipe that follows). Add more fortunes to the list. Copy down some of the ones you get at a Chinese restaurant.

- Answer the door. Opportunity is knocking.
- You will travel somewhere cool.
- You will travel somewhere hot.
- You will help someone.
- You will be a great leader.
- There is a great hair day in your future.
- You will meet a new friend.
- You will get a raise in your allowance.
- You will learn a new skill.
- You will receive a surprise.
- Trouble is headed your way.
- Let a smile be your umbrella.
- Good luck awaits you.
- Your wish will be fulfilled.
- Someone you don't know will bring happiness.
- You will receive an important letter.
- You have a secret admirer.
- You believe in yourself.
- You will do a good deed.
- Someone will tell you a secret.
- You will forget something important.
- You will celebrate something special.
- Someone with the initial "S" (insert your own letter here) is thinking about you.

INVISIBLE FORTUNES

WHEN YOU REALLY NEED TO BE hush-hush, make your messages with invisible ink! Well, it's not really ink. It's lemon juice. But it knows how to disappear. First, get a bowl and pour the juice in. Next, write out your secret fortune using a toothpick dipped in the lemon juice. After about thirty minutes, the juice should be dry. Hold the fortune near something warm (a radiator cover or a soft lightbulb, for example.) Once the paper is slightly warmed the "ink" should turn darker—revealing your magical message.

For more idea about writing and notes, turn to page 132.

HOW TO

MAKE YOUR OWN FORTUNE COOKIES

FORTUNE COOKIES ARE TRICKY TO get just right! A few things you need to remember before you bake:

Make sure that each spoonful of batter is spread out evenly on the baking sheet.

Instead of using the back of a wooden spoon to spread the batter, tilt the baking sheet back and forth as needed.

Use cold baking sheets so everything stays unstuck.

Although it's time consuming to make only two or three cookies at a time, it's the best way to go. Otherwise, cookies become stiff very quickly and when cooled are too brittle to bend into their familiar shape.

To handle the hot cookies, wear white, cotton gloves.

Don't forget! Very important! Get permission to cook and make sure an adult supervises you in the kitchen. I can think of nothing worse than having an accident while making fortune cookies! What kind of omen would *that* be?

Now, get your ingredients:

- 1 ¼ cup flour
- 2 tablespoons cornstarch
- ½ cup sugar
- ½ teaspoon salt
- ½ cup vegetable oil
- 2 egg whites
- 1 teaspoon water
- 2 teaspoons vanilla extract

And make the cookies!

1. Preheat oven to 350 degrees.
2. In a large bowl, sift together the flour, cornstarch, sugar, and salt.
3. Stir in the oil, egg whites, water, and vanilla.
4. On a well-greased, cold baking sheet, drop spoonfuls of batter into circles. (You might want to do 2 for the first batch and then more as you get better at folding them.)
5. Bake circles for 15 minutes, or until golden.
6. Have an adult help you remove the pan from the oven and immediately flip cookies onto your cotton-gloved hands.
7. Hold fortune in center of bendable cookie while folding cookie in half. Watch out if it's hot!
8. Grasp ends of cookie and draw gently down to crease at center of cookie. It should hold this shape while it cools.

100+

- Unicorns
- Mermaids
- Sprites
- Brownies
- The Shire
  (from *The Hobbit*)
- Watership Down
- Bigfoot
- Leprechauns
- Faeries
- C-3PO
- R2-D2
- Shrek
- Dumbo
- Puff the Magic Dragon
- Peter Pan
- Tinker Bell
- Jiminy Cricket
- Loch Ness Monster
- Peter Cottontail
- Mickey and Minnie Mouse
- Abominable Snowman
- E.T.
- Gryphons
- The Lost City of Atlantis
- Avalon
- The Bat Cave (in *Batman*)
- Bikini Bottom (home to
  SpongeBob, Patrick,
  Squidward, and friends)
- Candy Land
- Dinotopia
- The Emerald City
- Sim City
- Hundred-Acre Wood
  (Winnie the Pooh, Piglet,
  Eeyore, and everybody else)
- Mount Olympus
- Sesame Street (starring
  Elmo, Kermit, Oscar,
  Snuffleupagus and every-
  body else)
- *Where the Wild Things Are*
- Spiderman
- Wonder Woman
- Superman
- Barbie and the Twelve
  Dancing Princesses
- The Incredibles
- Woody
- Buzz Lightyear
- Hogwarts
- Ewoks
- Willy Wonka's factory
  (with all the Fizzy Lifting
  Drink, Everlasting Gob-
  stoppers, and more)
- X-ray Glasses
- Lightsabers
- Bedrock (home of the
  Flintstones)
- Jellystone National Park
  (home of Yogi Bear)
- Invisibility Cloak
- Platform 9 ¾
- Teleportation
- Quidditch
- Centaurs
- Pegasus
- Hercules
- Popeye (and Olive Oyl)
- The Indian in the Cupboard
- Gizmo (the good gremlin)
- Nemo
  (and Dory, of course)
- Lilliput
- The Care Bears
- The Smurfs

FANTASTIC
(AND FUN)
PEOPLE, PLACES AND THINGS
WE WISH WERE REAL

- Strawberry Shortcake
- Curious George
- The Time Machine
- The Mystery Machine
- Scooby Doo
  (and Shaggy, too)
- Magic carpets
- Magic wands
- Magic mirrors
- Genies in bottles
- Fairy godmothers
- Xanadu
- Gilligan's Island
- Shangri-La
- Angelina Ballerina
- Mary Poppins
- Babar
- ESP
- UFOs
- Imaginary Friends
- The Mad Hatter
- Alice in Wonderland
- Tweedledum
- Tweedledee
- Charlotte (the spider)
- Wilbur (the pig)

- The Force
- Gandalf
- The Cat in the Hat
- The Lorax
- Sneetches
- Heffalumps
- The Grinch
- Harold and his Purple
  Crayon
- Xena the Warrior Prince
- The Magic School Bus
  (with Ms. Frizzle aboard)
- Sailor Moon
- Sabrina, the Teenage Witch
- Buffy, the Vampire Slayer
- Camelot
- The Bionic Woman
- Narnia
- The Golden Compass
- Little Miss Muffet
- Snow White
  (and the dwarves)
- Sleeping Beauty
- Ariel
- Cinderella
- Little Red Riding Hood

- Goldilocks
  (and the bears, too!)
- The Old Woman in the
  Shoe
- Rapunzel
- Jumanji
- Supergirl (Oh, wait!
  That's YOU, isn't it?)

There are so many other people, places, and inventions from books and movies that could be included here. Make your own list. Try to think of places you'd like to explore, or other fantastic characters you wish you could invite to your next sleepover. I used to dream about Luke Skywalker (from *Star Wars*) asking me to marry him—in space. Wait. Did I really just admit that out loud? Sheesh. I'm baring my soul here. Your turn.

REVOL

FULL NAME:

PLANET EARTH

NICKNAMES:
Big Blue (because 97% of me is covered with water)

HOW OLD AM I?
I look great for my 4.5 billion years, don't you think?

HOW BIG AM I?
196,950,711 square miles (510,100,000 square kilometers)

HOT OR NOT?
Are you kidding!? HOT! Near my center, I'm about 7,000 degrees.

BASIC COMPOSITION:
Volcanic rock. But don't forget all the other stuff that's living on me! As of 2007, my human population is 6,627,854,547 people—and there are at least five to ten million kinds of insects and other animals here, too. (That's not total bugs or creatures by the way. You need to multiply those millions by millions to get a total critter count. Yeeps!)

Check out pages 174–176 for some things you can do to help keep me in the best shape I can be.

SOMETHING TO THINK ABOUT
Our planet has been here for 4.5 billion years. Dinosaurs were here for 250 million years. But Homo sapiens have only walked on Earth for 100,000 to 200,000 years! How on Earth (pun intended) are we supposed to think we're the center of anything when, compared to all that's come before, we've only been here for a blink of an eye?

HAS YOUR MOM OR DAD ever said these words to you? *The world doesn't revolve around you, dear. So stop acting like it does.*

Ha! Mine sure did. And you can laugh all you want, but for years, I thought— quite innocently—that the world did indeed revolve around me. Why not? I didn't know anything about orbits or gravitational pull or asteroids or whatever else is spinning out there in space.

Earth and I share a similar story—because for centuries of recorded history, Earth was named the precise center of the universe . . . even though it wasn't. How did scientists figure it all out in the end? Well, Earth's tale is far from over, but here are a few key moments along the way:

● Aristotle wrote in the fourth century B.C. that Earth must be a sphere because different stars could be seen as you move north and south, and the shadow of Earth on the moon during an eclipse was curved.

● In the second century A.D., Ptolemy made star catalogs. He said the solar system was like a carousel with Earth as the center. Planets, stars, the sun, and the moon were like the painted horses going around and around. Unfortunately, it didn't work that way. Although his wrong theory lasted for some 1,400 years, it was quickly booted by Nicolaus Copernicus. But (here comes the silver lining): If Ptolemy hadn't been so wrong, the next guy wouldn't have been so right. . . .

● "Right guy" Nicolaus Copernicus used math to explain how the sun, planets, and stars moved. He said the sun was the center of our solar system (thus naming it solar—*sun*— system). But he wasn't 100% right. This guy also believed Earth was flat. So there were still a lot of questions waiting to be answered.

● Johannes Kepler used elliptical orbits to predict planetary motion. When he wasn't predicting orbit paths, Kepler was predicting his next sneeze. He had a notoriously runny nose.

● Galileo Galilei proved that the sun was in the center of the solar system, and other planets (including Earth) orbited it. He was the first guy to spot craters on the moon by introducing the telescope into astronomy. He also discovered moons near other planets, too, like Jupiter.

● Isaac Newton proposed a theory of gravity to explain how the planets were held in place. Legend says he got hit on the head with an apple and cried, "Eureka! Gravity!" But the truth is, he probably just observed a falling apple (like so many other natural objects) and came up with his theory.

● Edmund Halley figured out that comets orbit the sun like planets do. Plus, he figured out the paths of *returning* comets, including Halley's Comet (named after him, of course).

DOT TO DOT

A GROUP OF STARS LOOKS LIKE the biggest connect-the-dots puzzle ever. Draw imaginary lines between them, and see a picture of an object, animal, or person otherwise known as one cool constellation.

But here's the weird part: Even though we see constellations as a pattern in our sky, their stars may not be near one another! Stars appear to have the same brightness, but each of the "dots" is actually a different distance from Earth. Although we see stars shining brightly, they are many light-years (one light-year = almost 6 trillion miles) away. That kind of distance is impossible to imagine. But all that distance is a good thing! Because stars are so far away, the sky moves and changes very, very slowly. And for centuries, sailors, astronauts, and all humans have been able to use the slow-moving stars as guides.

ASTRONOMY
vs.
ASTROLOGY

IMPORTANT! IN CASE YOU DIDN'T know this: Astronomy is the scientific study of stars. Astronomy and astrology are not the same thing! Scientists try to understand how stars are born and how they survive. They do not believe that things in space, especially ones positioned light-years from Earth, can affect our daily activities.

VS.

Astrologers think that stars, no matter how far away, determine our fates. An astrologist tries to predict the future or describe what people are like based only on their birth date and the position of stars.

3 COOL THINGS ALMOST EVERYONE CAN SPOT IN THE NIGHT SKY

When you look up at the sky at night, if it's clear outside, you can almost always count on a moon view. Sometimes it's full; other times it's crescent-shaped. You also probably know how to find the North Star, one of the brightest spots in a dark sky. But what else can you train your eyes to spot?

ANDROMEDA

- **WHEN?** November or December
- **WHERE?** High in the northern part of the night sky
- **WHAT?** The largest galaxy (bigger and more visible than the Milky Way galaxy), Andromeda can be seen without a telescope. It may look like a smallish, fuzzy star to the naked eye, but it's actually a vast spiral of light that is about seven times as big as our moon.
- **LEGEND?** In Greek mythology, Andromeda was the beautiful daughter of Cepheus and Cassiopeia. Likewise, this is known as one of the most beautiful sights in the night sky.

THE BIG DIPPER

- **WHEN?** Mid-summer
- **WHERE?** The northern part of the night sky
- **WHAT?** Shaped like a ladle, two of the stars in its "cup" point the way to the North Star. This is close to north on a compass, so it can help you find your direction in the darkness.
- **LEGEND?** The Big Dipper was known as the Drinking Gourd for slaves trying to make their way to freedom. They used it as a guidepost to find their way north to escape the bonds of slavery.

ORION

- **WHEN?** Very early morning, August through December; Evening, December through May
- **WHERE?** Rising in the east and setting in the west
- **WHAT?** Shaped like the giant figure of a hunter, the easiest way to spot this constellation is by its "belt." The belt is made up of three bright stars— Alnitak, Alnilam, and Minatka—that form one of the most recognizable patterns in the sky.
- **LEGEND?** The mythological hunter Orion is accompanied in the sky by his faithful dogs Canis Minor and Canis Major, waiting at the right "foot" of the great hunter.

MAPS OF THE STARS!

No, we're not talking about Hollywood stars. Check it out!

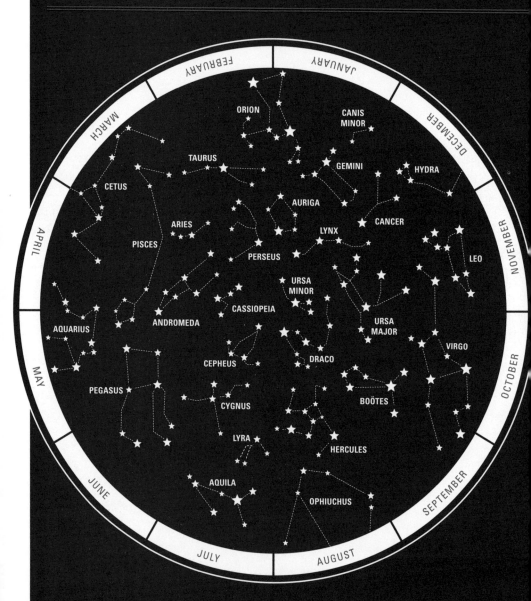

NORTHERN HEMISPHERE

NASA's (National Aeronautics and Space Administration) Web site has nifty printable star maps. Check it out. Soon, you'll be able to identify all the stars in your night sky.
Go to: http://spaceplace.nasa.gov/en/kids/
Click on PROJECTS
Click on STAR FINDER
Have a blast (or should I say have a blast-*off*)!

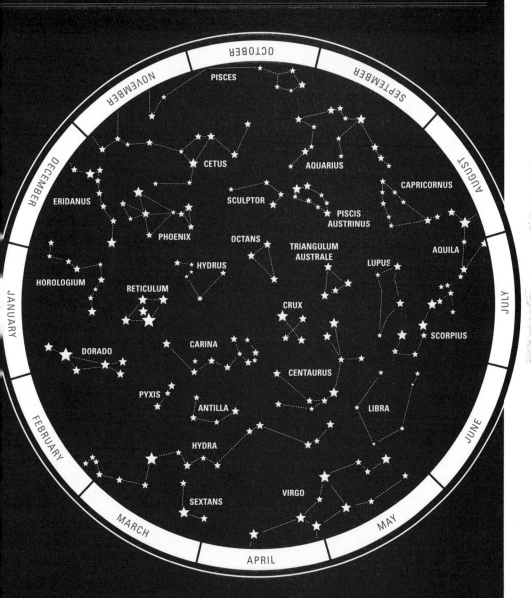

SOUTHERN HEMISPHERE

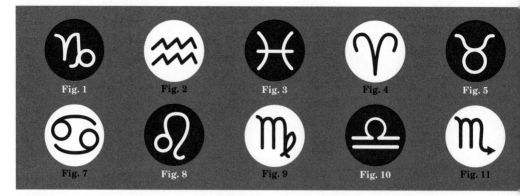

Fig. 1   Fig. 2   Fig. 3   Fig. 4   Fig. 5

Fig. 7   Fig. 8   Fig. 9   Fig. 10   Fig. 11

MORE THAN 3,000 years ago, the Babylonians used a twelve-month calendar based on the different phases of the moon. At some point, they divided the sky into twelve pieces*, naming each piece of sky after one of their months. Each month was assigned a unique animal or symbol called a zodiac sign. The word *zodiac* comes from the Greek *zidoakos*, which means "circle of animals."

CAPRICORN (Fig. 1)
The Goat 12/23–1/20
- Traits: Practical, responsible, wise
- Likes: Good manners, punctuality, expensive stuff
- Dislikes: Being embarrassed in public, surprises
- Most likely to: Be an accountant, jeweler, art dealer, or anything out of the spotlight
- Famous Capricorn Girls: Mary J. Blige, Kate Bosworth, Diane Keaton

AQUARIUS (Fig. 2)
The Aquarian 1/21–2/18
- Traits: Strong-willed, eccentric, dependable
- Likes: Fame, magic, surprises
- Dislikes: Show-offs, violence, aggressiveness
- Most likely to: Do something that requires innovation, like dance or invent
- Famous Aquarius Girls: Judy Blume, Alicia Keys, Oprah Winfrey

PISCES (Fig. 3)
The Fish 2/19–3/20
- Traits: Shy, caring, creative
- Likes: Make-believe, poetry, romantic places
- Dislikes: Dirty, crowded places and voices of authority
- Most likely to: Be in film, theater, TV, and advertising work
- Famous Pisces Girls: Drew Barrymore, Jessica Biel, Queen Latifah

ARIES (Fig. 4)
The Ram 3/21–4/20
- Traits: Active, takes risks, likes to explore
- Likes: Being liked, books, new clothes
- Dislikes: Being ignored, waiting, secondhand stuff
- Most likely to: Lead a group
- Famous Aries Girls: Mandy Moore, Mariah Carey, Posh Beckham

TAURUS (Fig. 5)
The Bull 4/21–5/21
- Traits: Materialistic, organized, cautious
- Likes: Nature, romance, doing the same thing over and over
- Dislikes: Chaos, change, being late
- Most likely to: Be an investment banker
- Famous Taurus Girls: Kirsten Dunst, Janet Jackson, Kelly Clarkson

GEMINI (Fig. 6)
The Twins 5/22–6/21
- Traits: Curious, charm-

---

* Some ancient stories say the Babylonians actually started with thirteen constellations in the zodiac, but they later dropped one called Ophiuchus.

Fig. 6

Fig. 12

ZODIAC ATTACK

ing, optimistic, coopera-
tive

- Likes: Gossip, talking on
the phone, hanging with
friends
- Dislikes: Being stuck in
the same place for too
long, getting bored
- Most likely to: Be a
teacher or politician
- Famous Gemini Girls:
Anne Frank, Angelina
Jolie, Paula Abdul

CANCER (Fig. 7)
The Crab 6/22–7/23
- Traits: Sensitive, nostal-
gic, dreamy
- Likes: Hugs, hard work,
romance
- Dislikes: Insults, rejec-
tion, betrayal
- Most likely to: Be a social
worker or chef
- Famous Cancer Girls:
Meryl Streep, Liv Tyler,
Lindsay Lohan

LEO (Fig. 8)
The Lion 7/24–8/23
- Traits: Show-off, popular,
proud
- Likes: Elegance, admira-
tion, loyalty
- Dislikes: Boredom, apolo-

gies, not being center of
attention

- Most likely to: Act, direct,
or sell something
- Famous Leo Girls: J. K.
Rowling, Jennifer Lopez,
Madonna

VIRGO (Fig. 9)
The Virgin 8/24–9/23
- Traits: Gentle, modest,
dedicated
- Likes: Working hard,
making lists, grooming
- Dislikes: Talking about
feelings, crowds, whiners
- Most likely to: Do something that seems hard to
most people
- Famous Virgo Girls: Shania Twain, Cameron
Diaz, LeAnn Rimes

LIBRA (Fig. 10)
The Scales 9/24–10/23
- Traits: Artistic, fair, opin-
ionated
- Likes: Looking good,
cleaning up, playing by
the rules
- Dislikes: Change, sloppi-
ness, loud arguments
- Most likely to: Be a
lawyer or diplomat
- Famous Libra Girls: Sere-

na Williams, Gwyneth
Paltrow, Kate Winslet

SCORPIO (Fig. 11)
The Scorpion 10/24–11/22
- Traits: Protective,
attached, determined
- Likes: A good fight, win-
ning, mysteries
- Dislikes: Nosy people,
competitors, flattery
- Most likely to: Be a detec-
tive or scientist
- Famous Scorpio Girls:
Jodie Foster, Hillary Rod-
ham Clinton, Julia
Roberts

SAGITTARIUS (Fig. 12)
The Archer 11/23–12/22
- Traits: Open, honest,
overly enthusiastic
- Likes: Flirting, moving
around, freedom
- Dislikes: Confinement,
doubt, tight clothing
- Most likely to: Be a per-
former, travel, and be
multilingual
- Famous Sagittarius Girls:
Miley Cyrus, Raven-
Symoné, Britney Spears

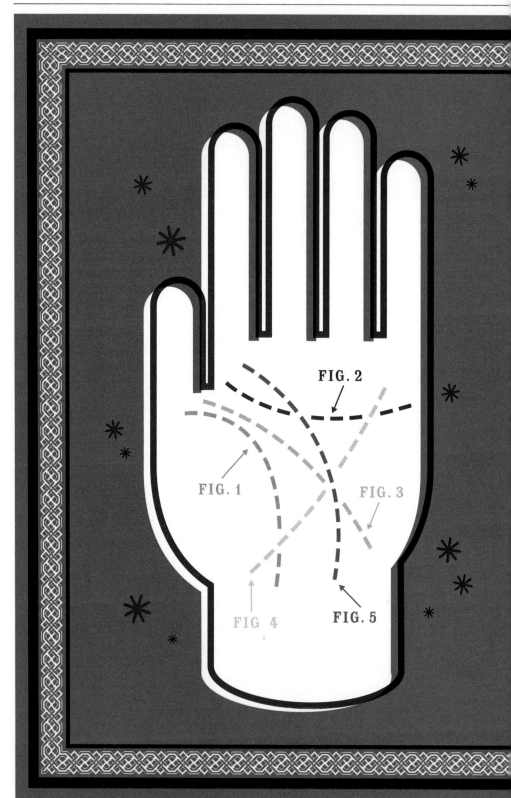

GIVE YOURSELF A HAND

PALMISTRY

DID YOU KNOW YOUR PALM IS LIKE a fingerprint and a snowflake? No two are exactly alike. But your palm tells the story of your life. Lines on the left hand show the past. Lines on the right hand show your future. Open your hands and take a look. What do you see?

"A wise person rules by his destiny . . . but is not ruled by it." —CONFUCIUS

LIFELINE (Fig. 1)
- **Long and curved:** Good health and life
- **Short and strong:** Energetic and strong-willed
- **Thin and wavy:** Health problems
- **Wide semicircle:** Enthusiasm for life
- **Straighter line:** Cautious

HEARTLINE (Fig. 2)
- **Long line:** Idealistic
- **Straight:** Hard to love
- **Curved and long:** Affectionate
- **Curved and going up:** Do anything for love
- **Short:** Overly emotional

HEADLINE (Fig. 3)
- **Head and lifelines linked:** Deep thinker
- **Head and lifelines separate:** Adventurous
- **Long and straight:** Good memory
- **Long and curved:** Imaginative
- **Light and wavy:** Can't concentrate
- **Short:** Indecisive

HEALTHLINE (Fig. 4)
No line actually means good health. A strong line means good sense. Heads up for a wavy health line. It could mean some health problems.

FAMELINE (Fig. 5)
Your fame line goes up the palm and ends at the ring finger. Do you have one? A broken line means ups and downs in your career, but a straight one means you will have a public life. Cover of *People* magazine anyone? Bring on the paparazzi.

DOIN' THE BUMP
PHRENOLOGY

WHAT PHRENOLOGISTS SAW INSIDE THE NINETEENTH-CENTURY HEAD

1	Hope
2	Self-esteem
3	Love of truth
4	Cautiousness
5	Friendship
6	True wit
7	Prudence
8	Courage
9	Parental love
10	Idealism
11	Imitation
12	Philoprogenitiveness (love of kids)
13	Secretiveness
14	Eventuality (knowledge that something is about to happen)
15	Language
16	Amativeness (love and attraction)
17	Sublimity (morals)
18	Veneration (awe)

WHAT PHRENOLOGISTS MIGHT SEE INSIDE YOUR TWENTY-FIRST-CENTURY HEAD

A	Wishing I were taller
B	Crushing on some boy in class who doesn't know my name
C	Gotta see the new episode of my fave show
D	Gotta memorize a monologue for drama club
E	Wishing I were more popular
F	Obsessing about the pimple on my chin
G	Wondering how I will tell Mom about the C+ on my report card
H	Studying for tomorrow's math test
I	Shuffling tunes on my iPod
J	Dreaming about the candy bar in my locker
K	Mentally planning my laps for the swim meet on Saturday
L	Cleaning my closet before Mom does it for me—and tosses everything out
M	Crushing on a different boy at lunch who does know my name
N	Wondering why no one has IMed me
O	Imagining what it would be like to be chased by paparazzi
P	Realizing I left my notebook in class
Q	Thinking about how much I love my BFFs

Here's a new word for you: *phrenology*. No, it's not green stuff that comes out of your nose when you have the flu. And it's not the name of a new flick over at the multiplex. Phrenology is the old-time practice of studying the bumps and lines on your head to determine character and personality traits. Not to be confused with craniometry, the study of skull stuff, or physiognomy, the study of your facial features.

While all this may sound like a bunch of gobbledygook, it's one example of a way in which people have tried to unravel some of the mysteries of the human mind. And no, current brain science doesn't really consider phrenology to be useful today. But it sure can be fun! The next time you and your friends are hanging out, check for bumps. It's just one more way to get inside each other's heads.

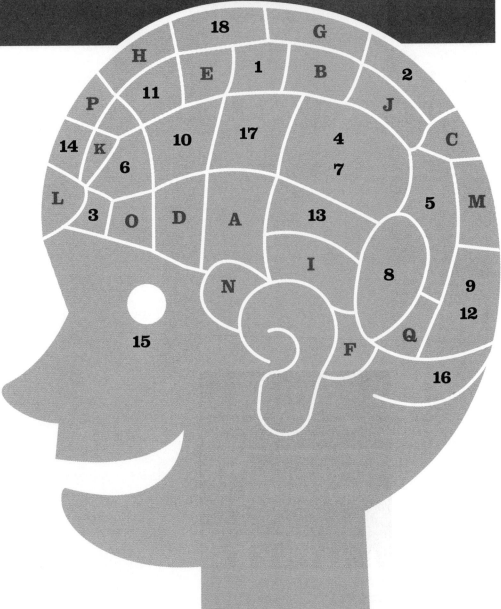

SPORTS SU

FOR CENTURIES, social conventions tried to tell women they were not as strong or agile as men. Thankfully, some women didn't listen! They stepped up, flexed their muscles, and set an example for the rest of us. It's been a slow but steady climb to the top of the record books, onto the Olympic podium, and into the hearts and minds of girls everywhere.

The timeline here shows a few ways in which women's sports have proven that girls can do whatever they want to do—even when faced with controversy and conflict. But remember this as you read some of these stats: Much of the progress in women's sports has taken place in the last twenty-five years. That isn't very long, is it? You may *think* women have had equality for a long time now, but the truth is . . . we're still fighting for it in a lot of places, including courts and stadiums all over the world.

What do you think women will do *next*?

776 B.C. Although women were not allowed at the first Olympics, they had their own Games of Hera, with foot-races just for women.

1567 Mary Queen of Scots is the first woman to play golf in Scotland. Her achievement is somewhat overshadowed by the fact that she plays her game only days after her husband Lord Damley's murder.

1784 Elizabeth Thible of France is the first woman to soar in a hot-air balloon.

1851 Amelia Jenks Bloomer invents the shorts that will bear her name (bloomers!)—and make it easier for women to run, jump, ride, and be more active in sports of all kinds.

1856 Catharine Beecher publishes the first exercise manual for women.

1873 A mile-long swimming contest is held in New York's Harlem River. Ten women compete, and the winner is Delilah Goboess. Her prize? A $175 silk dress.

1882 The first athletic games for women are held at the YWCA in Boston, Massachusetts.

1885 At age twenty-five, Phoebe Ann Moses (also known as Annie Oakley) becomes the sharp-shooting star of Buffalo Bill's Wild West Show. She could shoot a moving target while riding a galloping horse, shoot a cigarette out of her husband's mouth, and hit a dime in midair!

1895 Annie Smith Peck is the first woman to climb to the top of the Matterhorn. But what do the newspapers focus on? Her clothes! She wore knickerbockers, not a dress or a skirt.

1900 Women compete in a few Olympic events in Paris: croquet, golf, and tennis.

1902 Madge Syers of Britain enters the all-male world figure skating championships and places an incredible *second*! However, after her finish, officials announce that

PERSTARS

women are banned from the tournament. No way! It will be a few years until a separate women's event is planned in 1905. But Madge strikes back in 1908, winning the gold Olympic medal.

1917 Lucy Diggs Slowe becomes the first African-American woman to win a title in any sport. Her triumph? The American Tennis Association (ATA) tournament.

1918 Proving that women really *can* do it all, Eleanora Sears (who just happens to be a great-granddaughter of Thomas Jefferson) participates in all kinds of sports. She wins more than 240 career trophies in squash, baseball, golf, field hockey, auto racing, swimming, tennis, yachting, and speedboatracing. What is considered her most scandalous achievement? Sears rides astride her horse (rather than side saddle, the "ladylike" convention for women at the time) while playing polo.

1926 Gertrude Ederle is the first woman to swim across the English Channel.

1928 Sonja Henie brings a womanly touch to ice-skating, introducing ballerina-like moves and dance choreography. Girls everywhere are inspired to take up skating! Throughout her career, Henie wins more than 1,500 medals and trophies, including three consecutive Olympic Gold Medals.

1928 Women are finally allowed to participate in track and field events at the Olympics.

1931 Seventeen-year-old pitcher Virne Beatrice "Jackie" Mitchell becomes the first woman to play professional baseball—and what a start she has! While playing in an exhibition game for the Chattanooga Lookouts, she strikes out Babe Ruth and Lou Gehrig! Aghast, the baseball commissioner bans women from professional baseball for the next sixty years (the ban was lifted in

1992). His reason: Baseball is just too strenuous for women. His real reason: The sport can't risk having a woman like Mitchell strike out a man again!

1943 The All-American Girls Baseball League is formed to fill baseball stadiums emptied out by male players leaving for World War II.

1948 Alice Coachman is the first black woman to win an Olympic gold medal—in the high jump.

1948 Patty Berg and others found the Ladies Professional Golf Association (LPGA).

1953 Maureen Connolly is the first woman to win a Grand Slam (all four major tennis championships: the Australian Open, French Open, Wimbledon, and U.S. Open).

1960 Wilma Rudolph is the first woman to win three Olympic gold medals in track and field at the Olympic Games. It's an impressive feat made more incredible by the fact that she once had polio as a child—and needed leg braces to walk!

1964 Soviet gymnast Larissa Latynina finishes her Olympic career with eighteen medals—more than any other athlete in Olympic history.

1970 Diane Crump is the first woman to ride in the Kentucky Derby.

1972 The Constitution's Title IX of the Educational Amendments is passed. Girls in schools everywhere breathe a sigh of relief. (See page 97 for the whole story).

1973 Billie Jean King defeats Bobby Riggs in a tennis match that is dubbed the "Battle of the Sexes."

1974 Girls are (finally!) permitted to play Little League Baseball.

1974 Formation of the National Women's Football League, the first professional tackle league for women.

1976 Krystyna Choynowski-Liskiewicz of Poland is the first woman to sail around the world solo.

1978 Ann Meyers becomes the first woman to try out and sign an NBA contract for the Indiana Pacers (although she later won't make the cut

to the final team). In 1993, she is inducted into the Basketball Hall of Fame.

1982 Shirley Muldowney becomes the first person (woman or man) to win three National Hot Rod Association titles (in 1978, 1980, and 1982).

1983 Tamara McKinney becomes the first American female skier to win the Alpine World Cup overall championship.

1984 Joan Benoit-Samuelson wins the first women's Olympic marathon.

1985 Libby Riddles is the first woman to mush her way to an Iditarod (dogsled race) win.

1987 Jackie Joyner-Kersee is the first woman athlete to appear on the cover of *Sports Illustrated* magazine.

1991 The United States soccer team wins the first Women's World Cup.

1994 Speed skater Bonnie Blair wins five gold medals in three Olympics (1988, 1992, and 1994) and becomes the most decorated female American athlete in the history of the Olympic Games.

1994 Tennis great Martina Navratilova retires with an all-time record (male or

female) of 1,438 match wins.

1999 Two sisters dominate tennis: Serena Williams wins the U.S. Open; the next day, she and her sister Venus take the women's doubles title.

2002 Americans Jill Bakken and Vonetta Flowers win the first women's Olympic gold medal in bobsledding.

2003 Annika Sorenstam becomes the first woman to play in a PGA tournament in fifty-eight years.

2003 The University of Connecticut Lady Huskies rack up seventy straight wins—the second longest streak in college basketball history.

2005 Tennessee basketball coach Pat Summitt gets her 880th win and becomes the winningest (for both men and women) coach in NCAA history.

2005 Danica Patrick has a fourth-place finish in the Indianapolis 500—the best showing ever by a woman.

2006 Effa Manley, who played in the Negro Leagues Newark Eagles, is the first woman elected to the National Baseball Hall of Fame. She used her team to forward causes of the civil rights movement in addition to women's rights.

UP CLOSE:
BABE, BILLIE, MIA, AND JACKIE

SETTING THEMSELVES APART from the ranks of other women superstars are women whose actions on and off the court and field made a HUGE difference in the future of girls sports. This is not a stand-alone list by any means. You probably have your own personal female sports heroines. Go dig up their star stats and post them on your bulletin board for inspiration. We girls have to stick together!

WHO?	Mildred Ella Didrikson (nicknamed "Babe" after Babe Ruth)
FACTS?	Born 1911, Port Arthur, Texas; Died 1956, Galveston, Texas
HER STORY?	Babe is the first girl who proved that she could be as impressive an athlete as any man. She played and competed in every sport: basketball, track, golf, baseball, tennis, swimming, diving, boxing, volleyball, handball, bowling, billiards, skating, and cycling. From childhood, she had her goal set: to be the greatest athlete who ever lived. When asked if there was any sport she *didn't* do, Babe thought for a moment and said, "Yeah, dolls."
HER STYLE?	Tough and self-centered. Many said she was cocky about her abilities. But that didn't alienate George Zaharias, a wrestler who fell in love with Babe in 1938.
BIG WINS?	Olympic medals, basketball and golf tournaments, and 6-time Female Athlete of the Year
BEST ACHIEVE-MENT?	After winning a golf tournament in 1953, Babe learned she had a tumor—and the cancer spread to her lymph nodes. But fourteen weeks later, she was back on the golf course—and a year later she won the U.S. Women's Open by twelve strokes!
LEGACY FOR GIRLS TODAY?	Never give up. Don't be afraid to be strong and bold. Play more than one sport well—and be proud of it.

WHO?	Billie Jean King
FACTS?	Born 1943, Long Beach, California
HER STORY?	Ranked number one in tennis and listed in the top ten for seventeen years, King started a professional women's tour, sports magazine, and sports foundation. She won the famed "Battle of the Sexes" match against Bobby Riggs, making it clear that women could be jocks. She said, "In the '70s, we had to make it acceptable for people to accept girls and women as athletes. We had to make it okay for them to be active."
HER STYLE?	Determined, visionary, and willing to lead, King is a member of numerous Halls of Fame and was named one of the 100 Most Important Americans of the Twentieth Century by *Life* magazine.
BIG WINS?	King is the only woman to win the U.S. Open on all four surfaces (clay, grass, carpet, and hard court). She won twenty Wimbledon titles, including six singles. As a coach, she led the U.S. Olympic and Fed Cup teams to numerous wins.
BEST ACHIEVE-MENT?	Although her personal achievements on the tennis court rank among the best-ever players, it is her accomplishments *off* the court that count as her greatest contribution to women's sports. In 2006, the USTA National Tennis Center, home to the U.S. Open, was renamed the USTA Billie Jean King National Tennis Center.
LEGACY FOR GIRLS TODAY?	Demand gender equality in all sports.

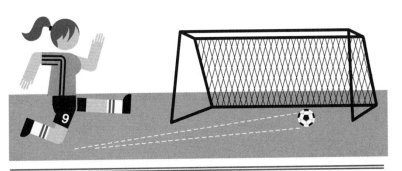

WHO?	Mariel Margaret Hamm (Mia)
FACTS?	Born 1972, Selma, Alabama (the same year that Title IX is enacted, see page 97)
HER STORY?	One of the best all-around female soccer players in the world.
HER STYLE?	Team player, pioneer, and believer in the abilities of young girls everywhere to be future sports leaders and stars.
BIG WINS?	The youngest player ever to be on a national team (she was fifteen); she retired in 2004 after winning two world championships, two gold Olympic medals, and many MVP awards. She was the first female player to reach the 100-goal mark. She scored a total of 158 goals throughout her career in international competition.
BEST ACHIEVE-MENT?	Demonstrating great leadership, she led her U.S. soccer team to a gold medal in the centennial 1996 Summer Olympics in Athens, Georgia. The coolest fact? 80,000 fans turned up to see it happen—the most spectators ever for a women's sporting event. In 2007, she was rightly inducted into the National Soccer Hall of Fame.
LEGACY FOR GIRLS TODAY?	She is a founding member of the Women's United Soccer Association—and an advocate for young athletes every-where.

WHO?	Jackie Joyner-Kersee
FACTS?	Born 1962, East St. Louis, Illinois
HER STORY?	One of the greatest Olympic athletes in history, Joyner-Kersee was one of the first generation Title IX girls (she was ten years old when it was enacted). Sports stars like Mia Hamm and other women athletes claim her as their primary role model.
HER STYLE?	She never flagged during competition: She fought back sickness, asthma attacks, debilitating heat, and more to triumph in sport—and in spirit.
BIG WINS?	Countless world track and field records (her 7,291 points in the 1992 Seoul Summer Olympics heptathlon still stands as the best ever), and nail-biting victories, including a long jump in the 1996 Atlanta Olympics that sent her from seventh place to the Olympic medal podium for a bronze medal.
BEST ACHIEVE-MENT?	Six Olympic medals—including three gold. Plus, wide-ranging philanthropic work, especially in her hometown of East St. Louis.
LEGACY FOR GIRLS TODAY?	There is no shame in being proud of your ability. Give it your all, even when you have to dig deep.

WHAT IS TITLE IX?

THE CONSTITUTION'S TITLE IX OF THE Educational Amendments of 1972 is landmark legislation that bans sex discrimination in schools, whether in academics or athletics.

𝔑𝔬 𝔭𝔢𝔯𝔰𝔬𝔫 𝔦𝔫 𝔱𝔥𝔢 𝔘.𝔖. 𝔰𝔥𝔞𝔩𝔩, 𝔬𝔫 𝔱𝔥𝔢 𝔟𝔞𝔰𝔦𝔰 𝔬𝔣 𝔰𝔢𝔵, 𝔟𝔢 𝔢𝔵𝔠𝔩𝔲𝔡𝔢𝔡 𝔣𝔯𝔬𝔪 𝔭𝔞𝔯𝔱𝔦𝔠𝔦𝔭𝔞𝔱𝔦𝔬𝔫 𝔦𝔫, 𝔬𝔯 𝔡𝔢𝔫𝔦𝔢𝔡 𝔱𝔥𝔢 𝔟𝔢𝔫𝔢𝔣𝔦𝔱𝔰 𝔬𝔣, 𝔬𝔯 𝔟𝔢 𝔰𝔲𝔟𝔧𝔢𝔠𝔱𝔢𝔡 𝔱𝔬 𝔡𝔦𝔰𝔠𝔯𝔦𝔪𝔦𝔫𝔞𝔱𝔦𝔬𝔫 𝔲𝔫𝔡𝔢𝔯 𝔞𝔫𝔶 𝔢𝔡𝔲𝔠𝔞𝔱𝔦𝔬𝔫𝔞𝔩 𝔭𝔯𝔬𝔤𝔯𝔞𝔪 𝔬𝔯 𝔞𝔠𝔱𝔦𝔳𝔦𝔱𝔶 𝔯𝔢𝔠𝔢𝔦𝔳𝔦𝔫𝔤 𝔣𝔢𝔡𝔢𝔯𝔞𝔩 𝔞𝔦𝔡.

Why was this so important? Before 1972, schools would regularly discriminate against girls or refuse to admit them altogether, making it difficult or impossible for them to succeed in their studies and sports. In 1972, a mere 9% of medical school graduates were women. In 1994, that number jumped to 38%. Since Title IX was enacted, female high school athletic participation has increased by a whopping 847%. In 1972, only 1 in 27 high school girls played varsity sports. By 2001, 1 in 2.5 high school girls played varsity sports.

WHAT DISABILITY?

Nothing is more inspiring than women (and men) who beat incredible odds and turn themselves into uber-athletes. In 1948, Sir Ludwig Guttman of Great Britain made a separate Olympics especially for the disabled, called the Paralympics. The number of athletes participating in Summer Paralympic Games has increased from 400 athletes from 23 countries in Rome in 1960 to 3,806 athletes from 136 countries in Athens in 2004.

Some of the sports categories seem familiar, but some have a twist to accommodate a person's disability, like sitting volleyball or wheelchair fencing, rugby, basketball, curling, and tennis. One of the most important things you can know about a Paralympics: these athletes are the real deal. They overcome disability, sure, but they have the same—if not more—guts and natural ability as non-disabled athletes. Although American sprinter Tony Volpentest has an artificial limb, he raced to a time 1.52 seconds shy of Donovan Bailey's 100-meter Olympic and world record. American swimmer Trischa Zorn has collected more than 41 Paralympic gold medals. Repeat after me: WOWZA.

Source: www.abilitymagazine.com

AT THE BARRE
BASIC BALLET POSITIONS

PROFESSIONAL BALLERINAS BELONG to an elite group, but many girls take ballet class at one time or another in their lives. Why do so many of us want to be ballerinas when we grow up—at least for a little while? Is it because we want to be lighter than a feather, flying through air? Is it because we all want to know what it feels like to spin around and never get dizzy? Or is it all that pink, tulle, and ribbons? Model Elle Macpherson said, "I wanted so badly to study ballet, but it was really all about the tutu."

The art of ballet dance officially began sometime around the late sixteenth century in Italy, but classical ballet became popular in the French courts in the seventeenth century. Into the eighteenth and nineteenth centuries, classical ballet evolved. By the twentieth century, Russian ballet showcased a wider range of technical strength and drama. Ballet was not just a pretty dance, it was about power, grace, and control.

Despite all the shifts, however, certain things about ballet do not change. Every move in ballet—classical or contemporary—is based on one of the five key positions for feet and hands.

FEET AND LEGS

First In this position, the feet are placed heels together and the legs are turned out so that the feet are as close to 180 degrees as the dancer is able.

Second Again the feet are in line like first position, but this time they are spaced apart; sometimes it is described as shoulder-width spacing and sometimes a foot's length apart.

Third In this position, the legs are turned out and the heel of one foot fits in front of the instep of the other foot.

Fourth This position is similar to fifth position (see below) but instead of the feet being tight together, they are spaced apart to the front and back. Again the description of the distance varies.

Fifth The feet are turned out, with one fitted snugly in front of the other. How much they overlap is dictated by the method being taught; in the Russian method they are heel to toe.

All feet and leg positions should be practiced in one of three ways:

1. Flat feet
2. Demi-pointe (half-toe, standing on the

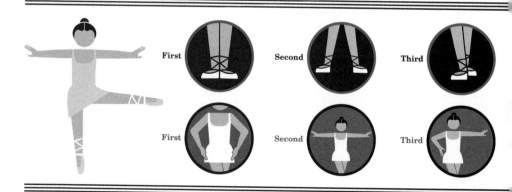

balls of the feet with the heel raised as high as possible)

3. En pointe (straight up on your toes)

ARMS AND HANDS

During all of your leg and foot positions, you must carefully watch the placement of your hands.

First The arms are held in front of the body slightly curved so that the tips of the fingers almost meet, resting on the thighs.

Second Both arms are held out to the side slightly below shoulder level. How curved they are depends on the style being taught; in the Russian method, they only have a slight curve.

Demi-second Demi is French for "half." This is a position, as the name says, halfway between first and second. The arms are lifted to about 45 degrees and held away from the body.

Third The hands and arms are kept in the same shape as first position, but raised up in front of the body to just below shoulder height.

Fourth In this position, one arm is in fifth position and the other in second. Which arm is in fifth position relates to which foot is in front. The choreography will dictate whether this will be the same arm as the front foot or the opposite arm.

Fifth The hands and arms are in the same shape as first position, but raised above the head. In this position the hands should be held with the palms turned away from the audience.

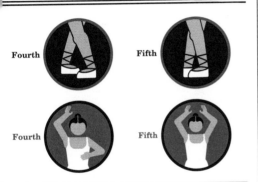

Fourth Fifth
Fourth Fifth

OTHER BALLET TERMS YOU SHOULD KNOW

As most ballet schools originated in France, terminology referring to jumps and bends are French words.

- Arabesque (*ara•besk*) Stand on the right leg while the left leg is raised straight out behind.
- Emboite (*em•bwaht*) Move forward while jumping on alternate toes.
- Jeté (*zhe•tay*) Leap from one leg to another.
- Pirouette (*peer•ooh•ett*) Turn or spin.
- Pas de chat (*pah de shah*) Jump to the side.
- Plié (*plee•ay*) Bend the knees.
- Relevé (*ray•leh•vay*) Rise up on the tiptoes.
- Port de bras (*por de bra*) Move the arms through various positions.
- Sauté (*sew•tay*) Jump.

WHAT'S YOUR POINTE?

The first pointe shoes were soft slippers, heavily darned at the toes, but today's pointe shoes are made of multiple layers of burlap, paper, and hardened glue.

How does a dancer dance on her toes? By contracting the muscles of her feet, ankles, legs, and torso, she is able to pull herself up on pointe. Inside the shoe, her foot is supported underneath the arch by a stiff sole or shank that encases the toes and lets her weight rest on a platform inside the shoe.

A prima ballerina can complete thirty-two Fouette turns while staying in the exact same spot on the floor. After the turns, her pointe shoe tip is actually HOT to the touch. It is also so worn out that it is used then only for rehearsals. Most ballerinas get ten pairs of pointe shoes from their dance company *per month*. In 2003, the English National Ballet went through 3,546 pairs of pointe shoes.

THE
FUNKY CHICKEN
& FRIENDS

SOMETIMES A DJ WILL TROT OUT the funny music to get a crowd dancing silly moves. Check out this collection of fad dances. You'll probably know a few. (I mean, is there anyone alive who doesn't know the Electric Slide?) For the ones you don't recognize, ask your mother or grandmother to remember. Maybe they can give you a little shake-your-hips demonstration of the ones they knew?

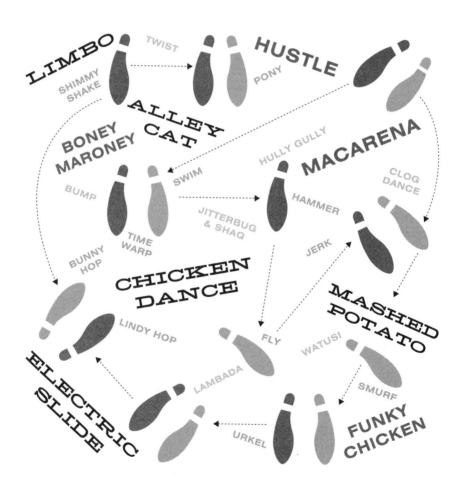

LIMBO — TWIST — HUSTLE — SHIMMY SHAKE — PONY — ALLEY CAT — BONEY MARONEY — HULLY GULLY — MACARENA — CLOG DANCE — SWIM — BUMP — HAMMER — JITTERBUG & SHAG — JERK — TIME WARP — BUNNY HOP — CHICKEN DANCE — LINDY HOP — FLY — MASHED POTATO — WATUSI — LAMBADA — SMURF — ELECTRIC SLIDE — URKEL — FUNKY CHICKEN

Singin' in the Rain All-time dancing great Gene Kelly sways with his umbrella under a street lamp and sings, "What a glorious feeling . . . I'm happy again!" as he leaps into a puddle. Nothing better! When planning a dance flick-a-thon, don't forget classics like this.

Dirty Dancing "Nobody puts Baby in the corner." See it and you'll know what I'm talking about.

Flashdance After hearing the title track, I admit that I ran through the streets of New York in a ripped sweatshirt, thinking I could dance like Jennifer Beals (the movie's star). Haven't you ever left a movie wishing you were the star at the center of all the drama? Sigh.

Center Stage Ballerinas duke it out for the best roles at a fictional ballet school.

Footloose Dancing is outlawed in this small town, but Kevin Bacon is about to change all that.

Top Hat, Shall We Dance, and *Swing Time* Rent black-and-white classics from the 1930s with Fred Astaire and Ginger Rogers, the greatest pair of dancers ever.

Grease Sandy in leather pants, the guys jumping around to "Greased Lightning," and the "Born to Hand Jive" dance scenes at the prom make this movie a must-see.

15 GREAT DANCE MOVIES TO SEE WITH YOUR FRIENDS

Newsies The true story of a courageous group of newsboys who become unlikely heroes when they team up to fight a mean old newspaper tycoon. Oh yeah, and they dance a lot.

Hairspray See the version from 2007, with John Travolta and Nikki Blonsky dancing their way around in Technicolor outfits and to-die-for wigs.

Strictly Ballroom A hilarious Australian flick about two dancers who come together to find their own dance style, with the best hair and makeup you'll never, *ever* want to have for yourself.

Billy Elliot Billy's a boy who can do ballet and tap dance so well you'll be cheering for him throughout the film.

Swing Kids Friends in war-torn Nazi Germany rebel against the times with swing and jitterbug dancing. Sounds like an odd mix of subjects, but it's a fascinating flip side (and footnote) to history—and the dancing is great.

High School Musical Though I'm sure everyone has seen this crew do their thing in HSM #1 and #2, it's worth repeated viewings. Just because we can't get enough Sharpay.

Save the Last Dance Emotional tale of a ballerina who uses hip-hop to become a better dancer.

Fame Join the kids from the New York High School for the Performing Arts as they dance in front of their school, and everywhere else for that matter. The movie's opening song wails, "I want to live forever!" Hmmm. Maybe dancing is the key.

HERE! HERE!
GIMME A CHEER!

Hip! Hip! Hooray! • Way to Go! • Let's Go, Team!

FAMOUS FOLKS WHO USED TO BE
CHEERLEADERS

WHO?	WHERE ARE THEY NOW?
Paula Abdul	*American Idol* Judge
Halle Berry	Academy Award–Winning Actress
Sandra Bullock	Actress and Producer
George W. Bush	President of the United States
Katie Couric	News Anchor
Jamie Lee Curtis	Actress and Author
Michael Douglas	Academy Award–Winning Actor and Producer
Dwight D. Eisenhower	Former President of the United States
Ruth Bader Ginsburg	Supreme Court Justice
Madonna	Pop Star and Author
Steve Martin	Actor, Author, and Comedian
Reba McEntire	Country Singer and TV Star
Mandy Moore	Singer and Actress
Franklin D. Roosevelt	Former President of the United States
Aaron Spelling	Legendary TV Producer
Meryl Streep	Academy Award–Winning Actress
Vanna White	*Wheel of Fortune* Hostess

BUST
A MOVE!
BASIC TERMS AND FACTS

• *Attack the Crowd:* Technique to get the audience involved in a cheer or song.

• *Base:* The person (or people) down on the floor who lift a flyer into a stunt.

• *Candlesticks:* Cheer motion where you extend your arms out in front of you with your fists facing each other as if you were holding a lit candle in each hand.

• *Cradle Catch:* An end movement where a base catches a flyer after tossing her in the air. The base holds the flyer under her thighs and around her back.

• *Cupie:* The base's arm is fully raised up and both of the flyer's feet are in the base's one hand. Also known as Kewpie or Awesome.

• *Double Hook:* A jump where one leg is bent in front of you and the other leg is bent behind you, while your arms are in a high V. Also known as a Pretzel, Abstract, or Table Top.

• *Facials:* Facial expressions that show how eager and involved you are, like winks, wide smiles, or head bobs.

• *Flyer (sometimes called floater):* The person who is elevated into the air by the bases; the person on top of a pyramid or stunt.

• *Herkie:* Cheerleading jump where one leg is bent towards the ground and the other is out to the side as high as it will go in the toe touch position.

• *High V:* Both arms are up, locked, in a V shape.

• *K Motion:* One arm forms a High V and the other arm rotates across your body on the right or left side (like a windmill).

• *Peel Off/Reload:* A squad splits into two or more groups to do the same motion, skill or step at different times.

• *Spankies:* Another word for briefs or underwear. Also called lollipops, bloomers, and tights.

• *Squad:* A group of cheerleaders.

• *Suck It Up:* When a flyer is up in a stunt, the base must suck it up, or hold it and not fall.

• *Tick-Tock:* When a flyer switches feet in a stunt.

• *Touchdown:* Motion with both arms held up high against your head.

• *Tuck:* Jump where you bring both knees up to your chest; sometimes precedes a flip.

HOW TO

ACE YOUR TRYOUT

CHEERLEADERS ARE, ABOVE EVERYTHING ELSE, *leaders.* They are meant to show the highest level of skill, sportsmanship, athletics, and spirit. If you're serious about becoming a cheerleader, you need to get serious about your health (cheerleaders are fit!) and your attitude (cheerleaders have positive energy!).

When going out for the cheering squad, there are a few things you want to do *ahead of time*:

• Get set to do more than yell and jump around. Familiarize yourself with basic cheers and cheerleading moves.

• You need to be physically strong. Regularly eat a balanced diet, exercise, and get a good night's rest.

• Learn specific jumps. You need to be able to do basic gymnastics and dance, and be a strong tumbler, too. Check local gyms, recreation departments, and colleges for classes you might take to better your skills.

• Learn about the sport you'll be cheering for. Ask questions, read books, watch videos, use the Internet. Never be afraid to say "I don't know" or "I don't understand," and "Can you show me?"

• Practice motions, cheers, jumps, and facial expressions, too. You want to leave a good impression. You might want to videotape yourself and then watch it to catch mistakes. Practice in front of a mirror.

On the day of the tryout, there are a few more things you need to do:

• Keep your hair away from your face and tuck in your shirt (in upside-down stunts, everything shows). Consider wearing a bow in the school colors. Wear clothes in your school colors, too.

• Don't wear jewelry, chew gum, or wear a lot of makeup.

• Try not to play around with your friends or talk too much.

• Keep that smile pasted on your face, no matter what. Think peppy.

• Make eye contact with the judges. Look ahead. Never look down or at the floor.

• Think sharp. Make sure all your motions are clean.

• Take your time when you say the cheers (and don't sing; say the words loud and clear).

• Ignore mistakes. Keep going. Use the opportunity to show you can recover from a mistake.

• Be confident. Believe in yourself. You can do it! Yeah!

BRING ON THE POM-POMS

Bow and Arrow

Daggers

Right L

Left L

Go or Punch

Hands on Hips

Touchdown

Low Touchdown

High V

Low V

T

Half T

Left Diagonal

Right Diagonal

Right K

Left K

HOW TO

DO A PERFECT CARTWHEEL

1. Make sure you have plenty of room. Start on soft grass, mats, or carpet while you perfect your moves.

2. Extend your arms straight above your head. Keep your hands turned in towards your head, with your arms against your ears. Reach for the sky, but keep your arms straight at all times.

3. Point one foot in the direction you will be going. Turn the other foot slightly outward, for better balance.

4. Pick a spot in front of you where you will land. Reach your hands out in the direction of the pointed foot. If you pointed your left foot, your left hand will touch the ground first (and vice versa). Your other hand will follow.

5. While the first hand is going down, the opposite foot should come up. Pretend you are landing on a straight line. Keep both hands on the same imaginary line that your feet started from. Just make sure to keep that leg straight.

6. Push yourself and kick powerfully so your legs come off the ground. Balance your weight on both of your arms, like a handstand, with your legs straight in the air, but out in a straddle/split position. Try to keep your back straight. This will help you to stay up; not to fall. What you want to look like is a bicycle wheel with its spokes turning one over the other.

7. Now that you've flipped around, land on the opposite foot. Do this facing the direction you came from, front leg slightly bent. You should be in the same position you started in, but with the opposite leg pushed forward.

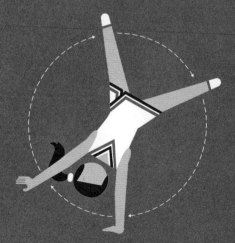

P.S. Don't forget to tuck in your shirt.

THESE GIRLS KNOW

The best part about being an animated action girl: Cartoons are invincible. They can do a zillion flips, and never get dizzy, and look ultra-cool while doing it. Here are a few popular (and not-so-popular) girls who've been animated to fame. Do you count anyone as your alter ego? Who would you want to be your best friend at school? Who would make your enemies run in the opposite direction?

	POWERPUFF GIRLS	KIM POSSIBLE
REAL NAME(S)	Blossom, Bubbles, and Buttercup	Kim Possible
HOMETOWN	Townsville	Middleton
OUTFIT	Multicolored dresses with black stripes	Stylin' black T-shirt and cargo pants
SUPER SKILL	X-ray vision and assorted super-strengths (plus, Bubbles speaks squirrel!)	She can do anything
X FACTOR	Chemical X	Kimmunicator
SIDEKICK	Professor Utonium	Wade the genius
EVIL VILLAIN	Mojo Jojo	Dr. Drakken
WEAKNESS	Their curfew	Ron Stoppable
QUOTABLE QUOTE	"And so, once again, the Powerpuff Girls save the day."	"What's the sitch?"
VOTED MOST LIKELY TO...	Save the day. Duh.	Save the world.

HOW TO KICK BUTT

PEPPERMINT PATTY	LARA CROFT, TOMB RAIDER	SAILOR MOON	PEBBLES FLINTSTONE
Patricia Reichardt	Lara Croft, daughter of Lord Henshingly Croft	Serena "Bunny" Tsukino	Later, Pebbles Flintstone-Rubble
Wherever the Peanuts lived, U.S.	London, England, and all over the world	Azabu Juban, Japan	Bedrock (and later, Hollyrock)
Tomboy look: striped shirt and sneakers	Ripped T-shirt and strap-on weapons	Odango hairdo & clothes with moons and ribbons	Designer cave dress circa 1 million B.C.
Superstar athlete	Fearless solver of traps and puzzles	Magic and moon-light attacks	Wearing a bone in her hair
Bat & ball	Archaeology smarts	The silver crystal	Dino the dinosaur
Marcie	Werner Von Croy	Tuxedo Mask	Bamm-Bamm
Lucy	Gangsters, super-natural beings, and prehistoric creatures	Dark Kingdom, Black Moon Clan, and others	Her Dad, Fred, when he gets mad
Doesn't get it	Reckless	Eating cake	Getting her pals Wiggy, Moonrock, and Penny into trouble
"You kind of like me, don't you, Chuck?"	"This is where I start to have fun."	"Moon prism power, makeup!"	"Abba Gabba Goo." (And later, "Abba Dabba Doosie.")
Crush on Charlie Brown.	Globe-trot.	Become sovereign of Earth by the thirtieth century.	Pursue a career in advertising. (She really did!)

HOW TO

TEAR A BOOK IN HALF

AMAZE FRIENDS WITH YOUR SUPER-GIRL STRENGTH!

START SMALL! YOU WILL BE ABLE to tear a huge telephone book in half eventually, but first try a smaller, thin telephone book that's out of date.

Sit in a chair. With both hands, hold the book firmly across the long, open edge. See fig A.

Keep your palms on one side and put your fingers on the opposite side, with the spine of the phone book on your lap/knee. See fig B.

Pull your fingers up and push your palms down, spreading out the long, open edge of the telephone book. The pages should be in a slanted position so that each one just slightly overlaps the one next to it.

Start to tear the pages, one at a time gradually, so you're not actually tearing the thickness of the whole book at once. See fig C. Once the pages begin tearing, the entire book should tear apart more quickly.

Twist your hands in opposite directions, slanting the pages as much as possible as you tear. See Fig D.

Watch your position! The audience can't see the slanted side of the book that's facing you. They think you're ripping apart a huge book. See fig E, the audience's view of you and fig F, the view from your side.

Once you've torn the book into two pieces, say to your audience, "But wait! There's more!" Then, tear the book into two more pieces. Your audience will be amazed! Note: This trick may take a little practice to get it just right. But don't rip apart all the paperback books on the bookshelf. Ask friends if you can use their old phone books.

If for some reason your superpowers fail you while executing this feat, simply shrug it off. Even supergirls have off days, right?

Fig. A　　Fig. B　　Fig. C

Fig. D　　Fig. E　　Fig. F

GETTING ELECTED

CLASS

PRESIDENT

IF MY RESEARCH IS CORRECT, I may possess the lamest slogan ever offered by a class presidential candidate. The year was sixth grade and I ran with the clever phrase, "Laura, We're For Her." Catchy? Um . . . nope. Rhyming? Sorta. The thing was, despite my sappy slogan, I put stickers with the slogan onto pencils that I handed out in class. And I frosted the slogan onto a batch of cookies. Now everyone knows that free cookies = victory, right?

What are some of the best pointers you'd offer a pal trying to get elected class president at your school? What winning strategies worked for you? Here are a few more of the tried and true:

- You need good ideas about how to bring the class together and get students involved. Organize your ideas. Create a list of "talking points" for yourself, so you are able to think clearly and answer questions.

- Be an awesome listener. You can't do all the talking.

- Don't stop smiling. Ever. Half-grins don't count. Teeth showing at all times! Oh, and with that in mind, you must remember to brush and floss a lot. You never know what's sticking out of your gums after lunch.

- Come up with a GREAT slogan. (Oh, and try to make your rhyme a little more exciting than mine.)

- Really care. No, really. CARE.

- Press the flesh. This means lots of hand shaking. It also means you should carry around a little container of that antibacterial gel because, well, you just never know.

- Make dozens of posters to plaster the halls. Just make sure you use bold, big letters, and add a photo of yourself looking class presidential (whatever that means!)

- During the election, don't try for any crazy fashion statements. You want to appeal to the widest base possible.

- Think about your campaign speech more than five minutes before you deliver it. In other words, you need to plan, write, rewrite, and practice in front of your friends. Being a presidential candidate is tough stuff. Just think how it'll be when you're actually elected president? You'll be making speeches all the time.

HAVING YOUR FIRST
(ALMOST) REAL JOB

CHANCES ARE THAT YOU GET SOME kind of allowance. Maybe Mom and Dad give you $5.00 a week just for being you. Or maybe you have to clean the basement, do the dishes, take out the trash, polish the car, and weed the garden before you even see fifty cents. Or maybe you get bupkus, nada, not a cent. Everyone's situation is different when it comes to making, saving, and spending money.

So when you wake up one day and decide, "I want a *real* job," you're probably thinking about the money part of it. If you work hard, you can add to that pile o' cash that's growing in your savings account. And that's true. But here's another truth: Getting a job is about a lot more than money. It's about independence, responsibility, experience, and self-confidence.

Deciding what kind of job you might want to take on is tricky. You have a lot of things to think about.

1 *What kind of services can you offer?* Make a list of all the things you can do and like to do. If you like plants, you could offer to water your neighbor's plants or mow their lawn. If you like dogs, you could walk your neighbor's pet. Are you crafty? Maybe you need to make something and sell it.

2 *Ask your family and neighbors what kind of things they need help with.* Maybe your neighbor needs someone to help them wash the car or clean out the basement. You're just the person for the job! These days, a lot of people have busy households and can always use an extra

hand. Don't rule anything out. Someone may need help doing a load of wash—or taking the dog for a long walk.

3 *How much time do you have?* Considering whether to take on a job depends on your other commitments. Will you have time to finish your homework, clean your own room, and get to soccer practice *first*? Those are your top priorities. It's a good idea to ask your parents for advice in figuring out how to make your schedule work. Sometimes weekends are a good time to take on small jobs, but weekends are also family time for a lot of people. And yes, you want to work, but you also need to play. Don't overschedule or overbook yourself. A lot of kids try to do too much. Give yourself a chance to just chill out, too.

4 *Make a real plan.* If you're serious about offering your services, then get serious about making a business plan and put it into action.

a. *Write down all the details of your business.* Describe what you want to do and how you expect to do it. For example, say you want to shovel driveways when it snows. How much money do you want to make? Are you trying to save for something specific? Write it all down.

b. *Make a list of all the materials you need.* If you're shoveling snow, you will obviously need a few important things: a good shovel and sturdy, warm gloves. What else?

c. *Identify your competition.* **Are** there other kids who shovel snow? Do some neighbors usually shovel themselves? Does someone hire a service to plow his driveway? Consider all the competition—and see what you can do to make your service better than their service.

d. *Where will your business be located?* It's easy to imagine your snow-shoveling business based in your house because you're not dealing with a lot of materials or products. But if you decide to embark on a business with a lot of stuff to store, Mom and Dad may not be so happy about its taking over the garage or your bedroom. You need to find the right place to make and store your stuff.

e. *Figure out your sales plan.* Figure out how much you would like to charge each house to shovel their driveway based on the size and time you will have to put into the job. Multiply that by the number of people in your neighborhood. Consider working on the next block, too. If your job is shoveling, you need to consider the fact that it may not snow—or it may snow *a lot.* Are you willing to work harder sometimes—or deal with no work sometimes? What will you do when it doesn't snow? Perhaps you need to be a raking *and* shoveling business. Maybe, in the spring and summer, you can offer to water and weed, too. Should you go into business with a friend or two in case the workload gets too big? Try not to get overwhelmed by all the possibilities. Start simple and build your plan as you go.

f. *Advertise your business.* Come up with a memorable name. Make a flyer to deposit in everyone's mailbox. (Just make sure you clear all the information posted on the flyer with an adult first.) Post or put a flyer on the local post office bulletin board. Hopefully, once your business gets going, customers will recommend you to their neighbors and friends. "Word of mouth" is the best kind of advertising.

g. *Prepare for the worst.* There will be times when you have no business at all. Someone may not need your services or maybe it's not snowing—even though your shiny shovel is just raring to pick up some newly fallen snow. Don't lose faith in your ability as a good businessperson or a smart worker. Don't give up. Re-evaluate your business plans and consider other jobs. Team up with a friend to brainstorm and get out of a slump.

5 **Don't ever forget your number one priority: YOU.** It may be tempting to work all the time. There's a chance your business plan may really take off and you're flush with cash. But you need to learn how and when to say "No, thanks" as well as "Yes." You can't do it all. Your homework, your sleep, your health — all of these things must come first. No matter what kind of job you do, keep tabs on your other responsibilities. Check in with your parents often. Take care of yourself.

6 **Be responsible about the money you do make.** Don't let money burn a hole in your pocket. Save some—or *all*—of it. Spend it on things that really matter. Take your time to value what you've earned and how you've earned it.

HOW MUCH?

Negotiating how much you will be paid for your time and services can be tricky. Here's a good rule of thumb: Find out the "going" rate for your type of service. What do local babysitters get paid? How much does the kid down the block get for each lawn he mows? Your salary will be based on age, experience, location, and obviously, your skills. The more you know, the more you get!

THINGS YOU CAN DO FOR

$ $ $

IF YOU'RE ARTISTIC . . .

- Make and sell stuff like greeting cards, pot holders, decorated T-shirts, flip-flops, or even friendship bracelets (see pages 197–198).
- Paint a mural on a child's bedroom wall using those fabulous art class skills!
- Paint wooden picture frames—and then personalize them for customers.

IF YOU LIKE GREEN STUFF (AND WE'RE NOT TALKING ABOUT MONEY, WE'RE TALKING ABOUT THINGS THAT GROW) . . .

- Plant or tend a garden for your neighbors. (One idea: In late summer/fall you could offer a yard cleanup and bulb planting service.)
- Plant watering (indoor or out).

IF YOU LIKE FOOD . . .

- Bake and sell cookies with cups of lemonade at a sidewalk stand.
- Offer to help neighbors serve food and clean up at a birthday or graduation party.

IF YOU'RE SUPER-ORGANIZED . . .

- Basement or garage picker-upper.
- Organize recyclable materials the day before curbside pickup.
- Help with laundry: washing, drying, and folding.

- Run errands for senior citizens or any neighbors who can't do it themselves. This works best if you have stores within walking distance, or if you can get a ride to the store from an adult. With permission, you could also take a local bus or train. Just figure its cost into the cost of your services.

IF YOU LIKE ANIMALS . . .

- Think about dog, fish, or other pet sitting (and feeding!) while someone is at work or on vacation.
- Dog walking.

IF YOU LIKE FLEXING YOUR MUSCLES* . . .

- Snow shoveling.
- Car washing/waxing.
- Sidewalk or patio sweeping.
- Leaf raking.
- Fence painting.

*Note: A lot of times it's the *boys* who get these gigs. But girls have just as much muscle! *And* they have a reputation for being thorough and neat. Emphasize what you can offer that girls and boys do differently.

IF YOU LIKE LITTLE KIDS . . .

- Mother's helper.
- Babysitting (read on for useful tips about this popular choice).

BABYSITTING

JUST ABOUT EVERYTHING YOU NEED TO KNOW

Congratulations! You're ready to babysit. Now what? Let's break it down.

THE KIND OF PERSON YOU NEED TO BE

Respectable: Listen to what the parents instruct you to do and respect their wishes.

Responsible: You need to show up on time, ready to get to work. Although most of the experience may turn out to be more like playtime, think about it as a job.

Loving: You must like kids. That's the number one job requirement. As if you didn't know. You also need to know *how* to act with kids.

Self-confident: The kids you are watching will be able to tell how you are feeling by your words and actions. Let them know you're feeling good about you.

Mature: If there is any kind of emergency, you need to be able to stay clear-headed and manage the scene, which includes tending to the sick or injured kid *as well as* continuing to watch the other kids, if necessary.

Well-Mannered: Set a good example by saying please, thank you, and excuse me.

Adaptable: Just when you think everything is under control, something crazy is bound to happen. One of the most likely scenarios: The kids will miss Mom and Dad. How will you deal with tears—sometimes hysterical, red-in-the-face ones? Plan to be comforting, entertaining, and safety-conscious all at the same time. And remember: Distraction is your best friend. When he or she starts bawling, try to get your charge interested in something else like a game or snack.

ADVERTISE YOUR SERVICES

- Lead off with a friendly message. (Fig. 1)
- Put your name in a bold, bright color to make it the focus. (Fig. 2)
- Add some quick points about your credentials (Fig. 3) with a message to call for more information. (Fig. 4)

- Put your phone number here, maybe in the same bold color as your name. (Fig. 5)
- End the flyer with a friendly closing note. (Fig. 6)
- Always check with a parent before advertising anything, especially your services.

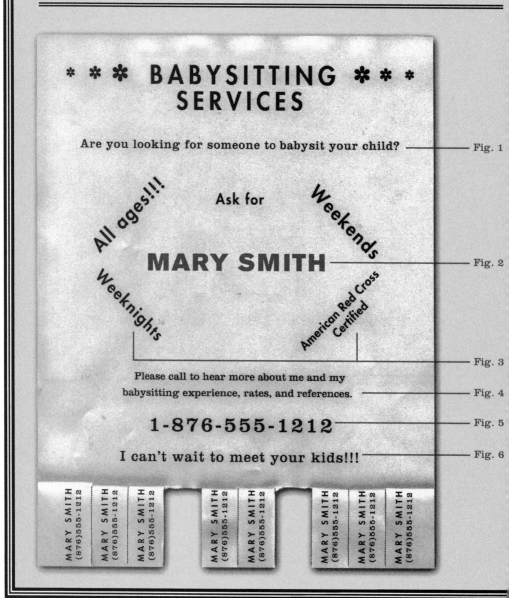

* * * BABYSITTING * * *
SERVICES

Are you looking for someone to babysit your child? —— Fig. 1

Ask for

All ages!!!

Weekends

MARY SMITH —— Fig. 2

Weeknights

American Red Cross Certified

—— Fig. 3

Please call to hear more about me and my
babysitting experience, rates, and references. —— Fig. 4

1-876-555-1212 —— Fig. 5

I can't wait to meet your kids!!! —— Fig. 6

MARY SMITH (876)555-1212

YOU GOT THE JOB, NOW GET THE FACTS

Before you start any babysitting job, meet with the parents and the child or children you'll be watching. You're the babysitter; the child is called your "charge." (That's because you're the one *in* charge! Got it?) There are essential questions to consider. Write information down on a babysitting "cheat sheet" so you can refer to it now and later. Trust me . . . the parents will be impressed by your attention to details.

☑ TIME
- How long will I be babysitting? When should I arrive? When should I plan to be picked up?

☑ CONTACT INFO
- Where will you be? How can I reach you? Ask for telephone numbers, including cell phones. Make sure they leave a list of emergency numbers, including the doctor, 911, and another adult who can help if there is any problem.

☑ FOOD & MEDICATION
- Do I have to serve a meal? When do I serve it? What do I make? Does the child have any eating problems/likes/dislikes/allergies? What about snacks and drinks? Am I allowed to cook with stove or microwave? Am I allowed to eat something from the fridge, too?
- Are there any things you usually do at mealtime like saying grace or playing a game at the table?
- Is the child in good health? If there is any chance that the child needs medication, you need to know the dose and the time it needs to be given.

☑ PLAYTIME
- Where can the children play inside the house? Outside? Will any friends be available for play dates while I am babysitting? Can the child use the computer or watch TV? What about video games—even hand-held ones? What can the child watch? Are there any toys or games that are off-limits?
- Ask about favorite games, books, and play spots for each kid you are watching. Are there any other favorites or play routines you need to know about?

☑ BED & BATHTIME
- Do I need to give the child a bath? Can the child do any of the washing herself? Can the child brush his teeth or does he need help? What clothes does the child get into after the bath?
- Do I need to put the child to bed? What does the child wear? What time is lights out? What is the usual routine? Does the child have a "lovey" like a pacifier or blanket that she needs to fall asleep?

☑ DIAPERING AND DRESSING
- Where are the children's clothes? Do I need to change diapers? Where are extra diapers, baby wipes, or powder?

☑ ALL AROUND THE HOUSE
- Does the child have any other special needs? Are there any other house rules that I should know about?
- Where are flashlights and batteries in case the power goes out?
- Where are the Band-Aids and antiseptic ointment in case someone gets a boo-boo?
- What else am I not allowed to touch or use in the house/apartment? Can I turn on the air conditioner or fan if it gets hot?
- Do I get a set of house keys? Are we allowed to go into the yard or to the playground?
- What else should I know about?

FAMOUS FIRSTS

1773
PHYLLIS WHEATLEY
- First African-American published poet
- Although she came to the United States, Wheatley's book of poems was first published in England.

1792
MARY WOLLSTONECRAFT
- First feminist author
- Her work, *A Vindication of the Rights of Woman*, talked about inequality between the sexes like no one had done before.

1849
ELIZABETH BLACKWELL
- First woman physician in the modern era
- When she applied to medical school in Geneva, NY, the school endorsed admission only because they believed she was playing a joke on them. Ha! Who got the last laugh?

1849
AMELIA JENKS BLOOMER
- First woman U.S. newspaper editor
- Founded *The Lily*, a semimonthly women's periodical in 1849.

1865
MARY EDWARDS WALKER
- First woman to receive the Congressional Medal of Honor
- This army surgeon was awarded the medal for her service during the Civil War, but in 1910, it was stripped from her because she

had not served active military duty. Half a century later, in 1977, the medal was reinstated by the Army board.

1866
LUCY HOBBS
- First woman dentist
- After marrying Civil War veteran James Taylor, Hobbs taught him how to be a dentist, too—and opened their dental practice together.

1869
ARABELLA MANSFIELD BABB
- First woman admitted to the bar (lawyer)
- In college, Belle (her nickname to family and friends) and her brother, Washington Irving, were the best students. She was valedictorian (top student) and he was salutatorian (second-best student).

1881
CLARA BARTON
- Founder of the American Red Cross
- During the Civil War, President Abraham Lincoln placed Barton in charge of the search for missing Union army men. Her group was able to locate 30,000 men!

1881
VICTORIA CHAFIN WOODHULL
- First woman U.S. presidential candidate
- Many people cite reasons why she should not officially be considered a candidate: She was under the age of 35, her name was

AND FOUNDERS

not put on the ballot, and, *of course*, she was a woman!

1887
SUZANNA MADORA SALTER
* First woman mayor
* After marrying Civil War veteran James Taylor, Hobbs taught him how to be a dentist, too—and they opened a dental practice together.

1888
LOUISE BLANCHARD BETHUNE
* First woman member of the American Institute of Architects
* During her career, she designed schools, factories, hotels, housing developments, and one of the first U.S. structures with a steel frame and poured concrete slabs, now commonplace.

1904
MARY MCLEOD BETHUNE
* First woman to establish a four-year college
* One of seventeen children of slave parents, Bethune went on to become vice president of the NAACP.

1910
BLANCHE STUART SCOTT
* First woman to fly an airplane (unofficially)
* In 1910, Scott was also the second woman to drive a car coast to coast.

1912
JULIETTE GORDON LOW
* Founder of Girls Scouts of America
* She is the eighth woman ever to be honored with a stamp.

1917
JEANETTE RANKIN
* First woman in Congress (Montana)
* Rankin was the only member of Congress to vote against the United States' entry into World War II—an unpopular decision that cost her a lot of support.

STRENGTH IN NUMBERS?
As of November 2006, there were 152 million females in the United States. Number of males? Only 148 million.
Source: www.history.com.

=================================

1917
KATE GLEASON
- First woman bank president
- The first woman to enter Cornell University's engineering program, she was good friends with suffragette Susan B. Anthony.

1922
FLORENCE E. ALLEN
- First woman judge
- Friends called her a "two-fisted" woman, meaning that she fought for her principles. When she was just eleven, her mother took her to hear Susan B. Anthony speak at a meeting celebrating the victory for women's suffrage in Utah.

1925
NELLIE TAYLOE ROSS
- First woman governor (Wyoming)
- Happy as a wife and mother, Ross inherited the governorship after the death of her husband; but found that politics suited her. Years later, she was named director of the U.S. Mint.

1931
JANE ADDAMS
- First woman to win the Nobel Peace Prize
- In 1889, she founded Hull House, one of the first settlement houses offering neighborhood services like day care, classes, and more.

1932
AMELIA EARHART
- First woman to fly solo across the Atlantic Ocean
- How weird is this: Earhart met Orville Wright (one of the brothers who flew the first plane) the year she disappeared! She also had a great relationship with Eleanor Roosevelt and planned on teaching her how to fly.

1933
RUTH BRYAN OWEN
- First woman foreign diplomat
- Daughter of William Jennings Bryan (famous Democratic politician), she was inducted into the Florida Hall of Fame in 1992.

1938
PEARL S. BUCK
- First woman to win the Nobel Prize for Literature
- Buck's won this (and the Pulitzer Prize, 1932) for her book *The Good Earth*, the story of a peasant farmer whose love for his land sustains him through hard and good times.

1930s
MAE WEST
- First woman to make $1 million per movie
- Starred with W.C. Fields in *My Little Chickadee* . . . and she wrote the screenplay, too!

1949
GEORGIA NEESE CLARK
- First woman treasurer of the United States
- She started her career as an actress in New York and spent ten years touring the country for $500 week.

1953
JACQUELINE COCHRAN
- First woman to break the sound barrier
- Also the first woman to: take off and land on an aircraft carrier; pilot a bomber; and the only woman in the Aviation Hall of Fame, among other achievements.

1963
VALENTINA TERESHKOVA
- First woman in space

- A crater on the far side of the moon is named after Tereshkova.

1967
MURIEL SIEBERT
- First woman to sit on the New York Stock Exchange
- What are the odds? Siebert's seat was one among 1,365 men's seats on the Exchange.

1975
JUNKO TABEI
- First woman to climb Mr. Everest
- She is also the first woman to have reached the summits of all the highest peaks on the seven continents.

1981
SANDRA DAY O'CONNOR
- First woman Supreme Court Justice
- An accomplished lawyer and jurist, O'Connor served on the court for more than twenty-four years.
- Fun Fact: In 2002, O'Connor was inducted into the National Cowgirl Hall of Fame!

1983
SALLY KRISTEN RIDE
- First American woman to fly into space
- She started up www.sallyridescience.com, a science company dedicated to supporting interest in science, math, and technology for girls.

1984
JOAN BENOIT SAMUELSON
- First woman to win an Olympic marathon
- Benoit originally took up long-distance running to help recover from a skiing injury.

1986
ANN BANCROFT
- First woman to cross the ice to the North Pole

- An avid naturalist, Bancroft led her family on mini-excursions into the Minnesota wilderness as early as the age of eight.

1992
MAE JEMISON
- First black woman to fly into space
- Jemison speaks fluent Russian, Japanese, and Swahili, as well as English.

1997
MADELINE ALBRIGHT
- First woman Secretary of State
- When Albright became a U.S. citizen in 1957, she was twenty and spoke four languages: Czech, her mother tongue, Serbo-Croat, French (from schooling in Switzerland), and English (learned in London, where the family evacuated to during World War II).

2003
JULIA ROBERTS
- First woman to earn $25 million for a movie
- Roberts has been named one of *People* magazine's most beautiful people in the world eleven times.

2007
NANCY PELOSI
- First woman Speaker of the House
- She grew up in a political family (her dad was mayor during her entire childhood); however, she waited until the youngest of her five children was a high school senior before she ran for Congress in 1987.

????
YOU
- First woman President of the Universe
- What's *your* greatest achievement so far? What do you have to say?

THE REAL MOTHERS OF INVENTION

ALEXANDER GRAHAM BELL invented the telephone. Thomas Edison discovered electricity. George Washington Carver could make everything from butter to plastic—all with a pile of peanuts.

So, what's wrong with this picture?

There are no women in it! And U.S. patent office records show that women have been just as active as men in developing useful objects and ways to do things. Some of the inventions are wild and crazy. In 1873, a woman invented sunshades to keep the sun out of her horses' eyes. At the Chicago Exposition in 1893, women presented inventions for a combined sofa and bathtub (yes, together), and a combination dress stand and fire escape. A woman named Bertha D. Lilly invented a collar and diaper for her parakeet in 1959. (Hey, it cut down on the mess in the birdcage.)

Of course, there are numerous inventions by women that have left a more lasting mark on our world. Some of these women have been inducted into the National Inventors Hall of Fame. A few of the standouts:

MARY DIXON KIES, 1809

- Weaving straw with silk
- Kies was the first woman to apply for and receive a U.S. patent in her own name. The New England hat-making industry adopted her patent for a process that wove straw with silk. At a time when the U.S. had stopped importing European goods (during and after the Napoleonic wars), her patent and ideas were invaluable. First Lady Dolley Madison credited Kies with giving a boost to the hat industry at a critical moment in history.

AMANDA THEODOSIA JONES (with Professor Leroy Cooley), 1872

- Vacuum process for preserving food
- Jones's important invention, the vacuum process for canning, paved the way for her Women's Canning and Preserving Company in 1890, the first business ever staffed and run by women only. Although the company failed, Jones went on to patent another important invention: the oil safety valve. This device ensured that a reasonable supply of oil went into lamps and other tools, reducing the danger of things catching fire.

JOSEPHINE GARIS COCHRAN, 1886

- Automatic dishwasher
- Socialite Cochran (sometimes spelled Cochrane) was tired of her servants chipping all her dishes, but she hated washing them herself. A solution? Invent a machine that safely washed dishes for her! At the Chicago Exposition in 1893, Cochran's incredible invention (the Garis Cochrane Dish-Washing Machine) was not only put on display, but was also put to use by almost every restaurant in the Chicago area. The company she founded to manufacture these machines later became KitchenAid.

GRACE HOPPER, 1943

- COBOL computer language
- Hopper created a program that translates instructions for a computer from English to machine language. Computer pioneer Howard Bromberg called her "a mathematician, computer scientist, social scientist, corporate politician, marketing whiz, systems designer, programmer," and,

always, a "visionary." But when did Grace really know she'd made it big? In 1996, the U.S. Navy named a ship after her—the USS *Hopper*, nicknamed Amazing Grace.

MARION O'BRIAN DONOVAN, 1949
- Disposable diapers
- Thanks to Donovan, you don't have to worry about washing and drying cloth diapers when you babysit. This stay-at-home mother revolutionized baby care with the creation of a moisture and leakproof diaper that used snaps instead of pins. How did she come up with the idea? She made the first one using a shower-curtain liner. It took her three years to get it just right!

BETTY NESMITH GRAHAM, 1956
- Liquid Paper
- Graham's mother was an artist and she wanted to be one, too, but after a bad divorce, she got a secretarial position instead. Frustrated with erasing her typing errors on the job, Graham revived some of her art techniques and began covering errors in ink with tempera paints. The formula caught on! Eventually, she began making her invention in her kitchen, with her son and other family members helping to mix it and put it into bottles.

STEPHANIE LOUISE KWOLEK, 1965
- Kevlar
- Kwolek's teachers encouraged her to pursue science and chemistry when she was a child. After years of school, she ended up in the lab at Dupont, asked to make long molecules called polymers that could be made into fabric or plastics. Always up for a challenge, Kwolek created Kevlar, a synthetic thread that is five times stronger than steel at the same weight. Kevlar is used in bulletproof vests, canoes, skis, boat hulls, firefighter suits, and radial tires. In 1995, she was inducted into the National Inventors Hall of Fame.

ANN MOORE, 1969
- SNUGLI, the baby carrier
- Moore, a nurse who lived in French West Africa for a time, got her idea for a baby "backpack" from watching African women carry their babies securely on their backs. SNUGLI reached enormous popularity with parents in the late 1980s. Today, Baby Bjorn and other carriers are popular with moms and dads everywhere.

GOT A BIG IDEA?

WHAT DOES A PATENT DO? IT legally clears the way for you—and only you—to own (and profit from) your invention for twenty years.

In addition to patenting your own clever inventions, you can enter contests and even go to invention camp. There are cool scholarships and awards available to kids of all ages, too, like the Partnership in America's Future (K-12), or the Duracell/NSTA Scholarship. NSTA stands for National Science Teachers Association, so ask your own science teacher to help you get the details you need. Check statewide for smaller contests that encourage young inventors, too.

Other great resources:
- www.uspto.gov (information on patents and trademarks)
- www.girltech.com (cool facts about girl inventors)
- www.invent.org/camp (how to go to inventor camp)

COOL TECH GIRLS

TECH GIRLS DO WAY MORE THAN GO online or work with computers. Jobs in engineering and technology include everything and anything: designing a rollercoaster, making weather predictions, developing new medicines, controlling and preventing pollution, and exploring new worlds under a high-powered microscope or in outer space. How do you get to be a tech girl?

When her husband, Washington Roebling, became ill in 1872, **EMILY ROEBLING** took over as day-to-day supervisor of Brooklyn Bridge construction. What a job! She had to supervise hundreds of men working dangerous conditions and long hours on the bridge, in addition to making sure all the construction was just right. Of course, she'd studied many engineering topics related to bridge construction, including mathematics, strength of materials, and cable construction. You can find her name on the plaque dedicating the bridge.

ADA BYRON LOVELACE, daughter of the English poet Lord Byron, designed the first "computer program" in 1843, more than a hundred years before the computer was even invented! Her program calculated certain numbers, called Bernoulli numbers. She also wrote a paper that predicted the development of computer software, artificial intelligence, and electronic music. Next time you think your imagination has gone wild . . . go with it. Ada did!

In the 1940s, movie star **HEDY LAMARR** had another major accomplishment: She held a technology patent. Her big idea: frequency hopping, or switching from frequency to frequency in split-second intervals over lines of communication (so messages could not be detected!). In World War II, her technology was used to transmit messages safely. Today, it is the foundation for wireless networks. Next time you talk on a cell, think of Hedy.

When she was only eight, a young girl named **VALERIE THOMAS** bought a book called *The Boy's First Book on Electronics*. Unfortunately, her dad didn't want to do the projects with *her*. In her all-girls school, no teachers encouraged Valerie to take advanced courses in science or math, but Valerie persevered! She attended Morgan State University and was one of two physics majors. Out of college, she landed a job with NASA and invented an illusion transmitter, a device that uses mirrors to produce optical illusion messages.

TECH-CRAZY FACT

The U.S. Department of Labor reports that the top five fastest-growing occupations are computer-related. According to the Pew Research Center-Internet and American Life Project, if current trends continue, Internet use is likely to equal that of the telephone (94%) or television (98%) within the next fifteen to twenty years.

So Are You a Tech Girl?

DO YOU LIKE USING COMPUTERS? Would you consider attending a summer robotics camp? Do you play video games? How would you design a video game just for girls? How many tech items do you use in one day?

Girl Scouts of America have patches that you can earn in just about every area, including technology. In order to earn the I.T. patch, you need to complete a short quiz. Some of the selected questions are below. To find out the answers, see the bottom of this page, or surf around for them on the Girls are I.T. Web site at www.girlsareit.org.

What does I.T. stand for?
The first PDA was created in what year B.C.?
Who was the first computer programmer?
What important technological invention arrived in 1969?
When was the first computer bug found?
What kind of bug was it?
In what year did "You've Got Mail" begin?
To see a nanochip, you must use what?

Answers: 1. Information Technology. 2. Apple Computers created the first PDA, the Newton Message Pad, in 1993. 3. Ada Lovelace (See previous page for more information on this pioneer). 4. The Internet (e-mail) came shortly thereafter, in 1971). 5. The first bug was found by Grace Hopper in 1945. 6. It was a moth—an actual bug that got trapped in her very large computer. From that moment on, the term stuck. Even if a computer problem was virtual, it was still called a bug. 7. In 1992, America Online changed the process so everyone could dialup and get e-mail, the most popular function on the Internet. 8. A microscope.

HANDY-DANDY E-CHAT DICTIONARY

DO YOU AND YOUR PALS TALK ONLINE or TEXT using shorthand? Many of these acronyms are in popular use all over the Internet. You can also make up your own online e-chat or invent your own emoticons (faces made from lines, dashes, and dots).

2C4W	Too cool for words		GR*	Great
AFK	Away from keyboard		GTG	Got to go
BCNU	Be seeing you		HHOK	Ha ha, only kidding
BFN	Bye for now		HIG	How's it going?
BIFF	Best Internet friend forever		HTH	Hope this helps
BRB	Be right back		IDGI	I don't get it
BTDT	Been there, done that		IYSS	If you say so
BTW	By the way		J/K	Just kidding
CSL	Can't stop laughing		J/J	Just joking
CUL8R	See you later		J/W	Just wondering
DBEYH	Don't believe everything you hear		KIT	Keep in touch
			LMK	Let me know
DGT	Don't go there		LOL	Laugh out loud
DLTM	Don't lie to me		LTNE	Long time no e-mail
DTRT	Do the right thing		LYLAS	Love ya like a sister
FC	Fingers crossed		NBD	No big deal
FTBOMH	From the bottom of my heart		N2M	Not too much
GL	Good luck		OMG	Oh, my goodness!
GMTA	Great minds think alike		QT	Cutie

SS	So sorry	^5	high five
TAL	Thanks a lot	<brrr>	That is sooo cold
TMA	Take my advice	<grrr>	I'm angry
TOOC	Totally out of control	@—)—(—	Rose (flower)
TOY	Thinking of you	:-#-	My lips are sealed
TTFN	Ta ta for now	>:-<	I am angrier than angry
VF	Very funny	(@@)	You're kidding
VVF	Very very funny	:-~(	I'm all choked up
WDYS	What did you say?	(: :)	Band-Aid
WML	Wish me luck	:-6	I'm sooo wiped out
YBS	You'll be sorry	0<| :-}}}	Santa Claus
YYSW	Yeah, yeah, sure, whatever	] - 8	Wearing sunglasses and
: -)	Happy		lip gloss
: -))	Very happy	-=#:-)/	Wizard and his wand
: -)))	Very, very happy	: - X	Sworn to secrecy
: - (	Sad	:-***	Smooches
=8-0	Shocked	<>)?	Huh?
{(i)}	Butterfly		
>^,,^<	Kitty cat		

Full disclosure: All of the above were used or invented in my From the Files of Madison Finn book series.

POINT & CLICK
REMEMBER THIS WHEN YOU GO ONLINE

YOU'VE PROBABLY HEARD SOME OF the bad stories about people who get tricked, lied to, or attacked online. Even when your computer has blocks on it to filter out material that is not suitable for you, the Internet can still be a very tricky and dangerous place. Though it is packed with vast amounts of facts, photos, and instant news . . . it is also a place that needs to be monitored.

A few very important **DON'T**s:

DON'T ever agree to meet someone in person that you have met online. If someone asks you to do this, tell Mom, Dad, or an adult <u>right away</u>. Maybe it will be someone you can see—under supervision—at a future date. But never agree to go somewhere alone. It's the equivalent of getting into a car with a total stranger.

DON'T ever give out your personal information. No exceptions. Although Web pages and blogs have become extremely popular, make sure you do not show your actual address or phone number. Don't e-mail it to strangers, either. And be careful of the photos you post.

DON'T ever spread bad rumors or bully someone. The increase in chat room environments has included an increase in bad behavior online. People make up things that are not true and then post it on message boards as if it's fact. Cyber bullies are even worse than bullies who get up in your face. Information that is spread virally (i.e. over the Internet) can reach thousands of people in a matter of moments. And the cyber bully can be a real coward, hiding behind his or her keyboard. Be aware. Take care.

NETIQUETTE

HAVE YOU EVER HEARD OF MISS Manners? She's newspaper columnist Judith Martin, who answers questions about how to be polite, have table manners, and all that important stuff that your grandmother always bugs you about. She's got a few things to say about cyber manners, too. "We have just as many ways, if not more, to be obnoxious in cyberspace," Martin says, "and fewer ways to regulate them."

Here are some things to think about before YOU communicate online:

• Never assume anything you write or do online is totally private. Once you've posted a message, you have no control over where it may go next. It could be forwarded to someone who shouldn't see it. OMG!

• Watch what you say. Although it's great to be able to send an instant note to someone, important details can get lost in translation. Like tone of voice. Maybe you're making a joke, but without your winking, in-person facial expression to back it up, the written joke falls flat. Be sure that what you write cannot be misinterpreted. You don't want to leave someone hurt or confused by what you've written.

• DON'T USE ALL CAPS. When you do that, it's the equivalent of yelling. GOT IT!!??

• Check your grammar and spelling, but don't correct other people's text. If you're in a chat room, people type quickly, so mistakes are bound to be made. Other people in the forum may be rushing, or coming from a different country.

• Triple-check your e-mail before you hit SEND. Once that button is pressed, there is no turning back. Make sure the message you send contains all the information you need—and is not offensive in any way.

• If you're on a Web site and have a question, be sure to check the FAQs (Frequently Asked Questions) page before asking it. A lot of times, sites have already answered the question many times before. Use resources that already exist.

HOW TO

WRITE A LETTER TO THE FUTURE

AT THE END OF EVERY SUMMER, my mind would race about the upcoming school year. What would it be like? Would all my friends be the same? Who would I like? Who would I *like* like? What other surprises would be in store for me? I solved my curiosity by doing something deceptively simple: Writing myself a letter now—about the future. Of course, this kind of letter can be written anytime. It's a great way to record predictions and wishes for the new year.

1 Address your letter to yourself.

2 Write a quick status report: where you are writing, what you are wearing, how you feel, who you like, what you're doing for the weekend.

3 Ask a bunch of questions. What's bugging you? What do you wish for? What do you need? Make promises to yourself. Anything goes!

4 Look outside yourself. Make observations or predictions about life in the outside world, too. If you're feeling really inspired, tear out some headlines. The letter can be a mini-time capsule.

5 Write down the name of at least one person who you want to get to know better, one person you hope to meet, and one person you want to help.

6 Seal the letter in an envelope and decorate it.

7 Pick a date to read the letter. Put that date on the envelope: Open After ____. Then put the letter in a safe spot, like your jewelry box.

8 Sometime in the future, open it up and a) laugh, b) gloat, c) wax nostalgic, d) feel proud, or e) all of the above. Then do it again.

BODY LINGO

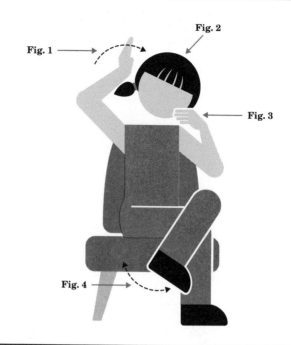

Fig. 1

Fig. 2

Fig. 3

Fig. 4

PATTING HAIR **Fig. 1** *Insecure*	**TILTED HEAD** **Fig. 2** *Interested*	**TOUCHING CHIN** **Fig. 3** *Making a decision*
LEGS CROSSED, FOOT SHAKING **Fig. 4** *Bored*	**LEGS APART, SITTING** *Relaxed*	**HANDS ON HIPS** *Aggressive*
BITING NAILS *Nervous*	**HANDS CLASPED BEHIND BACK** *Angry*	**RUBBING AN EYE** *Incredulous*
HANDS IN POCKETS, HUNCHED SHOULDERS *Bummed out*	**TAPPING FINGERS** *Impatient*	**RUBBING HANDS** *Cant wait*
TUGGING AT EAR *Indecisive*	**RUBBING THE NOSE** *Doubtful*	**ARMS CROSSED ON CHEST** *Defensive*

COOL LETTERING

Coming up with new ways to write the alphabet seems like the best possible way to disguise your own handwriting and to give your cards, letters, and art a dash of personality.

DOUBLE | TRIPLE

DOTTY | FUZZY

 |

WALKING | Loopy

SHADED | 3-D

PUT A PATTERN INSIDE YOUR BLOCK LETTERS! LIKE THESE

GRAPHOLOGY

Graphologists are experts who can identify forged (fake) documents. They can tell about someone's personality traits just from looking at handwriting. They look at different factors:

The pressure of letters. If you flip over a page that has writing on it, check for the impression left by the letters. Is it deep or dark? That means you have a lot of energy or confidence. Is the writing light? You may be shy or just feeling laid-back.

The size of letters. Small handwriting usually means you are research-oriented, methodical, and able to concentrate well. Large handwriting means you're outspoken and people-oriented.

Spacing of letters. Wide-open spaces between letters and words means you like your freedom. No space between letters and words means you put yourself under a lot of pressure.

Flourishes and embellishments. If you have a lot of loops and curls all over the place, you like to be the center of attention. See the list below for more specific explanations.

Slant of letters. If you write on an upward slant, you're feeling extra-happy. Slanted to the left? You are careful and cautious. Slanted to the right? Make way for success! If you don't slant but write straight up and down, you are very trustworthy.

A BRIEF HISTORY OF HANDWRITING ANALYSIS

There are references to handwriting analysis as far back as 4500 B.C.

Around 120 A.D., Roman historian Suetonius discussed Emperor Augustus's handwriting in his biography: "I have . . . observed this special peculiarity in his manner of writing: He does not divide words or carry superfluous letters from the end of one line to the beginning of the next, but writes them just below the rest of the word and draws a loop around them."

The first actual book devoted to handwriting analysis was published in 1622 in Italy by Camillo Baldi, a doctor of medicine and philosophy. It was called *How to Recognize from a Letter the Nature and Quality of a Writer.*

Modern graphology is now studied in university programs and used by jury selectors, forensic scientists, and others to determine an individual's state of mind. So the next time your teacher reminds you to cross your ts and dot your is, make sure you think about *how* you're doing it!

Ts crossed near the top Set for success. *t*	**Many loop-de-loops and dips** Steadfast and determined. *I'm very dedicated*	**Squished letters and words** Afraid of social events. *I'm kind of shy*
Ts crossed with an enormous swoosh Excited. Totally. *t*	**Big swoops on capital G and T** Overactive imagination. *G Y*	**Teeny, tiny letters** Good concentration. *I'm focused*
Ts crossed way down low Tired and blue. *t*	**A little loop inside your O** Are you lying? *O*	**Curly ends** So—emotional (sniff, sniff). *I'm a bit sensitive*
Perfectly dotted Is Little Miss Perfection. *i*	**Os open at the top** You're like Honest Abe. *O*	**Letters looped over like an umbrella** Protective. *I'm watchful of my siblings*
Is dotted with a dash instead of a dot Time to chill out. *i*	**Space between all your words** Fearless. *I'm not afraid!*	**Wavy lines of text** Soulful and loving. *Will you be my Valentine?*

Graphology researcher Andrea McNichol states that nearly 99% of all people in the general population will line up their letters at the left margin of a page. But a higher percentage of criminals will *not*. She claims this is because criminals refuse to literally "toe the line" in society. What do you think?

PASSING NOTES...
OR NOT?

THE DEBATE GOES ON: TO PASS A NOTE IN social studies class, or not to pass? Of course, your teachers would rather you paid attention and didn't pass anything around the room, but that might be a hard thing to do, especially when you are *just dying* to share a secret or ask a question of your pal in the third row, fifth seat over. My advice: Don't pass notes if you think it will seriously annoy your teacher. Be a good student above all other things. Don't mess with classroom karma.

BUT (oh, come on, there's always a *but*) . . . If the time is right and your friend is waiting for your note like a track star waiting for the relay baton, then here are some sneaky ideas:

- Fold a piece of paper into thirds so the top piece touches the bottom piece. Now, write a message on the edge between the two. When you open it up again, you'll only see half the word on either the upper or bottom portion. Your friend has to match it up to read your message.
- Make a decoy! Fold your note into a fan shape and pass it over to your friend. Upon opening the fan, she can read the message on the inside. Works best when the classroom is really hot. Does not work so well in January.
- Write your note on a tissue. Have your friend sneeze and pass the tissue to her. Just make sure you don't write on the tissue with permanent marker. It could get messy.
- Make a note "football." This is a variation on the paper airplane, but a little more reliable in terms of reaching its target. Don't forget to write the note inside *before* you fold.
- Stick the note in the side of your shoe. Kick the recipient's desk, and wait. That's your signal for your recipient to lean over and grab the note from your shoe (or sock). A-ha!
- Go for the tried and true: a paper airplane. But don't let your teacher catch the launch of this one. It'll be confiscated in a heartbeat.
- Write with invisible ink. See page 74 for more on this trick.

See page 74 for more on this trick.

HOW TO

MAKE A PAPER
FOOTBALL

1. Take an 8.5 x 11 sheet of paper and fold it vertically.

2. Fold it vertically again. You should have a long piece of folded paper.

3. Take the top-left corner and fold it diagonally.

4. Continue to fold the little triangle in the top downwards until there is a little rectangle in the bottom.

5. Fold the rectangle in to the little gap in the bottom to secure your paper football.

NOT-SO-PRACTICAL
NOTE-PASSING IDEAS

SLINGSHOT. A little obvious.

CARRIER PIGEON. A little messy.

FEDEX. A little over-the-top.

MORSE CODE. A little too secure? Not everyone speaks dash and dot.

REMEMBERING YOUR LOCKER COMBINATION

IF YOU'RE AFRAID OF FORGETTING your locker combination, try a memory trick to keep your brain abuzz. Write an encrypted number on the back of your lock with a permanent marker.

Encryption Option A: If your birthday is: 8 / 3 / 96 and your lock is 18 / 11 / 38, add the numbers together and write the total on the back: 26 / 14 / 134. When you forget your combo, subtract your birthday and—BINGO! You've got it.

Option B: Take your combination and add in a few 2s or 0s at the front, in the middle, and wherever else makes sense. How about adding 5 every second number? So if your combination is 18 / 11 / 38, your encrypted code would be 185115385.

Regardless of what combination you choose, pick something you can remember and use it consistently for *all* your locks.

OTHER TIPS:

Buy your lock a week before school, and practice at least five times per day.

Write down your combination twenty times in the AM. Do it again in the PM.

Make up a rhyme to memorize your combination. For example, if your combination is 3/12/28, say something like, "Three got me and twelve got thee, but twenty ate my honeybee." Sounds strange, but it works.

Write the combination in permanent marker on the inside of your backpack or somewhere else that's not so obvious where you can look at a moment's notice.

No matter what you do . . . do not tell anyone your combination, not even your best pals. Your locker should be your private, personal space at school.

Bonus! If all else fails! You can recover the combination online. Check out this very helpful site: *www.fusor.us/lockpick.html.*

OTHER WAYS TO IMPROVE YOUR MEMORY

WRITE THINGS DOWN: The act of writing something on a scrap of paper helps to cement the idea in your mind's eye (especially when you say out loud what you are writing). This way you are "seeing," "hearing," and "thinking" about the object or action. Most of your senses are engaged!

TEST YOURSELF: Test your short term memory for fun. Have Mom, Dad, or your little bro' put twenty random objects on a tray and cover it up (you can't peek yet!). They lift the cover (a scarf, a napkin) for exactly one minute. This gives you a chance to observe and hopefully memorize the objects there. Once it's covered up again, see how many you can recall. The more you practice this trick, the more you will recall.

USE AN ACRONYM: To remember a list of items, make up an acronym you will remember. An acronym is a word whose letters each represent the first letter of other words. One of the most popular memory acronyms I know is HOMES. This is an acronym used to recall all the names of the Great Lakes: Huron, Ontario, Michigan, Erie, and Superior.

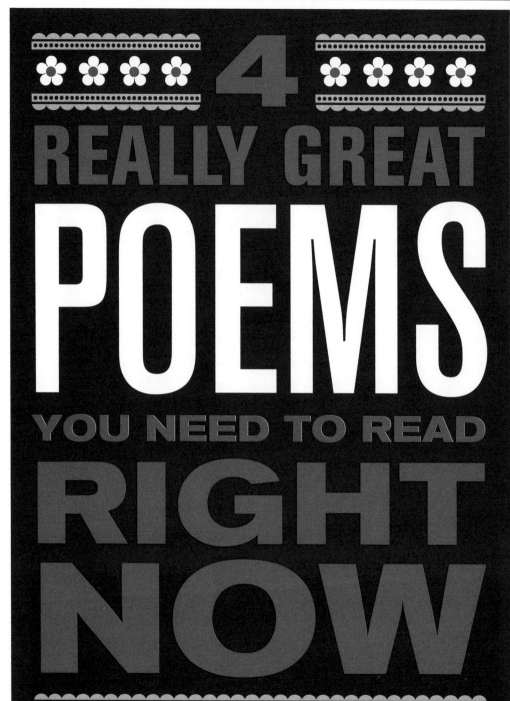

4 REALLY GREAT POEMS YOU NEED TO READ RIGHT NOW

SOME PEOPLE SAY THEY DON'T "GET" POETRY. But here's the thing: What are you trying to get? Poems are way more about your *gut*. How does a poem make you feel? I think poems can be firecrackers, getting us to fire up and think differently. Poems can also be blenders, churning up emotions and telling us that we're not alone. Poems offer us language and music and humor and everything in between. Here are four short poems by women poets. Read them once. Then read them again.

ELIZABETH BISHOP
I Am in Need of Music

I am in need of music that would flow
Over my fretful, feeling fingertips,
Over my bitter-tainted, trembling lips,
With melody, deep, clear, and liquid-slow.
Oh, for the healing swaying, old and low,
Of some song sung to rest the tired dead,
A song to fall like water on my head,
And over quivering limbs, dream flushed
    to glow!

There is a magic made by melody:
A spell of rest, and quiet breath, and cool
Heart, that sinks through fading colors deep
To the subaqueous stillness of the sea,
And floats forever in a moon-green pool,
Held in the arms of rhythm and of sleep.

SARA TEASDALE
I Am Not Yours

I am not yours, not lost in you,
Not lost, although I long to be
Lost as a candle lit at noon,
Lost as a snowflake in the sea.

You love me, and I find you still
A spirit beautiful and bright,
Yet I am I, who long to be
Lost as a light is lost in light.

Oh plunge me deep in love — put out
My senses, leave me deaf and blind,
Swept by the tempest of your love,
A taper in a rushing wind.

ELIZABETH BARRETT BROWNING
The Best Thing in the World

What's the best thing in the world?
June-rose, by May-dew impearled;
Sweet south-wind, that means no rain;
Truth, not cruel to a friend;
Pleasure, not in haste to end;
Beauty, not self-decked and curled
Till its pride is over-plain;
Love, when, so, you're loved again.
Whats the best thing in the world?
—Something out of it, I think.

VALERIE WORTH
Stars

While we
Know they are
Enormous suns,
Gold lashing
Fire-oceans,
Seas of heavy silver flame,
They look as
Though they could
Be swept
Down, and heaped,
Cold crystal
Sparks, in one
Cupped palm.

WRITE YOUR

ARE YOU A POET AND YOU DON'T know it? Maybe you just got inspired by the page before this one and you want to take a stab at some poems of your own. Or, maybe you've got something important to say and a poem just seems like the very best way to do it.

Here are different (and relatively simple) poem-starting ideas.

#1: LIST POEM

The list poem can be a proper list, like a shopping list or a list of favorite places to go in the summer, with one or two-word lines. But not all list poems are that short. Some are longer, describing things. You can make a list poem of people you love or things in your closet or feelings you have when you get good news. You can make a list of just about anything.

What I Dreamed About Last Night
The wind against the window
Swimming in the ocean
A window to nowhere
The boy who sits next to me in English
Swimming in the sky
A rock

A duck
A frog who talks
A princess without a castle
A castle
And you, whispering, whispering

Check out Elizabeth Barrett Browning's short list poem on the preceding page. She names a few things she considers the best in the world. What would you put on your "Best Things in the World" list?

Other list poem ideas:

- Homework tasks
- Things that smell good
- Things that taste good
- Things you wear
- Achievements
- Your grandmother's kitchen
- Things that make you squirm
- Famous people you like
- Things that are noisy
- Things that are cold
- Things that are hot
- Funny objects
- Bedtime things

OWN POEM

(OR TWO)

- Embarrassing moments
- Lucky things
- Things to do when I'm alone
- Mistakes I've made
- Things I love about my pals

#2: POEM OF ADDRESS

This is the kind of poem you want to write *to* someone or something. It doesn't have to be something alive or even something concrete. You could write a poem to your best friend, the mail delivery person, the soap in the bathtub, your glass of chocolate milk, or a puffy cloud. You could write an ode to unhappiness or to your bicycle.

In Sara Teasdale's poem of address on the preceding page, she writes to a person she loves. Who or what would you write to?

- An empty box
- A bunch of bananas
- The fog
- Lipstick
- Your teacher
- Bumblebees
- Skyscrapers
- Shoes

- Your hometown
- Your grandfather
- The baseball game you just won
- An octopus
- The beach
- Halloween
- War
- Peace
- Love
- Getting older
- Cutting your hair
- Your pet
- Sandwiches

Whenever you write any poem, be specific. Use words that employ all your senses. Come up with powerful descriptions. Elizabeth Bishop's poem about music on the preceding page uses language that—when read aloud—sounds mellifluous (that means like honey). Valerie Worth's poem *Stars* uses only a few words to describe stars, but each word has been carefully chosen. If you remember anything about poem-writing, remember this: less is usually more. Say a lot by choosing just the right words.

- In the English language, the single longest word that is spelled by displaying all of its letters in alphabetical order is "almost."

- If you spell out the names of every number from one to 999, you will find every vowel except A.

- What seven-letter word lets you spell out seven complete words in the same order in which their letters appear in the original word? The answer is "therein," which can be broken down into there, the, he, her, here, rein, and in.

- Which English word begins and ends with the letters "und"? The words "underground" and "underfund."

- The highest-scoring word in Scrabble is "quartzy." This will score 164 points if played across a red triple-word square with the Z on a light blue double-letter square. It will score 162 points if played across two pink double-word squares with the Q and the Y on those squares.

- The English word with the most consonants in a row is "latchstring."

- The word "girl" appears only once in the Bible.

- "Rhythm" and "syzygy" are the longest English words without vowels.

- The longest word in the English language, according to the *Oxford English Dictionary*, is "pneumonoultramicroscopicsilicovolcanoconiosis," pronounced (noo-muh-noh / uhl-truh / my-kruh-skop-ik / sil-i-koh / vol-key-noh / koh-nee-oh-sis). It is a sickness caused by the inhalation of very fine silicate or quartz dust.

- The second-longest word in the *Oxford English Dictionary* is "floccinaucinihilipilification," pronounced (flok-suh-naw-suh / nahy-hil-uh / pil-uh-fi-kay-shun) which is the act of estimating as worthless.

- The third-longest word in the English language is "antidisestablishmentarianism," which means opposition to the withdrawal of support for an established church.

- One out of every eight letters used in written English is an E.

- The dot over the letter i is called a tittle.

- There are only three words in the English language with the letter combination "uu," muumuu, vacuum, and continuum.

100+

MOST COMMONLY ~~MISPELED~~
MISSPELLED WORDS

MISPELED

You might want to copy this list into your English notebook, just in case.

acceptable	equipment	library	referred
accidentally	exhilarate	lightning	reference
accommodate	exceed	maintenance	relevant
acquire	existence	maneuver	religious
acquit	experience	memento	restaurant
a lot	fiery	millennium	ridiculous
amateur	foreign	miniature	rhythm
apparent	fourth	mischievous	sandal
argument	gauge	noticeable	schedule
atheist	generally	occasion	scissors
believe	grammar	occasionally	sensible
calendar	grateful	occur / occurred	separate
category	guarantee	occurrence	special
cemetery	harass	official	success
changeable	height	parallel	to / too / two
collectible	hierarchy	parliament	tomorrow
committed	ignorance	pastime	their / they're / there
conscience	immediate	pigeon	twelfth
conscientious	independent	possession	tyranny
conscious	indispensable	preferable	until
definite(ly)	intelligence	principal / principle	vacuum
disappear	its / it's	privilege	vicious
discipline	judgment	questionnaire	weather
drunkenness	knowledge	receive	weird
embarrass	leisure	recommend	you're / your

THE BUZZ ON

SPELLING BEES

OF THE EIGHTY-THREE CHAMPIONS in the annual Scripps National Spelling Bee, girls have won the most—so far. As of 2006, forty-three champs have been girls and forty have been boys. And what were the winning words? You might want to pull out your dictionary while you look at this list. Use it to practice for your own school bee.

1925: gladiolus	1950: meticulosity
1926: abrogate	1951: insouciant
1927: luxuriance	1952: vignette
1928: albumen	1953: soubrette
1929: asceticism	1954: transept
1930: fracas	1955: crustaceology
1931: foulard	1956: condominium
1932: knack	1957: schappe
1933: torsion	1958: syllepsis
1934: deteriorating	1959: catamaran
1935: intelligible	1960: eudaemonic
1936: interning	1961: smaragdine
1937: promiscuous	1962: esquamulose
1938: sanitarium	1963: equipage
1939: canonical	1964: sycophant
1940: therapy	1965: eczema
1941: initials	1966: ratoon
1942: sacrilegious	1967: chihuahua
1946*: semaphore	1968: abalone
1947: chlorophyll	1969: interlocutory
1948: psychiatry	1970: croissant
1949: dulcimer	1971: shalloon

How do you know if you are a spelling bee wannabe? You couldn't look at this list without taking out your dictionary.

1972: macerate	1990: fibranne
1973: vouchsafe	1991: antipyretic
1974: hydrophyte	1992: lyceum
1975: incisor	1993: kamikaze
1976: narcolepsy	1994: antediluvian
1977: cambist	1995: xanthosis
1978: deification	1996: vivisepulture
1979: maculature	1997: euonym
1980: elucubrate	1998: chiaroscurist
1981: sarcophagus	1999: logorrhea
1982: psoriasis	2000: demarche
1983: Purim	2001: succedaneum
1984: luge	2002: prospicience
1985: milieu	2003: pococurante
1986: odontalgia	2004: autochthonous
1987: staphylococci	2005: appoggiatura
1988: elegiacal	2006: Ursprache
1989: spoliator	2007: serrefine

For more on spelling bees, check out the official study site: www.myspellit.com. You, too, can be a word champion, otherwise known as a beater, conqueror, master, subduer, trimmer, vanquisher, whipper, or winner. *Whew.*

*There were no spelling bees held during World War II in the years 1943, 1944, and 1945.   Source: Scripps National Spelling Bee

20 WAYS TO JAZZIFY* YOUR JOURNAL

A JOURNAL DOES NOT NEED TO BE all words, although words are a great place to start, of course. Journals can be so much more: things you find on the sidewalk, photographs, doodles, pie charts, and just about anything that expresses your feelings and thoughts in some way. Adding art to a journal adds a whole other dimension of color, texture, and emotion.

You don't need an expensive leather, fur-trimmed journal to say what's on your mind. Any old composition notebook will do. (Hint: If you put packing tape on the spine, it'll stay together better.) Sometimes you can turn an old book into a new book, too, to make your journal. How? Go to a used bookstore and find a sturdy edition of some old, illustrated book you can get for a buck. Tape or glue pieces of wrapping paper, newspapers, magazine photos, drawings, and anything else you like onto the cover and the pages inside. There is something magical about covering up some of the words on the page—and leaving others. Inspiration guaranteed.

And now, without further adieu, the short list of twenty more cool ideas.

Drum roll, please. . . .

*Okay, so *jazzify* won't be showing up at any spelling bees in the near future. It is not actually a real word. But that doesn't matter—this is your journal. You're allowed to make up stuff in here—including *words*. Invent your own language if you want. Your entries will certainly stay secret if no one else is able to read them!

1 Glue an envelope into your journal and fill it with interesting bits and scraps: stuff you tear out of a magazine, a note from a friend, a piece of junk mail, or whatever else strikes your fancy.

2 Find a photograph of someone you've never met (and don't know). Write about that person. And yes, you have to make stuff up. Journals don't have to be a line-by-line reporting of your day. They can be free-flowing stories, too, about people you never met.

3 If you had to write down ten cool rules that you follow (or break!) in your life, what would they be? Write them here.

4 Draw a diagram of your room, labeling all the important places and objects.

5 Eavesdrop on someone's conversation in the lunchroom. Write down everything they say.

6 Write a letter to someone you admire. P.S. If you want to send it, for real, then send the original and paste a copy here.

7 Write down 100 things you want to do in your lifetime.

8 Find a picture of yourself as a young child. Make a copy and paste that into the journal. Now draw on it, in the style of a young child.

9 Close your eyes and write a journal entry without looking. Or, if you're a righty, write with your left hand instead. Lefties, try writing with your right hand.

10 Make a graph that charts your moods throughout the day or the week.

11 Write up a list of instructions for how to get through the school day.

12 Write about one single, inanimate object for a half hour. Describe it in detail without actually naming it.

13 Your closet is being reviewed by the glam police. What does the review say?

14 Write an entire journal entry in pig Latin. Or maybe cipher code. You decide. (Check out how to make a cipher on the next page).

15 Write down at least five things you would pack in your desert island suitcase.

16 Write your own recipe for creativity stew, whatever that means to you.

17 Collect flat objects from nature (leaves and flowers can be pressed in a hard book for a day or so) and paste them into an all-natural journal collage.

18 Make a list of the places you have ever visited or lived. Draw a map to show them.

19 Write one journal entry in the smallest letters you can write. Then make an entry in the LARGEST letters possible. That should be good for a few pages.

20 Cut a bunch of scraps from a magazine. Now make them into an interesting "this is me" collage, filled in with words between the pictures.

SECRET JOURNAL HIDING PLACES

Worst Case Scenario #1: Your younger brother discovers your journal and rips all the pages out.

Worst Case Scenario #2: Your older brother discovers your journal and scans the pages onto his computer so he can blackmail you.

Worst Case Scenario #3: Your mom finds your journal and she wants to see you later to "talk about it."

Yeeps! No matter which scenario comes up, one thing is clear: The most important thing you need to do when keeping a journal is to find a safe place to stash it. Some potential hiding places:

Under the mattress	Pro: Easy access. Con: Too obvious a hiding spot.
Inside the freezer	Pro: No one will ever find it under the ice cubes. Con: The ice cubes. Brrrrrr!
Your underwear drawer	Pro: Absolutely off limits to *everyone*. Con: You might forget it's there, too.
In your school locker	Pro: It gets mixed in with your other notebooks. Con: Someone discovers it and reprints your secrets on the front page of the school paper.
Locked up in a safe	Pro: Only you have the key. Con: Only you have the key—and it's missing.

HOW TO

MAKE A CIPHER CODE

- Draw a circle. Draw another circle inside the first one.
- Draw "pizza" lines to split the circle into twenty-six "slices."
- In the outer circle, write the alphabet.
- In the inner circle, write the alphabet again, but start A next to the outer circle's letter K or another letter.
- Switch to code mode when you write by substituting one alphabet for another.

HOW TO

WRITE THE BEST
THANK-YOU NOTES

EVER SINCE YOU COULD WRITE, you've probably heard it after every birthday, holiday, and sometimes other days, too: "Did you write your aunt a thank-you note for that _____?" My usual response to this question was a groan followed by a muffled, "Um . . . no. Do I have to?" And the answer to that was always a resounding: "OF COURSE YOU DO!"

Writing thank-you notes does not have to be tough stuff. There's a formula to it. Here's how to whip out a personalized and heartfelt note in ten minutes flat.

1. IN THE CARDS

Keep a cool supply of pens and note cards on hand. Lack of supplies is the number one reason most thank-you notes never even get started. And keep those cards small. You don't need to be wordy, just grateful. Postcards are even easier—and cost less postage, too.

2. NO CHEATING

Writing a thank-you in the body of an e-mail message is a nice sentiment, but it just doesn't mean as much. You need to send a real card.

3. SAY THE RIGHT STUFF

Address your note. Dear _____ .

Open with "hello" or any nice, informal greeting. For example, if you're a cowgirl, "howdy do" will do.

Right after that say "thanks," and how much you like the gift. "I love my sweater," or

"The books are great." Never say things like, "Thanks, but I already have one of those," or "I wish it were a different color, but I guess I'll live with it." (Helpful hint: If the gift was cash, don't mention money by name. Instead say, "Thank you for your generous gift.")

Add some detail about how you will use the gift—but make it genuine. Don't go overboard trying to convince the giver that you love it if you don't. Don't say, "Wow, I couldn't believe it when I opened up the package and saw that amazing electric blue sweater vest. I'll be the fashion queen at school." Say something true but noncommittal like, "Your gift arrives right in time for the cold weather. Thanks!"

End the thank-you note with a one-liner about getting back in touch. Maybe you can hint at a future conversation or meeting. For example, "I hope to see you soon," is pretty foolproof.

Sign off with one last thank you. You really can't say those two words enough. In a way, you could just create a card with a single message in huge type, all capital letters. It would be different—and get the job done.

Dear Cousin Jesse,

THANK YOU.

Love,

Me

One last note about your note: Try not to go off on any tangents. This is not the place to muse about what you're doing in school or at basketball practice or what you had for lunch. This is all about sending a proper thank you. Do it. Mail it. Done. And now Mom won't bug you.

YOURS TILL THE...

butter flies	friend ships
chocolate chips	candy canes
root beer floats	light bulbs
nail polishes	coffee cups
moon beams	season's greetings
ping pongs	wedding bells
candle sticks	Hershey's kisses
gum drops	heart aches
Web links	rain falls
ice skates	baby sits
home works	horse shoes
nose blows	trail mixes
peanut butters	pony expresses
scare crows	banana splits
pumpkin pies	ice creams
wind blows	carrot cakes
puppy loves	side walks
turkey gobbles	powder puffs
autumn leaves	Niagara Falls
potatoes mash	French fries
pumpkin pies	lemon drops
snow caps	sweater sets
mail boxes	Graham crackers
snow drifts	web sites
bees wax	dodge balls
duck quacks	door bells
pop stars	note books
life boats	orange ades
super stars	dew drops
spring rolls	shoe laces
flower pots	black berries
swimming pools	dust bunnies
road trips	smoke signals
globe trotters	ink wells
sun tans	soda pops
bubble gums	heart attacks
fire crackers	ice cubes
lip sticks	rain bows

THE GOOD, THE BAD, ANI

You're hitting the road with your family for a looooong car trip. But the thing you really want to hit . . . is your brother! Fear not. There are many ways to pass your car time without having to resort to backseat violence. You can whip out the electronic game or your iPod, but face it, even that is going to get boring after a while. So (drumroll, please) here are a few clever games that should keep you and your sibs in the fun zone—and keep the grown-ups in the car *very* happy indeed.

 = **BEWARE! MOM'S DRIVING!**

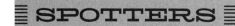

Look out the window and notice what's zooming by. See all those other cars' license plates? There are games to be played *everywhere*! Have everyone in the car look for license plates with certain letter or number combinations. Who can spot a plate with the numbers of his or her birth date or initials? Who can spot a plate with a sequence of at least three numbers (like 234 or 567)?

Who sees a license plate from out of state? The spotter with the most states wins.

Can you turn a license plate's letters into words for a funny phrase? For example, if you see the letters BMD on a plate, you might say, "Beware! Mom's driving!" Use this game idea with signs along the road, too. Who can make up a sentence for the longest sign word you see? Spot away!

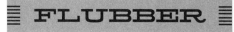

(or any nickname will do)

Does one of your little brothers or sisters—or anyone traveling in your car—have a fun or unusual nickname? Did you say the nickname was Flubber? Great! Use it and have some fun. One player picks an item that he or she usually sees along the road more than once (like a truck, bicyclist, shrubs, fence, etc.). Every time the player sees that item he or she yells out, "Flubber!" or whatever funny nickname was selected. All the other players in the car need to guess what object the nickname stands for. The first person to guess correctly gets to pick the next "Flubber."

GAMES!

THE TOTALLY ANNOYING

CAR CHARADES

YOU'VE HEARD OF THE "regular" version of this game. It can be challenging enough when you stand up. What if you had to play while *sitting* in a car?

The object is to guess the famous person, movie, book, or song while seatbelted in the car. You can only use hand or foot gestures (no words and no mouthing words) and fantastic facial expressions to offer clues.

Gesture to show *what* category you'll be doing (like movie, song, etc.).

Show how many words are in the title by holding up that number of fingers.

Start to pantomime the title. If you're acting out the entire title with one action, make a wide sweeping motion with your hand (trying, of course, not to hit your sister in the head.) If you're doing one word at a time, hold up fingers to also show which word you're acting out.

If the word is very tough, you may want to break it into syllables. Use the gesture for syllables (fingers pressed on hand) to indicate a) how many syllables, and then b) which one you're acting out. Each time you offer a gesture, make sure the others guess correctly before moving on.

To have someone guess non-acted-out words like "a" or the" you should pinch together your fingers to indicate small word. Then everyone guesses small words to see if they get the right one. Remember that each correct guess gets a pointed finger at the guesser to say, "You got it!"

You can use a karate chop motion to show a word that is shorter than one that may have been guessed, or stretch out an imaginary cord to show that the word guessed needs to be longer.

The person to guess correctly wins. That person will choose the next title in the game.

Use the hand signals to encourage, make faces to show when someone's wrong—you can use all body motions available to you. Unfortunately jumping is not a possibility since you're car-bound. What will you do instead?

= number of words in title	**= first word in title**
= small word	**= shorter word**

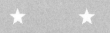

DESTINATION U

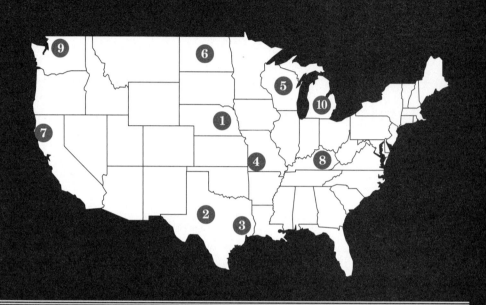

ALLIANCE, NEBRASKA
(Fig. 1)
Carhenge was created by
farmer Jim Reinders, who
wanted to build a memorial to
his dad, he used thirty-eight
cars rescued from farms and
dumps. At first, the town
wanted to rip it down, but
they soon realized it was a
regular tourist attraction.

KATY, TEXAS (Fig. 2)
A year-round exhibit built for
an estimated $20 million by a
former Hong Kong business-
man, Forbidden Gardens
includes a koi (fish) pond and
40,000 square feet of tiny
model palaces and people,
including a small-scale repro-

duction of Emperor Qin's
6,000+ man terra-cotta army.
Why in the middle of Texas?
Houston, just twenty-five
miles away, boasts the third
highest Asian population in
the U.S.

PARIS, TEXAS (Fig. 3)
Ooh! La! La! In the middle of
Texas, a state of oil platforms,
sits an enormous replica of
France's Eiffel Tower. But
this one's topped by a genuine, oversized cowboy hat.

SPRINGFIELD,
MISSOURI (Fig. 4)
Home to the world's biggest
fork! An advertising company
left it there when its previous

owner, a restaurant, went
belly-up. It stands as tall as a
three-story building. One
catch: The spoon appears to
be missing. Under suspicion:
the dish.

LAKE NEBAGAMON,
WISCONSIN (Fig. 5)
When he's not working at the
town dump, James Kotera is
working on his ball of
twine—one of the biggest
ever. He began his ball back
in the late 1970s. At last
count, the ball's weight was
nearly 20,000 pounds.

NKNOWN, U.S.A.

NEW SALEM, NORTH DAKOTA (Fig. 6)
Moo! Not only does this small town boast the largest cow anywhere in the world— named Salem Sue, the enormous cow measures thirty-eight feet high and fifty feet long and is made from six tons of fiberglass—New Salem also boasts a bevy of sports teams named . . . you guessed it . . . *the Holsteins.*

BAKER, CALIFORNIA (Fig. 7)
Somewhere in the high desert sits the world's largest thermometer. It's there to mark the place in the U.S. with the highest temperature ever recorded: In 1913 the mercury hit 134 degrees in Death Valley.

LOUISVILLE, KENTUCKY (Fig. 8)
Where can you find a 120-foot baseball bat? Just outside the Louisville Slugger Museum, of course. The gigantic bat was erected in 1995 and weighs thirty-four tons.

WINLOCK, WASHINGTON (Fig. 9)
If I were craving the biggest omelet ever, I would rush to Winlock, home of the world's largest egg.

ALLEN PARK, MICHIGAN (Fig. 10)
Roll with it! The world's largest tire sits near the Detroit Metro airport—all eighty feet and twelve tons of it. An urban legend says that once when it was moved, the tire broke loose and rolled across the highway.

NEXT STOP: MUCK

There are some pretty interesting names for some towns and cities around the world. How about a vacation in one of these hot spots?

- Anger, Ethiopia
- Antelope, Zimbabwe
- Asbestos, Canada
- Baa, Indonesia
- Bent, Iran
- Berry, France
- Black Tickle, Canada
- Blue Hole, Belize
- Boring, USA
- Cadillac, France
- Coffin Bay, Australia
- Deception Island, Antarctica
- Egg, Austria
- Energetik, Russia
- False Point, India
- Fish, Namibia
- Goodhouse, South Africa
- Heart's Content, Canada
- Hope, USA
- Horn, Iceland
- Karma, Niger
- Moodyville, Canada
- Mosquito Coast, Honduras
- Muck, United Kingdom
- Of, Turkey
- Ogre, Latvia
- Outlook, Canada
- Penny, Canada
- Pest, Hungary
- Polar Bear, Canada
- Pukë, Albania
- Putty, Australia
- Resplendor, Brazil
- Rich, Morocco
- Rum, Jordan
- Runaway Bay, Jamaica
- Salt, Spain
- Searchlight, USA
- Sauce, Argentina
- Show Low, USA
- Song, Thailand
- Speed, Australia
- Ten Degree Channel, India
- Thorn, Poland
- Turbo, Colombia
- Umbrella Mountains, New Zealand
- Wee Waa, Australia
- Wink, USA

CAR TUNES

The car radio can also be the source of a lot of fun on long road trips. You can channel your inner Kelly Clarkson and do "car-a-oke" as you sing along with a top-40 song, or just lip-synch making funny facial expressions. You can also play "Name that Car Tune." Here's how:

1. Get a grown-up to help out. He or she must be sitting up front to change radio stations.

2. Tune into a random radio station. Listen to a few seconds of a song and then lower the volume to see who can guess the song.

3. Try a speed round flipping between stations: As soon as one person guesses the song, quickly speed to the next one.

4. If you run into stations that are all advertising stuff or too much talk radio, then guess what kind of song will come up next (rock, country, etc.).

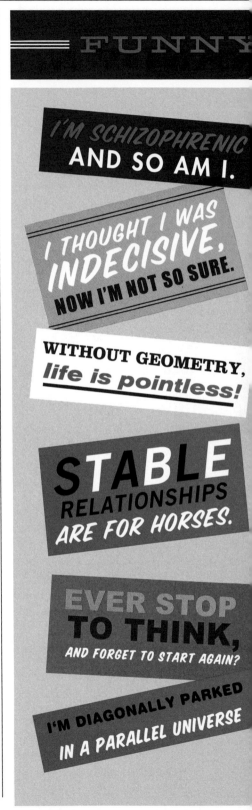

FUNNY

I'M SCHIZOPHRENIC AND SO AM I.

I THOUGHT I WAS INDECISIVE, NOW I'M NOT SO SURE.

WITHOUT GEOMETRY, life is pointless!

STABLE RELATIONSHIPS ARE FOR HORSES.

EVER STOP TO THINK, AND FORGET TO START AGAIN?

I'M DIAGONALLY PARKED IN A PARALLEL UNIVERSE

BUMPER STICKERS

ON YOUR MARK, GET SET, **GO AWAY!**

OUT OF MY MIND. BACK IN FIVE MINUTES.

My OTHER car is a *Rolls Royce*

National Spelling Bee **RUNNER-UP**

BE ALERT! THE WORLD NEEDS MORE LERTS.

WHEN LIFE HANDS YOU **GATORS,** MAKE GATORADE.

This vehicle STOPS at all **BINGO GAMES**

I USED TO HAVE A HANDLE ON LIFE, **BUT IT BROKE.**

MAY I TAKE YOUR

Menu of the ~~World~~ Weird

Appetizers

BAALUT
(The Philippines)
Fertilized chicken egg that's been buried in the ground for a few weeks (also known as "the treat with feet").

SEA SLUGS
(Korea)
Crunchy, served raw.

TAKOYAKI
(Japan)
Flour balls with octopus centers.

MONKEY TOES
(Indonesia)
Deep-fried toes eaten directly from the bone.

ALLIGATOR ON A STICK
(Southern United States)
Chunks of gator tail rolled in cornbread.

TURTLE EGGS
(Nicaragua)
Appearing like boiled ping pong balls, these eggs are served with hot sauce and a shot of rum.

Soups and Sides

BIRD'S NEST SOUP
(China)
Actual nest from the cave swallow, which secretes a strange-tasting liquid that holds the nest together like glue.

FISH-EYE SOUP
(Southeast Asia)
Scoop out an eyeball, suck out the juices, and spit out the cornea. Repeat.

SCRAPPLE
(United States)
Take all the leftover parts of a pig (lips, snout, organs), add a touch of cornmeal, and cook in a block. Served by the slice, fried.

GREEN ANTS
(Australia)
Munch on small green ants. To eat: Pick up the bug, squash the head, and take a bite.

HU HU GRUBS
(New Zealand)
Fat, white bugs that taste a little like peanut butter.

ORDER, PLEASE?

Menu of the ~~World~~ Weird

Main Course

SURSTRÖMMING
(Sweden)
Herring that's been sitting for a year (or more) in a barrel. You gut the fish on your plate and eat over potatoes and thin, hard bread. But don't forget to pinch your nose. The smell will knock you out.

GEODUCK CLAMS
(Northwest United States)
Also called "Gooey Duck," these clams with the very long necks are a little odd-looking.

SQUIRREL BRAIN
(Southern United States)
The squirrel's head is baked with the other parts of the body. To eat, crack the skull and dig out the brain. Tastes a little like mushrooms.

HAGGIS
(Scotland)
Sheep's stomach stuffed with oatmeal and sheep's organs and steamed, usually served with chappit neeps (also known as turnips).

BOREWORS
(South Africa)
Sheep or cattle intestines stuffed with spices and grilled.

TACOS SESOS
(Mexico)
You've had tacos with hamburger meat; now try them with cow brains. Talk about smart food.

TARANTULA
(Cambodia)
These roasted furry eight-legged critters are a delicacy in many places all over the world.

Dessert

PIG BLOOD PUDDING
(Trinidad)
Add pig's blood to rice and bread crumbs and you've got something different for dessert.

UBE ICE CREAM
(The Philippines)
Purple ice cream made from purple yams.

MOVE OVER, BIG MAC

ONE MENU THAT'S ENJOYED WORLDWIDE is the one found under the golden arches: McDonald's. But McDonald's *isn't* the same everywhere. Its menu changes depending on the country. Who knew?

MAHARAJA MAC—a Big Mac made from lamb or chicken (because Hindus cannot eat beef) and the *McAloo Tikki*—a vegetarian burger.

McLAKS—a sandwich made from grilled salmon and dill sauce.

McPOLLO, JR.—a chicken sandwich served with mashed avocado.

GREEK MAC—a sandwich of two burgers served in a pita with yogurt sauce, tomato, and onions.

McKROKET—a deep-fried roll with beef ragout that's served on another bun.

McOZ—made from Australian beef and beetroot—with Vegemite (yeast spread) on the side.

McSCHWARMA—a kosher version of the Big Mac (because meat and dairy cannot be served together).

CROQUE McDO—a hot ham and cheese sandwich prepared like a traditional Croque Monsieur, a French grilled snack served in cafés.

KOROKE BURGER—made from mashed potato, cabbage, and katsu sauce, and the **EBISU BURGER**—made from fish and shrimp.

RICE BURGERS—a regular beef patty that's served bun-free, between two patties of rice instead of bread.

INDIA

NORWAY

CHILE

GREECE

THE NETHERLANDS

AUSTRALIA

ISRAEL

FRANCE

JAPAN

HONG KONG

THE REAL KINGS

King	Company	Year	Best in Show	True!
Dr. James Baker (U.S.)	Walter Baker Chocolate	1780	Semisweet baking chocolate	After the Boston Tea Party in 1773, patriots drank Baker's chocolate instead of tea.
Stephen Whitman (U.S.)	Whitman's Candies	1842	Whitman's Sampler (1915), assortment of chocolates which let people "sample" the chocolates they liked best	Introduced America to cellophane, which was used to wrap the candy boxes.
John Cadbury (England)	Cadbury Limited	1847	Cadbury Dairy Milk chocolate bar and the first Valentine's Day box of chocolates (1868)	In 1854, the company received orders to be the official manufacturers of cocoa and chocolate to Queen Victoria of England.
Domingo Ghirardelli (Italy)	Ghirardelli	1852	Signature Squares	In San Francisco, where the chocolate factory is located, there is a landmark named after the chocolate company: Ghirardelli Square.

OF CHOCOLATE

King	Company	Year	Best in Show	True!
Milton Hershey (U.S.)	Hershey's Chocolate Company	1871	Great American Chocolate Bar (1900); and Hershey's Kiss in its silver foil (1906)	Hershey's makes twenty to twenty-five million Hershey's kisses per day.
Heinrich Nestle (Germany) who changed his name to Henri Nestle (Switzerland)	Nestle	1875	Nestle Crunch, the first candy bar to combine taste, texture, and sound (1938) AND chocolate chips (1939)	Nestle was a trained pharmacist who created baby formula for mothers who were unable to breastfeed.
Rodolphe Lindt (Switzerland)	Lindt & Sprungli International	1879	Lindor Truffles	Invented the "conche," a vessel designed to melt and blend chocolates.
Joseph Draps (Belgium)	Godiva Chocolatier	1926	Shell-molded chocolates and gold foil packages	Named after Lady Godiva, whose cruel husband promised to lower taxes if she rode naked in the streets. She did! Her boldness inspired Draps to name his chocolates after her.

JUST THE
CHOCOLATE
FACTS, MA'AM

A S A GIRL, I CAN SAY WITH FULL CONFIDENCE that most of my girlfriends (ages tween and up) would do just about anything for a handful of M&M's, myself included. But what is it exactly about chocolate that has had us in its spell for centuries?

Cacao beans were like cash in ancient Mexico. The Maya, Aztec, and Toltec civilizations used them to pay for supplies and taxes.

In the seventeenth century the first recorded case of "Death by Chocolate" occurred in San Cristobal de las Casas, in Chiapas, Mexico. The Bishop of Chiapas was found dead. Poison had been secretly added to his daily cup of hot chocolate.

Chocolate was such a luxury that Louis XIV of France, also known as the "Sun King," established a job called Royal Chocolate Maker to the King in the seventeenth century.

By the eighteenth century, every European country from England to Austria made products from the cocoa tree, or (in Latin) the Theobroma Cacao. Translated literally, that means "food of the gods."

During World War II, the U.S. government asked Hershey's to make a chocolate bar especially for soldiers. During the Persian Gulf War, Hershey was asked to make another candy bar that could withstand very high desert temperatures.

As of 2006, American consumers spent more than $7 million annually on chocolate-related products. Apparently, we each consume twelve pounds of chocolate per year. Do you remember eating that many candy bars?

American chocolate manufacturers use about 1.5 billion pounds of milk annually. The only people who use more are cheese and ice cream makers.

A single chocolate chip provides sufficient food energy for an adult to walk 150 feet. It would take about thirty-five chocolate chips to go a mile, or 875,000 chips for an around-the-world stroll. Ready?

Contrary to very popular belief, chocolate does NOT cause zits. Overactive oil glands, heredity, dead skin cells that lodge in pores, hormonal changes, and even stress are what cause acne.

Ten Excuses for Eating Chocolate

1.	I love it.	6.	I love it.
2.	I love it.	7.	I love it.
3.	I love it.	8.	I love it.
4.	I love it.	9.	I love it.
5.	I love it.	10.	I *really* love it.

(But who needs an excuse? Pass the Snickers, pronto!)

ONCE UPON A TIME, HORSES FREELY roamed all over the continents, except for Antarctica. But the Ice Age changed all of that. Horses disappeared from North America. Around 3000 B.C. in Europe and Asia, people began to tame horses, to domesticate them, and to use them to carry things. Horses made a big difference in people's lives. They could be used in war as weapons and transportation. Around 1519, horses finally reappeared in North America, brought there by invading Spanish conquistadores (conquerors).

Over time, horses have become a girl's best friend due to their strength and elegance. Here is a list of some of the most popular breeds.

Do you *collect* horses? I mean, of course, the pretend kind, the ones that sit on your shelf, pose for pony photo ops, and roam the range that is your bedroom floor. These are the top five favorite collectible horses available now from Breyer, the collectible horse company:

1. Black Beauty
2. The Black Stallion
3. Misty of Chincoteague
4. Spirit: Stallion of the Cimarron and Rain
5. Cloud's Legacy

Breyer Animal Creations® was founded in 1950 and makes more than five million model horses and accessories each year for play and collecting.   Visit   them   at www.BreyerHorses.com.

Rain®, Spirit: Stallion of the Cimarron™ © 2002 DreamWorks L.L.C.

- **American Saddle Horse:** The most beautiful show horse, which can learn to walk, trot, and canter for competition.
- **Appaloosa:** This spotted horse was used by American Indians to hunt buffalo.
- **Arabian:** Bred in the desert and swift, these were the horses that fought wars, carrying great leaders from history like Genghis Khan, Napoleon, Alexander the Great, and even George Washington.
- **Belgian:** Two Belgian horses could pull a massive load of 4,275 pounds, making them even stronger than a tractor.
- **Clydesdale:** This horse looks like it is wearing white fur boots; it's the national horse of Scotland.
- **The Morgan:** This fearless horse is often used by policemen.
- **Mustang:** As wild as a tornado, these horses live in the open range of the mountains and have jobs as bucking broncos for Wild West shows.
- **Palomino:** Queen Isabella is supposed to have sent five golden Palominos to New Spain (Mexico).
- **Percheron:** The horse you're most likely to see under the circus tent.
- **Quarter Horse:** Bred to race.
- **Thoroughbred:** A racer with a strong will, whose ancestry goes back to the three original sires: Byerly Turk, Darley Arabian, and Godolphin Arabian.
- **The Standardbred:** Horse you see at harness races.

EXTRAORDINARY HORSES

THERE ARE SO MANY REASONS TO love a horse. Their majestic beauty is inspiring. And you can gaze for hours into a horse's deep, brown eyes. Sigh. Some of the best horses from real life, books, and movies:

- **Black Beauty:** From the classic novel of the same name by Anna Sewell, about a Victorian horse sold to a series of owners (book; movie)
- **The Black Stallion:** "The Black" is a brave horse who rescues a boy from a sinking ship and then lives with him on a desert island (movie)
- **Seabiscuit:** A gifted, winning horse that beats the odds and captures the hearts of people during the Great Depression (real life; book; movie)

- **Kentucky Horse Park:** A Pilgrim horse is traumatized by an accident, but healed by "The Horse Whisperer" (book; movie)
- **Spirit, Stallion of the Cimarron®:** A free-roaming Mustang is caught by the U.S. Cavalry but learns to love again (movie)
- **Misty of Chincoteague:** Based on the ponies coming from Virginia's Assateague Island, a nature preserve; Misty was created by one of the best-loved authors of horse stories, Marguerite Henry (real life; book; movie)
- **Barbaro:** Winner of the 2006 Kentucky Derby who shattered his leg and later died, making his life and death one of the most heart-wrenching horse tales in years (real life)

WHAT A HORSE NEEDS TO BE HAPPY

A pasture to roam (without loose wire fences or rusty farm equipment).
Grass for grazing, and hay, too.
Unlimited supply of water.
Unlimited supply of minerals and salt. Horses need salt
    licks to keep their bodies working properly.
Shelter and shade.
A dry place to lie down.
Someone to watch for illness or injury.
Companionship with another horse or a sheep, dog, or goat.

HOW TO

GROOM YOUR PONY

INSIDE YOUR GROOM-ING TOOL BUCKET

- A curry comb or grooming mitt
- A stiff-bristled body brush
- Mane and tail comb (plastic lasts longer)
- Soft bristle finishing brush
- Hoofpick
- Soft cloth or sponge
- Clippers

Step #1: Be sure to place your tool bucket in an area where the horse won't knock it over.

Step #2: Secure the horse with a safely tied release knot.

Step #3: Clean the horse's hooves. Slide your hand down the left foreleg and squeeze at the tendon, gently saying "up," or whatever word will get the horse to respond. Hold the hoof carefully and use the pick to pry out dirt, manure, or anything else lodged in the areas of the foot. When done, place the hoof down gently. Repeat for all four hooves.

Step #4: Curry your horse. Start on the left side, using

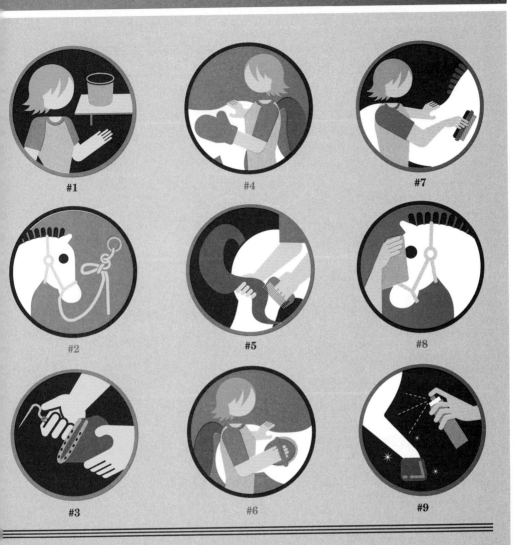

#1

#4

#7

#2

#5

#8

#3

#6

#9

the comb or mitt to loosen dirt on the horse's coat. Use circular motions all over the body. But use a lighter touch in the bonier areas of the horse's body. Take note: If the horse lays back his ears or swishes his tail, he's communicating with you. Stop brushing too hard.

Step #5: Comb out tangles in the mane and tail.

Step #6: Whisk away any more of the loosened dirt. Use the body brush.

Step #7: Use your finishing brush across the entire coat.

Step #8: Use the soft cloth to very gently clean the ears, muzzle, and eyes.

Step #9: Finish up with grooming spray (if you have it) or whatever other soft touches you have to give. Don't forget the kiss on his head at the end.

BABY ANIMALS

ANIMAL	BABY	GROUP
Alligator	hatchling	congregation, pod
Bear	cub	sleuth, sloth
Bee	larva	hive, swarm (in flight), bike, drift, grist
Camel	calf	flock
Cat	kitten	clutter, clower
Cheetah	cub	coalition
Crow	chick	murder, muster
Dog	pup	litter, pack, kennel
Dolphin	pup, calf	herd, pod, school
Duck	duckling	badelynge, brace, bunch, flock
Elephant	calf	herd, parade
Ferret	kitten	business, fesynes
Fish	fry, fingerling	draft, run, school, shoal
Fox	kit, cub, pup	skulk, leash
Frog	tadpole, polliwog	army, knot
Goat	billy	herd, tribe, trip
Gorilla	infant	band
Hamster	pup	horde
Hedgehog	piglet	array
Horse	colt (M), filly (F)	stable, harras, herd
Hummingbird	chick	charm
Leopard	cub	leap, prowl
Lion	cub	pride
Llama	cria	herd
Otter	whelp, pup	family, raft, romp
Oyster	spat	bed
Penguin	chick	rookery
Pig	piglet, shoat, farrow	drove, herd, litter
Pigeon	squab, squeaker	flock, kit
Rhinoceros	calf	crash
Shark	pup	school, shiver
Sheep	lamb, lambkin, cosset	drift, drove, flock, herd, mob, trip
Tiger	cub, whelp	ambush, streak
Turkey	poult	rafter
Turtle	hatchling	bale

POPULAR vs. WACKY PETS

POPULAR PET	WACKY PET	WHY SWITCH?
Cat	Alpaca	Although the alpaca takes up a teeny bit more space than a cat, these are calm, curious animals that are very easy to watch. Trade in your feline purr for an alpaca hum.
Dog	Hedgehog	Although her back is covered with spiny stuff, the hedgehog's belly is as soft as your dog's.
Hamster	Degus	A lot like chinchillas, degus like to chew on everything and take daily dust baths. For dinner, serve degus pellets, hay, and certain fresh veggies.
Fish	Wild Scorpion	You can reuse the fish tank for the new pet—but be sure to have spots (rocks, branches) where the scorpions can hide. You must keep the tank super-hot, but that's easier than keeping a fish tank super-clean.
Guinea Pig	Pot-Bellied Pig	Pigs are smart, easily trained, affectionate, and odor-free—and they do *way* more than their guinea pig cousins. They are, however, on a constant quest for food and they like to root with their snouts (which can cause damage). So, get thee to a pig-trainer, pronto!
Parakeet	Tarantula	Tarantulas are easy to care for and they don't need a lot of handling. Think about that next time you clean the birdcage. And what sounds cooler: exotic spider or little birdie? Even your big brother will think you've gone cool.

Worth noting: Some exotic critters are illegal in areas. Check with local regulations before getting an alternative pet.

6 MORE PETS, VIRTUALLY

- **FURBY:** An electronic toy that speaks Furbish, until you teach it English.
- **NEOPETS:** Virtual pets cared for online. You buy them food, toys, and accessories with Neopoints.
- **TAMAGOTCHI:** A handheld pet housed in an egg-shaped case that needs you to a) feed it, b) clean up after it, and c) have playdates with it.
- **MY LITTLE PET SHOP:** The VIP versions of these mini animals can interact online with other cyber pets.
- **WEBKINZ:** Stuffed animals that come with a special code on their labels to get into "Webkinz World" where you can "adopt" a virtual version of the pet for virtual interaction.
- **ROBOT DOG:** A robot built like Goddard from the series *Jimmy Neutron*.

A TO Z

AMAZING WOMEN WHO CHANGED THE WORLD IN THEIR OWN WAYS

"Life shrinks or expands in proportion to one's courage."
—Anaïs Nin, author

WHEN YOU'RE LOOKING TO GET inspired, or seeking someone different to write about for that next school essay, or just trying to impress (and inspire) Mom at the dinner table, consider these fascinating—and truly courageous—women from history. Many appear in school history textbooks; many do not. But in her lifetime, each woman here went out of her way to make the most of her talent and ability, to do something extraordinary.

P.S. Someday your name will belong on this list, too. Believe it.

ELEANOR OF AQUITAINE

- **BORN 1122—DIED 1204**
- **POINT OF ORIGIN:** Medieval France
- **BEST IN SHOW:** Strong and single-minded for a woman of feudal Europe, she is reported to have dressed like an Amazon warrior and ridden her white horse into the Crusades battlefields to boost morale.
- **TRUE!** Sponsored "courts of love," where men having trouble in love came before a tribunal of ladies with their questions. Based on an idea from her forward-thinking daughter, Marie de France.

NELLIE BLY

- **BORN 1864—DIED 1922**
- **POINT OF ORIGIN:** Pennsylvania, U.S.
- **BEST IN SHOW:** Journalist who fearlessly traveled where no American woman had gone before: to Mexico as a foreign correspondent; inside Blackwell Island for its bad treatment of mentally ill patients; and around the world in seventy-two days.
- **TRUE!** Born Elizabeth Jane Cochran, she was nicknamed "Pink" for the clothes she always wore. In later life, she invented and patented a steel barrel and became one of the country's leading industrialists.

RACHEL CARSON

- **BORN 1907—DIED 1964**
- **POINT OF ORIGIN:** Pennsylvania, U.S.
- **BEST IN SHOW:** Writer, scientist, and ecologist whose prize-winning book, *The Sea Around Us*, brought public awareness of the natural world and our responsibility to it.
- **TRUE!** One of Carson's biggest triumphs: taking on the big chemical companies. She testified before Congress about the dangers of pesticides, especially DDT, which was killing birds and wildlife.

DOROTHEA DIX

- **BORN 1802—DIED 1887**
- **POINT OF ORIGIN:** Maine, U.S.
- **BEST IN SHOW:** Traveling across the country, she campaigned for the rights of the mentally ill. She fought to increase the role of government in social welfare.
- **TRUE!** In the Civil War, Dix was appointed Superintendent of the Army of Nurses. Even after she was relieved of duties, she was remembered as an example of kindness to Union and Confederate soldiers.

MARY BAKER EDDY

- **BORN 1821—DIED 1910**
- **POINT OF ORIGIN:** New Hampshire, U.S.
- **BEST IN SHOW:** Influential American author, teacher, and religious leader, noted for her groundbreaking ideas about spirituality and health, which she named Christian Science.
- **TRUE!** A healer named Phineas Quimby introduced her to alternative medicine. After a bad spinal injury, she read the Bible and recovered unexpectedly. Inspired, she became the first woman to start her own religion!

ANNE FRANK

- **BORN 1929—DIED 1945**
- **POINT OF ORIGIN:** Germany during World War II
- **BEST IN SHOW:** The diary of her family's two years in hiding during the German Nazi occupation of the Netherlands was discovered by her father, Otto, and published after the war. To date, it has been translated into more than fifty languages and is perhaps the best known diary of the Holocaust.
- **TRUE!** Anne wrote, "In spite of everything, I still believe that people are really good at heart." She died of typhus with her sister Margot in a concentration camp, weeks before it was liberated.

MARTHA GRAHAM

- **BORN 1893—DIED 1991**
- **POINT OF ORIGIN:** Pennsylvania, U.S.
- **BEST IN SHOW:** Influential American dance pioneer, teacher, choreographer and the mother of Modern Dance.
- **TRUE!** For more than fifty years she created dances, choreographing more than 180 works—and dancing in most of them!

QUEEN MAKARE HATSHEPSUT

- **DIED 1458 B.C.**
- **POINT OF ORIGIN:** Ancient Egypt
- **BEST IN SHOW:** One of the most successful female pharaohs, she reigned twenty-two years, longer than any other woman of an Egyptian dynasty. She was a great "builder-pharaoh," constructing hundreds of projects.
- **TRUE!** Hatshepsut's royal titles included: King of the North and South, Son of the Sun, the Heru of Gold, Bestower of Years, Goddess of Risings, Chief Spouse of Amen, and the Mighty One. There were so many statues made of her likeness, that most museums in the world have at least one. The Metropolitan Museum in New York City has an entire room dedicated to her.

QUEEN ISABELLA I

* **BORN 1451—DIED 1504**
* **POINT OF ORIGIN:** Medieval Spain
* **BEST IN SHOW:** In her quest to make Spain Catholic, Isabella unleashed the Roman Catholic Inquisition, which sought to convert—or else expel—scores of Spanish Muslims and Jews.
* **TRUE!** Her influence is far-reaching for this period in history: She had five children who would greatly impact sixteenth-century history and she's the one who paid Christopher Columbus to set sail when he "found" the so-called New World.

QUEEN JINGA (SOMETIMES GINGA OR NZINGHA)

* **BORN 1583—DIED 1663**
* **POINT OF ORIGIN:** Matamba, West Africa
* **BEST IN SHOW:** A member of the ethnic Jagas, a militant group that waged an inspiring, thirty-year war against the Portuguese slave-traders.
* **TRUE!** Using both the strength and will of male leaders, combined with the gentleness of women, she formed clever alliances with foreign powers, and pit them against one another to free Angola of European influence.

HELEN KELLER

* **BORN 1880—DIED 1968**
* **POINT OF ORIGIN:** Alabama, U.S.
* **BEST IN SHOW:** Blind and deaf author with incredible accomplishments in the face of physical handicaps: learning Braille and lip-reading; receiving a cum laude degree from Radcliffe College; writing best-selling books; and lecturing around the world. She is one of history's best advocates and inspirations for people with disabilities.
* **TRUE!** The story of Helen's life, *The Miracle Worker*, won the Pulitzer Prize and two Academy Awards. Her teacher, Anne Sullivan, lived with and assisted Helen for nearly fifty years.

QUEEN LYDIA LILIUOKALANI

* **BORN 1838—DIED 1917**
* **POINT OF ORIGIN:** Hawaii, U.S.
* **BEST IN SHOW:** The last reigning monarch of the Hawaiian islands, who wanted to preserve the islands for her people, but had to relinquish her throne when the U.S. annexed the islands for themselves.
* **TRUE!** In additional to her political fame, Liliuokalani is also known for composing many Hawaiian songs, including the popular "Aloha Oe," or "Farewell to Thee."

RIGOBERTA MENCHU

- **BORN 1959**
- **POINT OF ORIGIN:** Guatemala
- **BEST IN SHOW:** Self-educated activist and social reformer whose fight for the rights of her country's peasants earned her a Nobel Peace Prize in 1992. She was the youngest and the first indigenous person to receive the prize.
- **TRUE!** Her father founded the CUC (Committee of the Peasant Union), but Rigoberta celebrated its cause, educating the massive peasant population against the guerilla fighters who were taking over her country.

AMALIE "EMMY" NOETHER

- **BORN 1882—DIED 1935**
- **POINT OF ORIGIN:** Bavaria, Germany
- **BEST IN SHOW:** Although she showed no interest in math as a small child, Emmy went on to be an esteemed mathematician who worked with algebra theorems. Albert Einstein said that she was, "the most significant creative mathematical genius thus far produced since the higher education of women began."
- **TRUE!** Emmy's father, Max, was a mathematics professor at Erlangen University. Although women were not admitted to the school, Emmy was able to take classes and become a mathematics professor in her own right.

GRACE O'MALLEY

- **BORN 1530—DIED 1603**
- **POINT OF ORIGIN:** Ireland during the Tudor re-conquest of England
- **BEST IN SHOW:** The daughter of a wealthy, seafaring family whose "tough girl" exploits are the stuff of Irish legend, she once met face-to-face with Queen Elizabeth I to petition the release of her jailed sons and half-brother.
- **TRUE!** O'Malley earned the nicknames "The Sea Queen of Connaught" and "The Pirate Queen" because of her brave and brazen role in the Irish rebellions of the time, which attacked English ships and fortresses near Ireland and Scotland.

EMMELINE PANKHURST

- **BORN 1858—DIED 1928**
- **POINT OF ORIGIN:** Victorian England
- **BEST IN SHOW:** One of England's greatest activists, she and her three daughters founded the Women's Social and Political Union (WSPU), aggressively fighting for women's rights, including suffrage, or the right to vote.
(continued)

• **TRUE!** Whenever a suffragette was released from prison, the WSPU would be there with a flower-decked wagon and a parade! Pankhurst also brought attention to the cause with pageants, torchlight processions, and hunger strikes. Many American suffragettes considered her their role model.

HARRIET QUIMBY

• **BORN 1875—DIED 1912**
• **POINT OF ORIGIN:** Michigan, U.S.
• **BEST IN SHOW:** America's first licensed female pilot and the first woman to pilot her plane across the English Channel; she made aviation accessible to *all* women.
• **TRUE!** Quimby was a noted journalist and author of five screenplays directed by the legendary D.W. Griffith. She met an untimely death when, while performing at an air show, she was pitched out of her plane. Her likeness was put on a postage stamp in 1991.

ELEANOR ROOSEVELT

• **BORN 1884—DIED 1962**
• **POINT OF ORIGIN:** New York City, U.S.
• **BEST IN SHOW:** The original First Lady activist during her husband Franklin Delano Roosevelt's presidency (1933–1945), Roosevelt was later made a delegate to the United Nations.
• **TRUE!** Her roster of volunteer and humanitarian efforts is unparalleled. She supported women's suffrage; volunteered for the Red Cross; helped provide financial aid to students through the NYA (National Youth Administration); worked with the NAACP (National Association for the Advancement of Colored Peoples); and drafted the Universal Declaration of Human Rights for the United Nations.

MARGARET SANGER

• **BORN 1879—DIED 1966**
• **POINT OF ORIGIN:** New York, U.S.
• **BEST IN SHOW:** A controversial figure, she fought for the rights of all women to have access to birth control; opened up numerous family planning clinics; and founded the American Birth Control League.
• **TRUE!** An avid defender of free speech, Sanger was arrested at least eight times while speaking publicly. She toured and lectured to as many women as possible—from halls and churches to socialites—getting millions of letters from women who sought advice and information.

VALENTINA TERESHKOVA

- **BORN 1937**
- **POINT OF ORIGIN:** Maslenikov, Russia (USSR)
- **BEST IN SHOW:** A Soviet cosmonaut who was the first woman to ever travel into space, aboard the *Vostok 6*.
- **TRUE!** Even though she had no formal space or flight training, Valentina was an amateur parachutist and engineer who beat out more then 400 applicants for the historic ride into space.

WINIFRED (FREDA) UTLEY

- **BORN 1898—DIED 1978**
- **POINT OF ORIGIN:** London, England
- **BEST IN SHOW:** Author, scholar, and leader of the anti-Communist movement who sought to usher in a new era of human freedom through political activity.
- **TRUE!** Formerly a Communist, she became a leader in the anti-Communist movement when her husband was arrested and disappeared in Moscow. She wrote pioneering theories on international events in China, Japan, Germany, the USSR, and elsewhere in the world.

ELIZABETH VAN LEW

- **BORN 1818—DIED 1900**
- **POINT OF ORIGIN:** Richmond, Virginia, during the Civil War
- **BEST IN SHOW:** Also called "Crazy Bet," she is known as one of the greatest spies of all time, serving during the Civil War.
- **TRUE!** Although born in the South, Van Lew worked for the Union, helping prisoners to escape. She ran a twelve-person spy ring, including a contact inside the Confederate White House. She got the nickname "Crazy Bet" because she would sometimes pose as a crazy person with overgrown hair. She was inducted into the Military Intelligence Hall of Fame.

SARAH BREEDLOVE WALKER

- **BORN 1867—DIED 1919**
- **POINT OF ORIGIN:** Louisiana, U.S.
- **BEST IN SHOW:** Born to a slave in the cotton fields of the South, Madame C. J. Walker (as she was popularly known) transformed herself from uneducated laborer to entrepreneur. America's first self-made, millionaire businesswoman, she was an innovator in the field of African-American cosmetics and hair care; and pioneered corporate responsibility and charity.

(continued)

• **TRUE!** Walker created her own beauty products, including Madame Walker's Wonderful Hair Grower, a scalp conditioner and healing formula, when she began to lose her hair at a young age. Selling her product door to door, she eventually built her own factory, hair and manicure salon, and training school, settling outside New York City.

XENOBIA, QUEEN OF PALMYRA

• **DIED AROUND 274 A.D.**
• **POINT OF ORIGIN:** Syria
• **BEST IN SHOW:** Upon the death of her husband, she became ruler of the empire and conquered Egypt with her brains and beauty.
• **TRUE!** Well-educated, she knew Greek, Aramaic, Egyptian, and Latin; the works of Homer, Plato, and other writers from Greece; and enjoyed hunting animals and drinking. At the end of her life, Xenobia lived in luxury and became a prominent philosopher, socialite, and Roman matron. Many prominent Romans are counted as her descendants.

ROSALYN YALOW

• **BORN 1921**
• **POINT OF ORIGIN:** New York, U.S.
• **BEST IN SHOW:** Co-winner of the Nobel Prize in Physiology or Medicine in 1977, Yalow was one of the most valuable research scientists of the twentieth century.
• **TRUE!** Although her prize-winning procedure (called radioimmuneassay; used to detect levels in the bloodstream) had commercial potential, Yalow and her partner did not patent it. They wanted to develop it for the people, not for financial gain.

MARGARETHA ZELLE

• **BORN 1876—DIED 1917**
• **POINT OF ORIGIN:** Leeuwarden, Holland
• **BEST IN SHOW:** Born Margaretha Zelle, she was a free-spirited dancer recruited in World War I as a German spy and given the name Mata Hari.
• **TRUE!** Many believe that Mata Hari may have been a double-agent, spying for Germany and France. Her dead body was left unclaimed, so she was delivered to the Museum of Anatomy in Paris for medical studies.

SO YOU WANNA SAVE THE WORLD?

10 THINGS YOU CAN DO RIGHT NOW

1 Don't open and close the fridge too much. A refrigerator uses almost five times more electricity than a television. Every time you open the refrigerator door, up to 30% of cold air escapes.

2 Recycle your cans and bottles. Recycling just one aluminum can saves enough energy to keep the television on for three hours.

3 Turn off your computer monitor when not in use for more than twenty minutes, and your computer when not in use for more than two hours. Consider getting a laptop. A laptop uses half the energy of a desktop computer.

4 Don't throw away plastic bags into the regular garbage. Worldwide, an estimated four billion plastic bags end up as litter each year. Tied end to end, that's enough to circle Earth sixty-three times. When those bags get loose, they kill hundreds of thousands of sea turtles, whales, cows, goats, and other animals who accidentally ingest them.

5 Take off your shoes when you enter the house. Every chemical and pesticide from the street and lawn comes inside with you when you walk in!

6 Don't let the tap run while you brush your teeth. Did you know that more than 70% of Earth's surface is covered by water, but less than 1% of it is drinkable? Conserve!

7 Recycle at home. Organize plastics, paper, and metals separately. Have them ready on garbage day for the recycle truck to pick up. If no recycle truck comes to your part of town, check your city's Web site to see if your location can be added to the route. If not, look for a listing of local recycling drop-off spots in your city.

8 Drink tap water instead of bottled water. In addition to the energy cost of producing, bottling, packaging, storing, and shipping bottled water, there is a huge environmental cost as the millions of bottles are disposed-with nowhere to go.

9 Totally avoid Styrofoam. It does not break down in the environment. At all. Plus, it contains chemicals that can build up in the body and cause health issues over time and with continuous exposure (even in small amounts).

10 Take shorter showers or ask Mom or Dad to install a low-flow shower head, which will limit the hot water and conserve more energy.

Sources: Con Edison NY, Health.com, treehugger.com

WHAT IS GLOBAL WARMING

IN THE PAST FIFTY years, humans have overloaded the atmosphere with heat-trapping gasses from cars and factories and power plants. More carbon dioxide is now in Earth's atmosphere than in the past 650,000 years. This carbon stays in the atmosphere, acts like a warm blanket, and holds in heat. That's why it's called "global warming." All this warming means that we're facing severe weather, extreme temperatures, and rising sea levels due to the melting of polar ice sheets. Ever wonder what it would be like if New York City was underwater? It's not impossible.

TAKE A GREEN SEAT

GROW A GRASS CHAIR IN YOUR BACKYARD. Take an old wooden chair and cover it with sod. Once it's grown, you won't be able to move it considering the more than 1,000 cups of soil it needs, but you'll be able to say that you're the proud owner of the greenest chair on the block. Of course, *mowing* the thing is another thing altogether, isn't it?

EVERYTHING
YOU WANT TO KNOW ABOUT
BARBIE

- *Who invented Barbie dolls?* Ruth Handler, co-founder of Mattel, in 1959.
- *What does Barbie stand for?* Barbara Millicent Roberts. The doll is named after Barbara, Ruth's daughter.
- *What does Ken stand for?* Ruth's son, Ken, inspired the Ken doll, which was produced in 1961.
- *Where are Barbie dolls supposed to live (besides your closet!)?* According to Mattel, Barbie attended Willows High School in Willows, Wisconsin.
- *Does Barbie have any sister dolls?* Five! Their names are Skipper, Tutti, Stacie, Kelly, and Krissy. She also has a best doll friend named Midge.
- *What was Barbie's first career?* Teenage fashion model. (She's had more than eighty doll careers altogether from rock star to presidential candidate.)
- *What special Barbie doll was introduced during the Gulf War in 1992?* Army Barbie.
- *Has there ever been a Barbie doll in a wheelchair?* Yes. In 1997, Mattel produced Share-a-Smile Becky, a fashion doll like Barbie who uses a wheelchair.
- *What's going on with Barbie dolls around the world?* Every second, two Barbies are sold somewhere on this planet. She's available in more than 150 nations. She has also been sold as forty-five different nationalities, including Quinceanera Teresa (Mexico), Spanish Barbie, and Freundshcafts, or Friendship Barbie (German).
- *How many outfits have been created for Barbie's closet?* Since her first appearance, close to one billion different fashion items have been created for Barbie and her whole doll family.
- *What unusual thing did Barbie dolls get for the first time in 2000?* Belly buttons!
- *What dolls have recently overtaken Barbie as the number one selling fashion doll?* Bratz dolls, with oversized heads, glam and rock looks, and flashy accessories.

SOLVE A MYSTERY LIKE NANCY DREW

WHEN I WAS NINE OR TEN, THE thing I loved most in life was getting a new Nancy Drew book. I ingested those suckers like candy. If I had to name anything I wanted to be when I grew up, it was a girl detective, just like Nancy. After all, how else would I be able to:

• Have the coolest friends ever who would drop everything and come sleuthing with me like George and Bess?

• Drive in a blue roadster at high speeds along gravel roads, in pursuit of the bad girl/guy/beast/ghost?

• Carry a flashlight everywhere just in case I need to shine a light on a sticky situation—or maybe throw some shadow figures on the wall?

• Trespass, break and enter, pick locks, and other sneaky stuff—without ever having to get in an ounce of trouble?

• Have an unlimited bank account so I can jet or ride all over the place collecting clues and getting a tan?

• Join my friends on wild adventures around River Heights, all while waiting for Ned Nickerson to notice that I *like* like him?

• Guess secret passwords in a snap, especially to places like Larkspur Lane, the Lilac Inn, Red Gate Farm, the 99 steps, and all those other quaint but oh-so-dangerous hot spots?

• Know everything there is to know about old clocks, ciphers, mysterious letters, tapping heels, crumbling walls, whistling bagpipes, moss-covered mansions, and everything else mysterious?

You just can't be a girl detective until you read all of Nancy's books. Here is a handy dandy checklist for the first thirty books in the series:

1. *The Secret of the Old Clock*
2. *The Hidden Staircase*
3. *The Bungalow Mysters*
4. *The Mystery at Lilac Inn*
5. *The Secret at Shadow Ranch*
6. *The Secret of Red Gate Farm*
7. *The Clue in the Diary*
8. *Nancy's Mysterious Letter*
9. *The Sign of the Twisted Candles*
10. *The Password to Larspur Lane*
11. *The Clue of the Broken Locket*
12. *The Message in the Hollow Oak*
13. *The Mystery of the Ivory Charm*
14. *The Whispering Statue*
15. *The Haunted Bridge*
16. *The Clue of the Tapping Heels*
17. *The Mystery of the Brass-bound Trunk*
18. *The Mystery at the Moss-covered Mansion*
19. *The Quest of the Missing Map*
20. *The Clue in the Jewel Box*
21. *The Secret in the Old Attic*
22. *The Clue in the Crumbling Wall*
23. *The Mystery of the Tolling Bell*
24. *The Clue in the Old Album*
25. *Ghost of Blackwood Hall*
26. *The Clue of the Leaning Chimney*
27. *The Secret of the Wooden Lady*
28. *The Clue of the Black Keys*
29. *The Mystery at the Ski Jump*
30. *The Clue of the Velvet Mask*

If *you* dream of being a girl detective, there are a few unofficial tips for solving your mystery Nancy-style.

✦ *Make a list of clues!* Call it your sleuth "cheat sheet." It's like those guys on CSI when they crawl through a crime scene jotting notes onto a pad—even the smallest detail can mean something big. Nancy knows how to take notes.

✦ *Beware red herrings!* No, I'm not talking about a kind of fish. I'm talking about the big dupe, the wool pulled over our eyes, the one that got away: Clues that lead us the wrong direction. How to avoid a herring? Follow each clue as far as it will go before jumping to any conclusions. And if you reach a fork in the road, a good detective will find some way to follow both paths—just in case. That way, you'll never be misled.

✦ *Know your cast of characters!* This is true of any adventure or mystery. You need to know who you're talking about, who you're talking to, and what everyone needs to accomplish. Keep a running list of possible suspects for each mystery you pursue, taking notes about appearance, attitude, and more.

✦ *Learn how to spot a villain!* One dead giveaway will be the villain's name. Benny No

Good should be pretty obvious, right? And then there's the villain's voice: deep and raspy like gravel.

✦ *Light the way!* Yeah, you might as well carry that flashlight after all (and a pair of backup batteries, too). Detective work in the dark is tough stuff. As a groovy girl detective, you need to be enlightened (ha, ha, get it?) at all times.

✦ *Look out!* Beware of danger ahead! Nancy and her crew were always coming up against trouble in some form. Sometimes it was a one-way ticket to peril, like the time she was hopelessly lost in the mountains outside Shadow Ranch; or the time she nearly toppled off a ladder; or the hundred or so times she was pelted by rocks, attacked by someone's pet, or nearly hit by a car. What if that were you? Then what would you do?

✦ *Make up a clever alias!* Don't use a name too close to your own, though, just in case someone recognizes you. Combine the new name with a new look, too: Add a wig, makeup, and whatever props disguise you while you're on the case.

6 INSPIRING WOMI

THERE ARE WAYS OF seeing the world, and then there are ways of seeing the world: painting, sculpting, sketching, shaping, and living through art. However, the history of women in art is sketchy at best before the eighteenth century. There are many reasons why this is true.

For one, women's primary artworks—weaving, embroidery, lace-making, and manuscript illumination—were unsigned, so we have few records of women's achievements in that area. Not to mention the problem with names! When women married, which they usually did at a very young age, they took their husband's names, creating a discontinuity of identity for these artists. Sometimes, too, paintings by women have been attributed improperly or women worked in art workshops where their identities remained unofficial while the name of the master artist (usually male) appeared on the canvas.

Despite all of this, there are many great women artists (and patrons of art) who we do know and admire.

These women put themselves out there bravely to paint, draw, take photos, and support the arts, even when it wasn't the popular choice.

MARIE TUSSAUD
- **Lived:** 1761–1850
- **Home:** Strasbourg, France
- **Her Story:** Her mother worked for a doctor skilled in wax modeling and he taught Marie how to model, too. During the French Revolution, she was arrested and her head shaved for execution by guillotine, but she was saved from death at the last minute. The condition? She was forced to make wax death masks of leaders like Robespierre, Marie Antoinette, and Marat, before they were killed.
- **Style:** Sculpture
- **Medium:** Wax
- **Famous Work(s):** During her lifetime, she personally sculpted many famous people in wax, including Voltaire and Benjamin Franklin. Madame Tussaud's Wax Museums remain popular tourist attractions all over the world today.

JULIA MARGARET CAMERON
- **Lived:** 1815–1879

- **Home:** Born in Calcutta, India, but lived in London, England
- **Her Story:** Cameron did not take a single photograph until she was forty-eight years old, when her daughter gave her a camera as a gift. Even more amazing, within just one year, she was a member of the photographic societies of London and Scotland, getting acclaim for her work. She smartly kept records of every photograph she took, which is why so much of her work remains intact today.
- **Style:** Closely framed portraits and allegorical photos based on religious works
- **Medium:** Photography
- **Famous Work(s):** Portraits of her family and friends, including Julia Jackson (her niece and the mother of author Virginia Woolf); Victorian society including Alfred Tennyson, Charles Darwin, Lewis Carroll, and Edward Lear.

MARY CASSATT
- **Lived:** 1844–1926
- **Home:** Born in Allegheny City, Pennsylvania, but later moved to Paris, France
- **Her Story:** The only American invited to exhibit with a

WHO LOVED ART

group of independent artists later known as the Impressionists, she painted average women like herself out and about in Paris, or at home, taking tea, reading, sewing, writing letters, and engaging in common activities. In 1880, she began to paint mothers with children, which became her signature theme.

- **Style:** Impressionism
- **Medium:** Oils, pastels, printmaking, Japanese woodcuts
- **Famous Work(s):** *Mother and Child (Baby Getting up from His Nap)*, c. 1899

KÄTHE KOLLWITZ
- **Lived:** 1867–1945
- **Home:** Born in the Province of Prussia, now known as Kaliningrad, Russia
- **Her Story:** Strongly influenced by her grandfather's fierce religious beliefs and her young brother's death, Kollwitz suffered from anxiety. Her parents' solution to that problem? Art! Her father saw her talent and enrolled her in art school. During World War II, despite being harassed by Nazis, she remained in Berlin to continue her life's work.
- **Style:** Naturalism and

expressionism
- **Medium:** Drawing, etching, lithography, woodcut
- **Famous Work(s):** She embraced all people affected (and afflicted) with poverty, hunger, and war, and her art shows the human condition (and inhuman conditions) in Germany during the first half of the twentieth century.

GEORGIA O'KEEFFE
- **Lived:** 1887–1986
- **Home:** Born in Sun Prairie, Wisconsin, but later settled in Santa Fe, New Mexico
- **Her Story:** She studied art from an early age, but soon realized she did not want her art to be traditional. After a friend sent a series of O'Keeffe's abstract charcoal drawings to photographer Alfred Stieglitz, O'Keeffe arrived on the New York art scene, exhibiting her work. She later fell in love with Stieglitz and began creating some of her most famous images of large-scale flowers. Her stark art was in great contrast to the chaotic art of the time. Later, when she moved to New Mexico, she painted images of the Southwest.

- **Style:** Abstract, bold colors, landscapes
- **Medium:** Oils, charcoal, pencil, watercolor, clay
- **Famous Work(s):** *Black Iris* (1926), *Poppies* (1927)

FRIDA KAHLO
- **Lived:** 1907–1954
- **Home:** Coyoacán, Mexico (near Mexico City)
- **Her Story:** Born Magdalena Carmen Frida Kahlo y Calderón, she contracted polio at age six and was in a bus accident at age eighteen that left her with numerous painful injuries. After the accident, Frida turned to painting full-time. Her works are often stark expressions of the pain she endured. As a young artist she met and married famous painter Diego Rivera. Kahlo painted with themes almost exclusively about women: women's bodies, birth, death, and survival. She herself was the subject of at least one-third of her paintings.
- **Style:** Surrealism
- **Medium:** Oils on canvas
- **Famous Work(s):** *The Two Fridas (1939)*

YOU NEED TO HEAR

LISTEN UP! YOU NEED to turn on the CD player and turn up the radio. There are some groovy girl bands, rockers, and divas out there just waiting to be heard.

- Mahalia Jackson
- Marian Anderson
- Billie Holiday
- Nina Simone
- Janis Joplin
- Tina Turner
- Celia Cruz
- Madonna
- Ani DiFranco
- Stevie Nicks
- Donna Summer
- Mariah Carey
- Celine Dion
- Patti Smith
- Joan Baez
- Aretha Franklin
- Laura Nyro
- Shania Twain
- Whitney Houston
- Agnetha Faltskog
- Alicia Keys
- Sarah Brightman

- Dusty Springfield
- Ella Fitzgerald
- Sarah Vaughn
- Björk
- Patsy Cline
- Kate Bush
- CeCe Winans
- Feist

- Edith Piaf
- Judy Garland
- Uum Kulthum
- Minnie Riperton
- Tori Amos
- Christina Aguilera
- Annie Lennox
- PJ Harvey
- Debbie Harry
- Dolly Parton
- Joan Jett
- Gwen Stefani
- Mary Wells
- Bette Midler
- Renée Fleming
- Pat Benatar
- Amy Winehouse
- Queen Latifah
- Ethel Merman
- Anita O'Day

5 CAN'T-MISS, ALL-GIRL BANDS

- The Go-Gos
- The Bangles
- Indigo Girls
- The Dixie Chicks
- Diana Ross and the Supremes

20 ROCKING GRRRL TUNES

- *Angelina* - Louis Prima
- *Barbara Ann* - The Beach Boys
- *Billie Jean* - Michael Jackson
- *Sweet Caroline* - Neil Diamond
- *Planet Claire* - The B-52s
- *Jack and Diane* - John Cougar Mellencamp
- *Donna* - Richie Valens
- *Come On, Eileen* - Dexy's Midnight Runners
- *Georgia* - Ray Charles
- *Gloria* - U2
- *Iris* - The Goo Goo Dolls
- *Jenny from the Block* - Jennifer Lopez
- *Proud Mary* - Ike & Tina Turner
- *Michelle* - The Beatles
- *Nikita* - Elton John
- *Rosalita* - Bruce Springsteen
- *Roxanne* - Police
- *Veronica* - Elvis Costello
- *Meet Virginia* - Train

THE PERFECT POP STAR NAME

Using the letters in your real name, discover what your new stage name could be. Take the first letter of your last name and find its corresponding star name in LIST A. Then take the letter of your first name and find its star name in LIST B.

LIST A		LIST B	
a.	Whitney	a.	Flowers
b.	Maggie	b.	Lee
c.	Delta	c.	London
d.	Chynna	d.	York
e.	Emerson	e.	Winter
f.	Lola	f.	Kite
g.	Brandy	g.	Fine
h.	Robyn	h.	Shay
i.	Shannon	i.	Bay
j.	Candy	j.	De Ray
k.	Lolita	k.	Best
l.	Tina	l.	Smile
m.	Tatum	m.	Stardust
n.	Fiona	n.	Dawn
o.	Cherry	o.	May
p.	Alyssa	p.	June
q.	Emma	q.	April
r.	Monique	r.	Tiger
s.	Krystal	s.	Fox
t.	Kiki	t.	March
u.	Raquelle	u.	Summers
v.	Joni	v.	Angel
w.	Summer	w.	St. James
x.	Cyndi	x.	La Donna
y.	Kara	y.	Roxy
z.	Bette	z.	Diamond

THINGS TO WRITE A SONG ABOUT

Your hometown, your best friend, the boy you like, the boy you don't like, rainbows, rain, religion, clouds, cliques, birds, a baseball game, loneliness, fear, the most embarrassing thing that ever happened to you, your Grampa, your dog, waterfalls, chocolate cake, outer space, movie stars, cowboys, pizza, a concert, and, of course, all of your deep feelings.

AMERICAN

FOR BE

HAVE YOU EVER WATCHED *American Idol* and thought one of the following things: a) I can do that, b) I wish I could do that, or c) That should be me? Have you ever stood in front of a mirror clutching a hairbrush and struck a pose like you were onstage at a live concert? Do you dream about applause and people holding signs that say VOTE FOR ALLYSON (or whatever your name is)?

Okay, take a deep breath. You have been diagnosed as having acute *American Idol*itis. It's not a big deal,

provided that you begin to take your interest in becoming a world-famous recording artist seriously. But you have to face some hard facts about breaking into the biz: It's a one-in-a-billion shot.

Are you a ready to face the music?

Ask yourself: Can I really sing? This question is not as easy as it sounds. You've seen the clips of people with the worst voices in the universe claiming they are actually superstars. Please. It's okay to love singing and have ter-

rible pitch. Just don't delude yourself into thinking you'll be the next Mariah Carey. Be content to sing because you love it.

Find out what you really love to sing. It's great to channel your inner Gwen Stefani. Just try other kinds of music, too. Find out what makes you grin or sigh with feeling. It could be a Broadway show tune or an operatic aria—or something else you don't expect.

Train your voice. Understand that you have muscles that

IDOL

GINNERS | BREAKING INTO THE BIZ

can be developed in the same way athletes train their muscles. Singing is fairly easy, with tiny muscles involved in coordinating the voice and subtle exercises required to develop their coordination. But like everything, it takes practice to get strong.

Increase your vocal range—and do your own thing. If you're really serious about making music (at least for now), then take voice lessons from a trained professional. Learn to sing in a higher register. Hold your notes for longer. Find something original to make the song "your own."

Always be prepared. Two of the key things you need to break into show business are determination and organization. Even if you're just practicing to audition for the school production, take your time to learn audition times, location, and requirements. When the details are handled, you can spend more time focused on . . . SINGING!

Find an agent. Chances are that you won't get any professional gigs unless a talent agent sends you out on auditions. How to get an agent? There are numerous books and Web sites that list agencies. Or just check the local Yellow Pages. Send a sampling of different agents your demo (a recording of your singing), along with a photo (a black-and-white headshot is the most professional), and a compelling letter to see if anyone is interested in representing you.

PLANN
ULTIMATE

Slumber-ific

[slum•ber•if•ik] adj.

Of, or pertaining, to the best slumber party ever.
Warm, fuzzy feeling you get while attending a slumber party with your best buds.
Alternative sleepover adjectives: awesome, major, cool, great, and FUN.

MY SLEEPOVER PARTY TO DO LIST

1 First things first: Pick a theme. Check out the ideas on the next page.

2 Make your invitation list. Try to keep your guest count low. No more than four or five of your closest pals.

3 Make and mail your invitations. Information you need to include:
* Theme of party
* Party location
* Date and time when party starts and ends (you need a pick-up time for the next morning)

4 Decide on a menu: dinner and breakfast.

5 Create or download a "soundtrack" for the party.

6 Purchase supplies.

7 Clean up your bedroom or basement-wherever the party will be held.

8 Make decorations or party favors.

9 Stock up on camera and film to capture the event.

10 Work out chaperone rules with Mom, Dad, or whomever is in charge.

11 Get a brand-new pair of PJs (of course).

12 Fluff up your sleeping bag and get set for FUN.

ING THE
SLEEPOVER

Dream Theme:
STARLET

Invitation:
Make mini-movie clapboard with black construction paper and white pencil or chalk; or make a mini -replica of the Hollywood sign.

Main Activity:
Watching movies! Everyone dresses up in their most glamorous pajamas and settles onto the sofa and pillows for a three-flick fest.

Other Stuff to Do:
Make a red carpet catwalk, complete with fashion modeling (ask guests to come prepared with some glamorous things to wear). You could have everyone choose a movie star name out of a hat, too. Let everyone else at the party guess who's who.

Food:
Fifteen different flavors of popcorn: try butter, salt, parmesan cheese, or cinnamon sugar. Taste test and make your own combinations.

Decoration:
Silver and gold streamers.

Goody Bag:
Glam sunglasses for all guests for that Hollywood look.

Dream Theme:
CASTAWAY

Invitation:
Write your facts on a piece of plain, brown craft paper rolled up into a scroll and tied with a piece of twine-and don't forget to play off the idea of the TV show Survivor. Write at the top of the invite: Who will survive my party?

Main Activities:
Obstacle course, scavenger hunt, puzzles (with a timer to see who is the fastest), and other funny challenges like the ones you see on TV.

Other Stuff to Do:
Make a tiki totem pole or tie-dye T-shirts together.

Food:
Think about the challenges on TV shows like Survivor and Fear Factor. Plan your menu accordingly. Take ordinary foods and give them funny names like spaghetti that gets labeled as Worm Pie or something just as gross.

Decoration:
Think outdoors—big huts, tiki torches (fake ones, please), and other stuff you'd see on a desert island.

Goody Bag:
Rubber snakes aren't too girly, but a shell necklace is just perfect.

Dream Theme:

SPA-TACULAR

Invitation:

Make the invite in the shape of a face or flower, something fresh.

Main Activity:

Spa central: Pedicures and manicures, washing each other's hair and then styling it silly, giving each other makeovers. Set up different "beauty stations" so everyone gets a chance to experience everything.

Other Stuff to Do:

Sample scavenger hunt-have everyone look for mini -samples throughout your house.

Food:

Fruit smoothies or homemade granola for breakfast!

Decoration:

Set the scene like a real spa: lemon water in pitchers, fresh towels, mellow music playing in the background.

Goody Bag:

Little soaps shaped like hearts, small-sized tube of body lotion, teeny tube of body glitter, hair clips, or even a jar of nail polish or nail art pens.

Dream Theme:

FEELING SPORTY

Invitation:

Paper shaped like sports equipment looks cute and fun. Or try an invite based on a newspaper sports page, with a headline: PARTY TIME AT SHERRY'S HOUSE and sports lingo to describe all the activities.

Main Activity:

Playing soccer or swimming or doing anything athletic. You can plan an "Olympics" right in your living room with balloon volleyball, a long -jump, and a hoop shoot into a garbage can.

Food:

Since you're being sporty, try to eat healthy: Gatorade sports drink, orange segments, fruit salad, Power Bars, or bottles of water are good for starters. Then you need to have fresh vegetables and salad. If you want to serve pizza, make it fresh!

Decoration:

Netting, signs (like Football Crossing).

Goody Bag:

Cool laces for your sneakers, a terry-cloth headband, and maybe a fun plastic flying disc.

30 GREAT MOVIES TO WATCH WITH A GROUP OF GIRLS

1. *The Breakfast Club*
2. *Bring It On*
3. *A Cinderella Story*
4. *Confessions of a Teenage Drama Queen*
5. *The Princess Diaries*
6. *The Princess Bride*
7. *Sixteen Candles*
8. *Mean Girls*
9. *Gone with the Wind*
10. *The Parent Trap*
11. *Freaky Friday*
12. *The Shop Around the Corner*
13. *Sense and Sensibility*
14. *Bend It Like Beckham*
15. *The Philadelphia Story*
16. *Little Women*
17. *The Secret Garden*
18. *Legally Blonde*
19. *Sabrina*
20. *Grease*
21. *Never Been Kissed*
22. *Splash*
23. *Clueless*
24. *Beaches*
25. *Say Anything*
26. *Ella Enchanted*
27. *Mermaids*
28. *Now and Then*
29. *Fried Green Tomatoes*
30. *Father of the Bride*

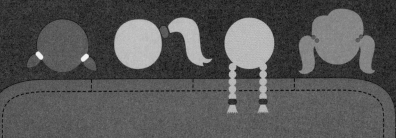

HOW TO

GIVE SOMEONE A GROOVY

TIP BY TIP
WHAT YOU NEED TO KNOW

- Nail painting is an art and takes lots of practice. If you are willing, have your friends practice and experiment on your nails—and vice versa.
- Go super smooth for your base coat. It will be much easier to draw a design if the surface is smooth.
- If you're painting toes, you need to put dividers between each toe (a rolled up paper towel works well; weave it in and out between each toe). This will keep the toes from smudging as you paint.
- When you use the paint, dip the brush into the bottle, then wipe it against the inside of the bottle to get just the right amount of polish. Keep the coats thin!
- Apply your stroke of polish down the middle of the nail, starting at (but not on) the cuticle and brushing upwards. Then paint the sides with the remaining polish.
- Wait until the first layer has dried, then put on a second coat. But don't do more than two coats. It will get messy.
- If you make any smudges, dab them with nail polish remover on the edge of a cotton swab.
- Get yourself specially made nail rhinestones and stickers to add to your pedicure or manicure when you're done.
- Always paint nails in a well-ventilated room. You don't want to breathe in the polish fumes for very long.
- When using nail polish and removers, use alcohol-free whenever possible. Alcohol dries out your skin and nails.

What do you do if you spill nail polish on the carpet?
Don't panic. There are solutions to this problem besides moving a chair over the spot to hide it. You could use acetone nail polish remover, which works, BUT (and this is a big but) you may risk ruining the carpet. Acetone is strong stuff. Instead, try a *non-*acetone remover and a little elbow grease. And don't forget to neutralize whatever solution you use with a little water so it doesn't leave a stain. Your best idea of all? Don't do nails on carpet. Paint atop an old towel, newspaper, or on a tiled floor.

MANICURE (OR PEDICURE)

PAINT A GARDEN
ON YOUR FINGERS AND TOES

WHAT YOU NEED:
- Pale blue or pale peach/pink nail polish
- Assorted nail art pens (brown, yellow, orange, pink, green, purple, etc.)
- Clear topcoat
- Cotton swabs and polish remover (just in case!)

1. Paint the entire nail the background color you want. Let it dry completely before you add any colors.
2. Pick your favorite design and the nail. **Sunflower (Fig. 1)** Using your brown nail art pen, paint a half-circle shape over the corner of the tip of the nail. Color in. Let dry completely. Use your bright orange or yellow nail art pen to paint triangle shapes around the brown circle (the petals of your sunflower).
   Wildflower (Fig. 2) Using your pink pen, draw a circle on the nail and fill in the color. Then use the purple nail art pen to draw teardrop-shaped petals around the circle. When the center has dried, dot it with the yellow art pen and outline the petals in yellow. If you have space, draw a stem with the green nail art pen.
3. When the design has dried, apply one coat of clear topcoat to seal it.

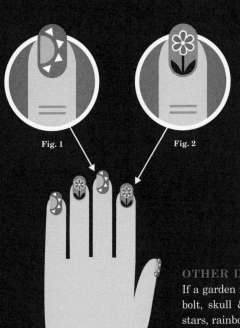

Fig. 1   Fig. 2

OTHER DESIGN IDEAS
If a garden isn't your thing, try alternative art: a lightning bolt, skull & crossbones, kitty, fish, sunshine, moon and stars, rainbow, smiley face, rose, or a yin yang symbol. You can also stay super-simple with swirls and letters. If you're attempting a cool design, try it out on paper first and *then* apply to your nails. Paintbrush in a pinch: Unbend a bobby pin and use the rough end as a painting tool.

HOW TO

MAKE 3 AWESOME FRIENDSHIP BRACELETS

Make a bracelet for yourself, an ankle wrap for your BFF, or a collar for your kitty! Each bracelet shown here should take between 10 and 30 minutes to make. Get your materials at any craft or sewing store: supply of many-colored embroidery floss, scissors, measuring tape or ruler, safety pin, masking tape, and beads (optional). You will also need a tape or a clipboard with a secure clip to hold the bracelet while you weave it.

KNOT! KNOT!

- Keep embroidery floss organized. Wrap it around flat pieces of cardboard to keep it from getting knotted and useless.
- For each bracelet, a measurement of each thread is indicated. This length of thread should be folded in two and knotted at the top. This "overhand" knot is where you pin/tape/hold the bracelet and where you tie the bracelet onto your wrist when it's done. Leave at least two inches to tie it off.
- The more strands of floss you use, the fatter the bracelet will be.
- As you weave, continue to push up the knots to keep the bracelet smooth and tight.
- Know your basic friendship knots.

BASIC FRIENDSHIP KNOT

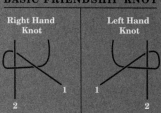

Right Hand Knot   Left Hand Knot

| Fig. 1 | Fig. 2 | Fig. 3 | Fig. 4 |

DIAGONAL STRIPES

Use three colors of strings, three strings of each color, each about three feet long.

1. Start with the overhand knot. Arrange your strings in the order you would like to see your stripes. (Fig. 1)

2. For your first knot, use the first strand on the left and make a basic knot over its neighbor string, twice. (Fig. 2)

3. Take that same knotting string and continue making double basic knots over each of the other strands in the row. (Fig. 3)

4. Now you're ready for row two. Do the same as above using the new first string on the left as your knotting string. (Fig. 4) Continue this way until the end of your bracelet. Tie it off by joining the bottom to the top with another overhand knot. Trim the loose ends if you want.

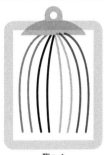

| Fig. 1 | Fig. 2 | Fig. 3 |

RAINBOW

Use four colors of string— two strands of each color, each about one yard in length.

1. Start by making the overhand knot and securing the strings, paired off by color, on your clipboard or table. (Fig. 1)

2. For this project, the two strings of the same color will be used together as if they're one string.

3. Start with the first two strings on the right and use them together to do the basic knot around all the other strings held together as a group. (Fig. 2) Pull the knot tight. Repeat these knots until you have a single color slide about one inch long.

4. Then use the next pair of strings to knot around all the others for an inch length, also. (Fig. 3) Continue this way until your bracelet is as long as you wish. End your bracelet as usual with the overhand knot.

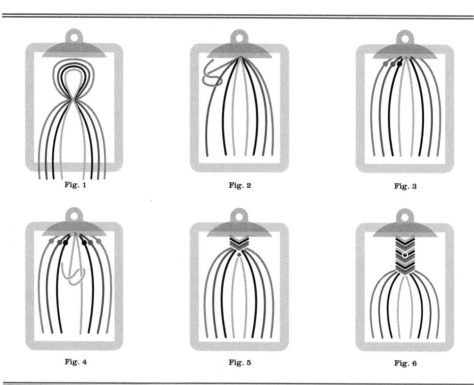

Fig. 1   Fig. 2   Fig. 3

Fig. 4   Fig. 5   Fig. 6

VERY Vs

You start this bracelet a little differently from the others. Use four different color strands, each at least six feet in length. Holding all four strands, fold them in half and make an overhand knot forming a loop in the middle. (Fig. 1) Slip this loop under the clipboard gripper or tape and you will have eight strings to work. Arrange the strings in a mirror image (see diagram). It's time to knot!

1. Start by doing the basic knot twice, knotting the first string on the left over its neighbor (Fig. 2) and then over the next string and the next until you reach the center (Fig. 3). Now do the same starting with the first string on the right.

2. When you reach the center (the two center strings should be the same color), make another double basic knot with the right hand string over the left (Fig. 4). Wow! Row one is complete. Time for row two.

3. Do row two exactly as you did the first row, and then row three, row four, etc. (Fig. 5) Do all the rows until you finish your bracelet. (Fig. 6) Tie it off, trim the ends, and wear proudly!

Bead Variation

This is the perfect bracelet to add beads. When you have finished the center joining knots, simply slip the strings through a bead and then knot again. Continue making V rows without joining the center knots until you've gotten to the bottom of the bead, then continue V rows, making the center joining knot just as you did above until you want to add another bead, then repeat.

THE INCREDIBLY UNSCIENTIFIC
BUT SURPRISINGLY ACCURATE

FOR GIRLS ONLY

SUPERQUIZ

IS THERE A SCIENCE TO QUIZ-TAKING? Many experts think so. Myers-Briggs Type Indicator (MBTI) test has been used for many years to identify cool things about people's personalities. The famous test, created by researchers Katharine Cook Briggs and Isabel Briggs Myers, is based on the teachings of philosopher Carl Jung. Jung introduced important concepts to psychology. He coined the words "introverted" (shy or reserved) and "extroverted" (outgoing) to explain why people act the way that they do.

Meyers believed that although we are all born with the same basic personality traits, we prefer some qualities more than others. Think about it like this: although you have two hands, you probably prefer one hand over the other to write, eat, or bat a ball. (Unless of course you're ambidextrous, meaning that you use both hands!) Meyers decided there were four main areas of our personality. She decided that those four qualities could be combined in numerous ways; sixteen possible ways, in fact!

Now, you're probably wondering where you fit on this spectrum. Which crazy combination of letters (personality traits) represents you?

Unfortunately, the Myers-Briggs test isn't meant to be used by girls or boys under the ages of fourteen. (That's because up until that point your personality is still taking shape.) But, fear not! In the absence of the actual test, I've developed this uniquely unscientific For Girls Only (FGO) quiz.

It's a teeny bit like the MBTI. There are four parts. Answer all of the questions in each part, tally your answers, and total your points on a separate piece of paper. After getting your number totals, you will then get four different letters; one for each part. It is the combination of these letters that reveals your personality profile.

Whew. Sound complicated? It really isn't. Think of it as Meyers-Briggs Lite. Although it's not the real deal, I hope you will be pleasantly surprised by the quiz results. Follow the directions (in order) and most importantly... have FUN.

PART ONE:
FASHION AND STYLE

Below are 40 questions about your clothes and personality (as you see it). Answer each one based on the following scale:

c Totally (1 point) c Sort Of (2 points) c No Way (3 points)

1. My dream job is to be a fashion designer.
2. I usually follow trends.
3. I always stop to look when I pass a mirror.
4. I change clothes more than once a day.
5. My wardrobe is bigger than Barbie's.
6. Frizzy is not cool.
7. I wish designer labels filled my closet.
8. Thrift shops are off limits.
9. If I look good; I feel good.
10. My outfits always match.
11. If I were a shoe, I'd be the cutest pair of flats ever.
12. My screen name is FASHIONGRL (or something like that)
13. If I had a credit card, I could shop all day long.
14. On my dresser: jewelry box with twirling ballerina inside.
15. In my jewelry box: charm bracelets and rings.
16. I would never get a tattoo.
17. My friends and I dress a lot alike.
18. I always compliment my BFF on her outfits.
19. I love it when someone compliments me.
20. I cannot live without my lip gloss.
21. Sneakers are for gym class.
22. I get invited to every party.
23. I could host the show *What Not to Wear*.
24. I believe in bling.
25. Sometimes I wear makeup.
26. Sometimes I dream about being a model.
27. Favorite four-letter word? SALE.
28. I carry scented lotion in my backpack.
29. Happiness is a great haircut.
30. My parents sometimes call me Princess.
31. I like to decorate my locker or bedroom.
32. I paint my nails.
33. I borrow things from my mom.
34. I tear pictures of models out of magazines for ideas.
35. Everyone wishes they had my sense of style.
36. When in doubt, dress up.
37. I wish I could walk the red carpet.
38. On my birthday wish list: perfume.
39. I get a new wardrobe every season.
40. Being "Best Dressed" in the yearbook is my goal.

Your Total _____
If your total is less than 40, you are C for Casual
If your total is more than 41, you are F for Fashionista
If your total is 125+ or above, you are Fashionista Plus Plus, which means that you'd spend all day looking in a mirror and dressing up in diamonds if you could. Helpful hint: maybe it's time to drag out the sweatpants and just kick back? Your call.
Your letter _____

PART TWO:
ATTITUDE

What's your self-esteem like these days? Take a close look at the following 10 questions and choose your answers.

1. **You just found out that there will be a pop quiz—and you haven't studied or done the reading assignment. How do you feel?**
   a) My palms are sweaty; I'm a mess!
   b) Huh? What? My mind has gone blank!
   c) I quickly try to review the assignment and prepare as best as I can.

2. **When my crush says hello in the hallway, I feel:**
   a) Happy and excited, in a heart-beating-faster way.
   b) OMG. I could just scream!
   c) Relaxed and serene. Just call me yoga girl.

3. **If someone is rude to me or cuts me in the lunch line, this is I what I say:**
   a) Nothing. I avoid conflict wherever possible.
   b) "Hey, what do you think you're doing?!"
   c) "Way to be friendly."

4. **If a teacher asks me to "come and talk" after class, I immediately think:**
   a) Ack! I'm in deep trouble!
   b) Yay! I'm a superstar!
   c) Gee, I wonder what's up?

5. **While waiting on a long line, what do I do?**
   a) I haven't got time to wait. I'll come back later.
   b) Stare at everyone. Talk to someone.
   c) Just wait.

6. **Whenever someone compliments me, I feel:**
   a) Like a ~~million~~ trillion bucks!
   b) Totally embarrassed.
   c) Sort of good; sort of uncomfortable.

7. **When I write my name down on a piece of paper, the letters look:**
   a) Pretty, open, and round cursive. In other words, *perfect*.
   b) Scribbly, and unreadable.
   c) Like I wrote it in 2nd grade.

8. **If I had to describe the way I think people see me as a critter, here's what I'd be:**
   a) A Bengal tiger.
   b) A butterfly.
   c) A Labrador retriever.

9. **If someone says something that upsets me, I reach for:**
   a) An ice cream sundae.
   b) A box of tissues.
   c) A telephone.

10. When my friends start talking about someone else (in not a nice way), I immediately think:

    a) They're entitled to their opinions, even if they are wrong.

    b) I wish I could think of something mean to say about them, too. Revenge can be sweet.

    c) That is so not cool. But I'll just let it go. Sigh.

---

    1. a=1 b=2 c=3
    2. a=3 b=1 c=2
    3. a=1 b=3 c=2
    4. a=1 b=3 c=2
    5. a=3 b=2 c=1
    6. a=3 b=1 c=2
    7. a=2 b=1 c=3
    8. a=1 b=3 c=2
    9. a=2 b=3 c=1
  10. a=1 b=2 c=3

Your Total _____

If your total is less than 16, you are
   R for Reserved

If your total is more than 17, you are
   O for Outgoing

Your letter _____

OUTGOING

16

RESERVED

PART THREE:
FEARS AND EMBARRASSMENT

There's nothing worse than being afraid or being embarrassed. Unless, of course, you get afraid or embarrassed at the same time! Below are 30 statements. Answer Y (for yes, if it's true) or N (for no, if it doesn't apply to you).

1. I am afraid of snakes or anything that slithers.
2. If my hair looks messy, I freak out.
3. I remain calm during tests.
4. I have burped in public and survived to tell the tale.
5. Someday I could climb Mount Everest.
6. My worst nightmare is failure.
7. I dream about winning an Academy Award.
8. Whenever I eat, food gets on my shirt.
9. I usually ride the rollercoaster more than once.
10. I would love to be photographed by the paparazzi.
11. There is nothing worse than parents telling "when she was a baby" stories.
12. Ghosts are real.
13. I snort when I laugh.
14. I have had toilet paper stuck to my shoe.
15. I am super-ticklish.
16. I feel better being part of a clique.
17. I've shown up to a school dance in the same outfit as a classmate.
18. I was hit in the face with volleyball during gym class (or something like that).
19. When I fall, I usually pretend to be fine, even if I'm not.
20. I have worn shirts inside out by mistake.
21. I heard a rumor about myself once.
22. I've waved to someone—only to discover he or she doesn't know me.
23. When I see a spider, I usually scream.
24. I've gotten cafeteria applause for tripping with a tray of food—splat!
25. I lost my bikini top in the pool/ocean/water.
26. I have trouble speaking in public.
27. I would totally run for class president.
28. I have no trouble talking to boys in social situations.
29. I don't mind shopping for a bra with my mom.
30. When I get embarrassed, my cheeks turn scarlet.

1. Y= 1 N=2	11. Y= 1 N=2	21. Y= 1 N=2
2. Y= 1 N=2	12. Y= 2 N=1	22. Y= 1 N=2
3. Y= 2 N=1	13. Y= 1 N=2	23. Y= 1 N=2
4. Y= 2 N=1	14. Y= 1 N=2	24. Y= 1 N=2
5. Y= 2 N=1	15. Y= 2 N=1	25. Y= 1 N=2
6. Y= 1 N=2	16. Y= 1 N=2	26. Y= 1 N=2
7. Y= 2 N=1	17. Y= 1 N=2	27. Y= 2 N=1
8. Y= 1 N=2	18. Y= 1 N=2	28. Y= 2 N=1
9. Y= 2 N=1	19. Y= 2 N=1	29. Y= 2 N=1
10. Y= 2 N=1	20. Y= 1 N=2	30. Y= 1 N=2

Your Total _____
If your total is less than 31, you are E for Easily Embarrassed
If your total is more than 32, you are D for Daring
Your letter _____

PART FOUR:
FRIENDSHIP

You can tell a lot about your own personality from the friends you hang with—and the things you do with them. What qualities do you look for in a friend? What's the nicest thing you ever did for someone—or that someone did for you? Select the multiple choice option that suits you best and add up your points.

1. **A day late, you realize that you missed your friend's birthday. What now?**

    a) You get an enormous bunch of Mylar balloons, a stuffed Teddy Bear, a homemade cake with the words BEST FRIEND IN THE UNIVERSE on top and surprise her a day late.

    b) You find out what everyone else got her and vow to do the same.

    c) You text message her: "Sry I missed ur bday. It's not a big dl, is it?"

2. **If your friendship was a movie, what would it be called?**

    a) *Just Like Sisters*

    b) *Let's Hang Out*

    c) *See You Next Year*

3. **Your friend had a huge fight with her mother. She calls you up for advice and wants you to tell her what to do. Now what?**

    a) Although you want to help her to feel better, explain that you can't tell her what to say or do. But you are here to be a great listener.

    b) Change the subject. There's no use in getting her more upset.

    c) Ignore her.

4. **What qualities are most important to you in your friendship?**

    a) Honesty, trust, and compassion.

    b) Common interests and sense of humor.

    c) Someone who lets me borrow all of her cool clothes.

5. **You catch your friend cheating on a science test. When your friend begs you not to tell, what do you do?**

    a) Convince her to turn herself into the teacher before it becomes a huge deal, blown out of proportion.

    b) Tell her you're sorry, but you can't keep a promise like that.

    c) Avoid your friend for a while. You can't be associated with a cheater.

6. **Your friend just told you a huge secret. What do you do with the information?**

    a) Lock it up and throw away the key.

    b) Write it in my journal and then tell one or two people.

    c) Talk about it a lot so eventually, you've blabbed the secret to almost everyone you know.

7. **It's the holiday party at school. Your friend shows up in the ugliest dress you've ever seen. Do you tell her?**

    a) No way. You don't want her to feel self-conscious!

    b) You make a little joke about the reindeer pattern on the dress fabric, but that's it. Otherwise, you let her wear it with no trouble.

c) Absolutely! Friendship = honesty. You want her to know what people really think, even if feelings get hurt.

8. **You suspect that your friend has been talking about you behind your back. How do you deal with the situation?**

a) Tell her what you've heard—and how much it hurt. See how she reacts when she sees how clearly she has hurt your feelings.

b) Catch her red-handed in the act of talking again. Then lay on the guilt trip.

c) Tell her you no longer want to be friends.

9. **A classmate has a big birthday party. Everyone has received an invitation—except your friend. What do you do?**

a) Boycott the party. If your friend can't go—you won't go.

b) Ask the person having the party why your friend didn't receive an invite. It might just be an oversight.

c) Tell your friend that she can come anyway. Who cares?

10. **During art class, you develop a crush on a cute guy—and then your friend says she likes him, too. What do you tell your friend?**

a) Tell her you agree that the guy's cute and maybe you can both like him. After all, it's not like anyone's going on a date.

b) Even though you feel competitive, you don't say anything. Better for her to think she's the only one who likes the guy.

c) "He's mine. Back off."

11. **How good a listener are you?**

a) You make time out of each day to ask your friend how she's doing— and actually listen when she tells you.

b) If your friend calls you, you talk for a little while.

c) You'd rather just send an IM or e-mail later.

12. **You borrowed one of your friend's favorite shirts—and spilled a diet soda down the front of it. Now what?**

a) You confess to the spill right away—and promise to get her a new shirt.

b) You don't mention it when you return the shirt. If there's a problem; she'll tell you.

c) Act like the spot was there before you wore the shirt.

13. **Someone in line for the cafeteria cracks a mean joke about your friend. She isn't there to defend herself. What do you say?**

a) You loudly say, "Stop talking about _____." Plain and simple. A good friend like you is a good defense.

b) You tell the person to stop, but you say it quietly, so you're not one hundred percent sure if the kid even hears you.

c) You don't say anything. Better not to get involved.

14. **If you are sick in bed with a cold, your friend will usually do what?**

a) Get your homework and bring it over to your house right away. She does everything she can to make you feel better!

b) Make some joke about bringing

over a container of chicken soup;
and check in on you by phone later
that day.

c) Stay far, far away. She doesn't want
to get sick, too.

15. **You both decide to hang out one Sat-
urday, but you want to stay at home
and study for a test while your
friend wants to go to the movies.
How do you resolve this conflict?**

a) You figure out a way to do both.
Study for an hour and then head to
the movie.

b) Go to the movie and then come
back to study.

c) You don't resolve it. You do neither.
She wants to have her way.

16. **Your friend decides to sit at a different table during lunch. How do you
feel?**

a) Not worried. She's allowed to have
other friends. You'll see her later.

b) A little jilted. She is your best pal,
after all. What's she up to?

c) Angry. How dare she leave you at
the other lunch table by yourself?

17. **You've been away all summer long.
When you get home, your friend is
giving you the cold shoulder. What
do you say?**

a) Tell her you missed her and ask to
spend some fun time together
before school starts. You can find
out what's bugging her then.

b) Get mad and call her up. Demand
to know what happened.

c) Blow her off. Two can play this
game.

18. **You're in a school play together. On
stage, your friend forgets an important line. Everyone is waiting. You**

know the line. What do you do?

a) You whisper the line, hoping that
she'll pick up the cue.

b) You stand still and try to send her
psychic signals. She'll remember
the line eventually, won't she?

c) You crack up.

19. **The ultimate day with your best
friend would be:**

a) Anything. Just being together is the
best part.

b) Doing as many activities as possible
with other friends, too.

c) The "ultimate" day is just me,
myself, and I.

20. **You've had tickets to go see a play
and now the day is finally here! As
you are getting ready to leave, the
phone rings. Your friend is in tears.
What do you do?**

a) Lend her support but tell her that
you can only talk to her about
what's happened after the play.

b) Tell her to deal with it. Things happen.

c) Shout, "I can't talk now. Sorry!" into
the receiver and then hang up.
Whatever it is can wait.

Mostly As—give yourself 3 points
Mostly Bs—give yourself 2 points
Mostly Cs—give yourself 1 point

Your Total _____
If your total is less than 40 you are L for Laid
Back
If your total is more than 41, you are T for True
Blue
Your letter _____

EVERYTHING GREAT
ABOUT TAKING A

FOR GIRLS ONLY

QUIZ

1. You can share this quiz with friends and laugh when the answers are right on the mark—or off base. Because that's what friends do best: cry, laugh and *understand* each other when no one else can.

2. No quiz is a crystal ball. It only records a few bits and pieces of you (ie. not the *whole* you). It only tells you how you're acting or feeling or existing *this* week. Results change from day to day. You have a lifetime of experiences—and quizzes—ahead of you. So don't give this one too much weight.

3. Any quiz responses are valid. All the letter types that define you after taking this quiz are good. Whoever you are on the spectrum is just fine. There's no judgment or criticism here. There is no "right" score.

4. Despite the fact that it isn't a perfect explanation of your future, a quiz like this *can* be a big help, even if it's just to cheer you up. And remember: you have the power to change any quiz result you may not like. Don't forget that. Re-take it, I say! That's why they invented erasers.

5. Quizzes are like potato chips. We can say they don't matter (and they really don't), but they still reel us in with their salty, wonderful, crunchy, and delicious answers. Hmmm. Is anyone else hungry?

Enough stalling! Turn the page and find out your personality type!!!!
Sorry. I meant to say, "Please turn the page? Thank you."*

*Never forget your manners, girls.

Still curious about the real MBTI? Look for more information online at www.myersbriggs.org.

YOUR FOR GIRLS ONLY PERSONALITY TYPE:

CASUAL FASHIONISTA	EASILY EMBARRASSED DARING
RESERVED OUTGOING	LAID BACK TRUE BLUE

CREL
You're a combination of Casual/Reserved/Embarrassed/ Laid Back.
You shrink away from stressful situations and can hardly get through the day without one embarrassing moment, which is made triply hard by the fact that you don't have a lot of close friends to give you some recovery time. You're could use some big change—to fix your fashion problems, to help you to speak up, and give you more incentive to fight for the friends you do have. Don't let things pass you by!

CRET
You're a combination of Casual/Reserved/Embarrassed/ True Blue.
Although you tend to be a little shy and even quiet, you are a steadfast friend. You get embarrassed easily, but that's okay because you surround yourself with good friends to help you feel better about what's going on. Let them help you to stand up and speak out. Don't be afraid to say what you feel or think. Friendship is the key!

CRDL
You're a combination of Casual/Reserved/Daring/Laid Back.
You're a study in contrasts. You like to wear low-key clothing, but your personality can be a little wild. You have to be careful not to step on anyone's toes because your daring nature can sometimes get in the way. You sometimes put your friends second, when they should be first. Try mixing it up a little bit more. Next time you step out…find someone to share the experience. Rock on!

CRDT
You're a combination of Casual/Reserved/Daring/True Blue.
Everyone likes your style: a combination of easygoing and daring that keeps friends interested in you. You have an appreciation for the quiet and loud things that make friendship work. Even more importantly, your sense of loyalty is sky high. You want to make a difference, but you don't need to hog the spotlight. You're happy to share it! Way to go!

COEL
You're a combination of Casual/ Outgoing/Embarrassed/Laid Back.
Although you're no fashion plate, you try to assert yourself in all sorts of other, simpler ways. Sometimes this means that you take small risks that don't always pay off. Don't worry, though. You don't get too hung up on the details. It's the big picture that counts—and you're setting a course for success.

COET
You're a combination of Casual/ Outgoing/Embarrassed/True Blue.
It's hard to keep your friendships on track because sometimes you want so much to do everything the right way—that you get too intense. But there's no denying: your sensitivity makes you a great listener—and, as a result, a special friend. Pay attention to those gut feelings. They are great guideposts for you!

CODL
You're a combination of Casual/ Outgoing/Daring/Laid Back.
You like to stay comfortable; never formal, even though you love a party. You're not

touchy-feely, though, so friends probably don't come to you with their deepest secrets or strongest feelings. It depends. Mostly, you're here for a fun time. Enjoy the ride.

CODT

You're a combination of Casual/ Outgoing/Daring/True Blue.

Although you'd rather hang out in sweatpants than a dress, you are a girl's best friend: always plotting some fun activity, rarely letting things get you down or embarrass you, and sticking by your friends through thick and thin. Someone like you who marches to her own drummer always finds a profound path in life, too. Chances are you'll be the one to discover a cure for cancer or write a Pulitzer Prize-winning novel. You're the quiet trailblazer. Kudos!

FREL

You're a combination of Fashionista/Reserved/Embarrassed/ Laid Back.

You make a huge fashion statement when you walk into a room—but it's your clothes and style doing all the talking for you. When it comes to baring souls, you're a little tight-lipped. You'd rather stay calm and quiet. In some ways, even mushy feelings embarrass you. But your dramatic exterior and reserved attitude sometimes don't mix, but you keep things interesting. You could give lessons on being—and staying—cool.

FRET

You're a combination of Fashionista/Reserved/Embarrassed/ True Blue.

You love to dress up, although you don't have any attitude about it. You're the first one to jump in when there's trouble. And although you may get embarrassed easily yourself, you're quick to rescue a friend if she gets embarrassed, too. You put the "true" in true blue. Everyone could use a friend like you!

FRDL

You're a combination of Fashionista/Reserved/Daring/ Laid Back.

Bold colors. Cool accessories. You've got the sense of humor to go along with all the bold statements you make. Everyone wants to be around you, too, but you tend to lay lower than the rest. You're more reserved than outgoing, after all. Your daring side combined with your tendency to be low-key about your friend's needs, may make you seem insensitive at times. But you're in it for the long haul. Friends forever!

FRDT

You're a combination of Fashionista/Reserved/Daring/ True Blue.

Although you know how to work a great outfit or hairdo, and although you like to take risks, you have a reserved side to you, too. It's this side that keeps you in check—and makes you more thoughtful. It's this part of your personality, too, combined with the "true blue" part, that makes you a fantastic listener. You're an ideal combination of girly-girl and tough—the kind of friend you can count on for almost anything. How did you get to be so great?

FOEL

You're a combination of Fashionista/Outgoing/Embarrassed/ Laid Back.

Sometimes friends might think you're in it all for show. You like the hot new outfits and feel a need to be noticed. In fact, you need attention so much that you'd even take a negative experience just to get noticed! You'll turn a nothing moment into a dramatic scene or make comments that might not be as kind to your friend as they should be. Remember to show people all the sides of you—out and in. It's not just about your shoes. It's about your heart—and yours is HUGE.

FOET

You're a combination of Fashionista/Outgoing/Embarrassed/ True Blue.

You're like the girl all dressed up to go to the party: you have the right dress, the right attitude, and you love your friends. But then, at the party, some of your insecurities show through a little. You need to trust all of the other qualities—and believe in yourself enough to toss those fears and embarrassments into the trash. You have so much to offer!

FODL

You're a combination of Fashionista/Outgoing/Daring/ Laid Back.

You've got the sparkle. You've got the quick wit. You're not even afraid of spiders! But here's the thing: sometimes you let all the stuff outside of you push down the feelings inside of you. You have so much to offer a great friendship. Make sure you're practicing your listening skills and taking seriously this great friend who needs you. Fly your banner high and be the leader everyone knows you can be.

FODT

You're a combination of Fashionista/Outgoing/Daring/ True Blue.

Nobody's perfect, although you are certainly trying very hard to be that way. Relax! You're usually stylin' and you're always up for adventure. You're not afraid to take risks and you're the best friend a girl could hope to have. Just make sure there's room—and time—for you. Keep a journal. Don't be afraid to be introspective once in a while.

EVERYTHING GREAT ABOUT TAKING A GIRL QUIZ

1. You can share it with friends and laugh when the answers are right on the mark—or off base. Because that's what friends do best: cry, laugh and *understand* each other when no one else can.

2. You know it's not a crystal ball. Not only does a quiz record just a few bits and pieces of you (ie. not the *whole* you), but a quiz like this only tells you how you're acting/feeling/existing *this week*. Results could change from day to day. And you have a lifetime of experiences—and quizzes—ahead of you. So don't give it too much weight.

3. All the quiz responses are valid. All the letter types are right. Whoever you are on the spectrum is just fine. There's no judgment or criticism here. There is no "right" score.

4. A quiz like this can be a big help. Sometimes we don't realize we're doing something annoying or goofy until we answer a few questions, tally our scores and see our result. But you have the power to change any result you don't like. Don't forget that. You have the power to believe in you. Use it.

Still curious about the real MBTI? Look for more information online at www.myersbriggs.org.

BIBLIOGRAPHY

Steven Caney's Kids' America © 1978 by Steven Caney. Workman Publishing. New York, NY.

Anna Banana: 101 Jump Rope Rhymes © 1989 by Joanna Cole, Ill. By Alan Tiegreen William Morrow & Co, Inc. New York, NY.

Album of Horses by Marguerite Henry, Ill. By Wesley Dennis. © 1951 by Rand McNally & Company, © 1993 Aladdin Paperbacks Edition.

The Curious Kids' Activity Book Boredom Busters © 1997 by Avery Hart and Paul Mantell. Williamson Publishing Company, Charlotte, VT.

Women Invent! © 1997 by Susan Casey. Chicago Review Press. Chicago, IL.

Scholastic Guides: How to Write Poetry ©1999 by Paul B. Janeczko. Scholastic Inc., New York, NY.

The Kids Guide to Fortune Telling © 1998 by Louise Dickson, Ill. By Pat Cupples. Kids Can Press, Ltd. Buffalo, NY.

Hopscotch, Hangman, Hot Potato & Ha Ha Ha: A Rulebook of Children's Games by Jack Maguire © 1990 by the Philip Lief Group. Simon & Schuster, New York, NY.

Folklore on the American Land © 1972 by Duncan Emmerich. Little Brown & Co. New York, NY.

Oxford Atlas of the World 12th Edition.

The Love magic book © 2003 by Gillian Kemp. Little Brown & Co. New York, NY.

Nike is a Goddess: The History of Women in Sports, © 1999 by Lucy Danziger.

The Book of Lists for Kids by Sandra and Harry Choron, © 1995 by Sandra Choron, Houghton Mifflin Co. Boston, MA.

Clever Letters: Fun Ways to Wiggle Your Words by Laura Allen © 1997 by Pleasant Company, Pleasant Company Publications, Middleton, Wisconsin.

The Encyclopedia of Dreams: Symbols and Interpretations by Rosemary Ellen Guiley © 1993 by Rosemary Ellen Guiley, Berkley Books, New York, NY.

"I Am In Need of Music" by Elizabeth Bishop from *The Complete Poems: 1927-1979,* and *"Stars"* by Valerie Worth from *All the Small Poems and Fourteen More,* reproduced with permission from Farrar, Straus, & Giroux.

ASSORTED WEB SITES:
www.Popculturemadness.com
www.Roadsideamerica.com
www.Snopes.com
www.Worldcocoafoundation.org
www.Costumegallery.com
www.About.com
www.Womeninworldhistory.org
www.Greatwomen.org
www.Rd.com (Reader's Digest)
www.spaceplace.nasa.gov
www.womenssportsfoundation.org
www.northnet.org/stlawrenceaau
w/timeline.htm
www.poemhunter.com/org
www.discoverychannel.com/uk
www.mcdonalds.com
www.weird-food.com
www.womeninworldhistory.com
www.globalfundforwomen.org/cms
www.fashion-era.com
www.school.discoveryeducation.com
www.amic.com
www.girlscouts.org
www.gettech.org
www.engineergirl.org
www.mathpower.com
www.whitehouse.gov
www.usolympicteam.com
www.dictionary.com
www.sleepfoundation.org
www.britannica.com

Thank you for reading this FEIWEL AND FRIENDS book.

A special thanks to HEADCASE DESIGN for making this

G·R·E·A·T

BOOK

The Friends who made *For Girls Only* possible are:

Jean Feiwel
PUBLISHER

Liz Szabla
EDITOR-IN-CHIEF

Rich Deas
CREATIVE DIRECTOR

Elizabeth Fithian
MARKETING DIRECTOR

Elizabeth Noland
PUBLICIST

Holly West
ASSISTANT TO THE PUBLISHER

Dave Barrett
MANAGING EDITOR

Nicole Liebowitz Moulaison
PRODUCTION MANAGER

Jessica Tedder
ASSOCIATE EDITOR

Allison Remcheck
EDITORIAL ASSISTANT

Ksenia Winnicki
MARKETING ASSISTANT

Find out more about our authors and artists and
our future publishing at www.feiwelandfriends.com.

OUR BOOKS ARE FRIENDS FOR LIFE

trary to Friends' order, only one of the parties was a member. When both parties to a marriage engagement were members in good standing, there was usually no reason why they might not apply to the meeting, and receive permission to marry under its authority, but there were some exceptions. Marriage between first cousins or others of close relationship was forbidden by the rules of the Society. Parental objection may have been a bar to a marriage in meeting in some cases. In other cases the couple married out of meeting for no other reason than to accomplish their purpose more quickly and without the formality which was necessary to a marriage in meeting.... [2]

The examples of Friends' records used here come from the Monthly Men's Meeting of Smithfield, Rhode Island, and from the same meeting of Hampton, New Hampshire. The following are typical entries taken at random from the minutes:

(SMITHFIELD)

—28th of 1st Mo 1802
   This meeting Recd a Certificate of Removal from Swanzy Monthly Meeting in favor of Job Chace his wife Sibel and their Children whose names are Earl, Cromwell, Pillena Joanna and Lamira Chase which being read Excepted and ordered Recorded.

—29th of the 4th Month, 1802
   This Meeting Recieved a Certificate of Removal from South-kingstown Monthly Meeting in favor of Alice Rathborn which being Read is Excepted

—Monthly meeting 30th of the 9th Mo 1802
   The women inform that they have come to a conclusion to Disown Rhoda Smith with which this Meeting unites.
      Smithfield preparitive Meeting informed this that Reuben Shearman Desires a Marriage Certificate to Uxbridge Monthly Meeting. Chad Smith and William Buffam are appointed to take the necessary care theirin and if nothing appear to hender prepare a Certificate and bring to next Monthly Meeting

---

2. Thomas W. Marshall, "Introduction" to Encyclopedia of American Quaker Genealogy, Vol. I, ed. by William Wade Hinshaw, 1936 (Baltimore: Genealogical Publishing Co., 1969 reprint), pp. ix-xi.

—Monthly Meeting 25th of the 11th Mo, 1802

Smithfield Preparatives Meeting inform this that Daniel Inman
Proposed Laying his Intention of Marriage with Abigail Mowry
before this Meeting he producing a Certificate from Uxbridge
Monthly Meeting. And they appeared in this Meeting and De-
claired their Intentions accordingly and were Directed to next
Monthly Meeting for an answer.

—Monthly Meeting 30th of the 12th Mo, 1802

Smithfield preparitive Meetg informed this Meetg that Elisha
Shearman was in the practice of Keeping Company with one
not a Member of our Society in order for Marriage Where-
upon Rowland Rathborn Joseph Bartlet Seth Kelly and Stephen
Aldrich Are appointed with such others as the womens Meetg
may appoint to make a visit to the family endeavoring to feel
after the mind of Truth theirin and Report their Sence thereon
to next Monthly Meetg

Daniel Inman and Abigail Mowry appeared in this Meetg
and Continued their intentions of Marriage and Recvd and
Answer accordingly and Zaccheus Southwick and Daniel Smith
are Appointed to have the Necessary Care theirof according
to Discipline and Report to next Monthly Meeting.

This Meetg is informed that James Clemence a member
theirof is gone to live a few monthes in the verge of Bolton
Monthly Meetg and Desires a few lines to Certify his right of
Membership, the Clerk is Directed to furnish him with a
Coppy of this Minute

—M M at 27th on 1st Mo 1803

The Committee on the Case of Elisha Shearman inform that
they have had an opportunity with him and that he is married
out of the good order of friends and Does not appear to them
to be in Sutable Disposition of mind to Make friends Satisfac-
tion. This Meetg after Solidly Considering the same Do with
the unity of the womens Meetg Disown unity with him as a
Member and Elisha Kelly and Rowland Rathborn Are appointed
to inform him their of his right to appeal Draft a Testimony
of his Denial and report to next Monthly Meetg.

The Committee on the Case of Philip Walden request for
his Children report that some care has been taken in sd Matter but not being ready to make full report at this time Sd
Case is referd under the same friends Care and Directed to
Report to next Monthly Meetg.

The Committee to have Care of Daniel Inman and Abigail

Mowry Marriage report that according to their observation it was Conducted in an orderly Manner and that the Certificate is Delivered to the Regester

—M M on 28th of 4th Mo, 1803
The Committy appointed to Prepare a Certificate for Joseph Bartlette to uxbridge Mo Meeting in order for marriage presented one wich Being Read with Some alteration is agreed to and Sined by the Clark.

—6th Mo, 30th, 1803
This Meeting appoints Caleb Pain to read the Testamony of Denial aginst Elisha Shearman at a publick Meeting in this Place and lodge the same with the Regester to be recorded and report to our next Monthly Meeting.

—11 Mo, 24th, 1803
The Women presented a Testimony of Denial against Waty Bartlett formerly Buffum which was read and agreed to in this Meeting.

—4th Mo, 26th, 1804
The Committee appointed to prepare a Removal Certificate for Elisha Thornton Jur to Newbedford Monthly Meeting presented one which being read with some Alterations is approved and signed by the Clerk.

—6th Mo, 28th, 1804
Our Beloved Friend Jonathan Wright attended this Meeting with a Certificate from hopewell Monthly Meeting in Virginia dated 6^{d} of 2th Mo, 1804—Expressive of their Unity with him as a Minister, whose Company and Gospel Labors have been exceptable to us.

(HAMPTON)

Joseph Dow deceaced this Life ye 4th of ye 2th Month 1703
Eastor Green Desesed Y^{e} 24th of Y^{e} 7th Month 1703
Abraham Green Juner dyed ye 11th of Y^{e} 3th month 1703
Thomas Lankster & Y^{e} widow Musey Kiled ye 19th of Y^{e} 6th mon 1703
Jeams Pearintun Lost at sea Y^{e} 12 day of the same: 1718: in his 55 year
Hannah Pearintun: daughter of James Pearingtun and Lydia his wife Born the 14th day of Y^{e} 2 mo: 1708

Lydia Mussey Pearintun Born ye 10th day of ye 9th mo 1671
1737: The: 3 day of the 10th mo Lydia Pearintun dyed in her:
66 year.

* * * *

A Record of the Births of the Children of Jonathan Hoag and
Comfort his Wife as Followeth (viz)——
    Peter Hoag: Son of the afore Said Jonathan Hoag
    and Comfort his wife Born the: 21 Day of y^e:
    12th month Called February------------------ 1738/9
    Hephsabe born the: 25th of ye 9th mo Called
    November----------------------------------- 1741
    Hussa born the 10th day of the seccond month
    April-------------------------------------- 1744
    Anna born the 1st day of the Sixth month Called
    August------------------------------------- 1745
    Mary born the 10th day of the Sixth month Called
    August------------------------------------- 1747
    Abraham born the 25th day of ye 7th mo Called
    September----------------------------------1748
    Isaac Born ye: 7th day of the 7th mo; Old Stile
    Called September--------------------------- 1752

* * * *

1742
    Whereas Jonathan Hardy son of John Hardy of Hampton in
the Province of New Hampshier in New-England and Lydia his
wife And Bathshabe Stanyan daughter of James Stanyan of Hampton in the province afore said And Ann his wife haveing publickly
decleared their Intentions of takeing Each other in Marrage before severall monthly meeting of the people Calld Quakers in
hampton and Almsburg according to the good order useed amongst
them: Whose proceedings there in after deliborate Considiration
Thereof: they appearing Clear of all others Relateing to marrage
And haveing consent of parents and Relations Conserned were
approved by the said Meetings - - -
    Now these are to Certify all Whom it may Consern that for
the full Accomplishing of their sd Intentions this fourteenth day
of the seventh month called September Anno Domini one Thousand Seven hundred and forty two: They the Said Jonathan Hardy
and Bathshaby Stanyan appeared in a Publick assembley of the
aforesd People (and others) Meet to gather for that purpose at

our meeting house at hampton afor'sd And sd Hardy takeing sd
Stanyan by the hand openly Decleared that he took Bathshabe
Stanyan to be his Wife Promiseing through the Lords assistance
to be unto her a Kind and Loveing husband untill it Shall please
God by Death to seperate us: (or to that Effect) and then and
their in sd assembly sd Stanyan publickly decleared that she took
Jonathan Hardey to be her Husband promiseing through the Lords
assistance to be unto him a true and faithfull Wife untill it shall
please God by Death to seperate us or words to ye same Import.
And the Said Jonathan Hardy and Bathsaby Stanyan as a farther
Confirmation thereof did hereunto Set their hands (she according
to the Custom of Marrage assumeing the name of her husband)
And wee whose names are hereunto Subscribed being present at
their Solomnizeing of Said Marrage and Subscription as afore sd
have here unto set our hands as witneses the day and year above
written - - - - - - - -

		Jonathan Hardy
		Bathshaby Hardy
Phebe dow	Philip Rowell	
Elizabeth dow	Jonathan Hoag	James Stanyan
	Winthrop Dow	Joseph Stanyan
	Abraham Dow	Merry Newbegin
	Nathan Hoag	Rebeckah Hunt
		Jonathan hoag jr
		Comfort Hoag
		Elizabeth Hunt

F. THE ROMAN CATHOLIC CHURCH

The Roman Catholic Church probably has as good records as any other
denomination. The sacramental records (registers) of the church are ex-
ceptional in the completeness of the information they contain. By church law
the records were carefully kept and well preserved—and these laws were
strict.

There is, however, some difficulty in doing research in the records of
the Roman Catholic Church. Reasons for these difficulties include:

1. Historically the records have been kept in Latin.

2. There are few indexes (not so different from most other
churches).

3. Most records are still in the parishes and little effort has been
made to centralize them.

4. Church law stipulates that the records may be searched only by
the priest and that the priest will issue a certificate (not a copy of the
original record).

PRESBYTERIAN BAPTISM RECORDS

Though some dioceses are bringing in the records from the parishes for microfilming, this has not essentially changed the policy of restricted usage. The filming is only for preservation purposes and not for research. It is a hopeful sign, however, that this is the beginning of some centralization activity and that some day there may be a change in the research and access policy relating to at least the older records.

G. OTHER CHURCHES

We have not pretended to cover the entire spectrum of church records in this discussion. This would be an impossible task within the limits of our work. You are, no doubt, acutely aware of many of our omissions and probably feel that many other religions and sects might be profitably discussed. We have passed over the records of the Orthodox Eastern Church, the Presbyterian Church, the Methodists (including the Methodist Episcopal Church which became so strong after the Revolutionary War), and the Anabaptists and their offspring (including the Mennonites, the Amish Mennonites and the Hutterites). We have also neglected the Reformed Church groups (Calvinistic) which came out of Holland (the Reformed Church in America and the Christian Reformed Church), the German Palatinate (the Reformed Church in the United States, which later became the Evangelical and Reformed Church), Hungary (the Free Magyar Reformed Church in America) and France (the Huguenots). And no attention has been paid to the various splinters from the Lutheran Church which came to America from central Europe. These include the Brethren Churches (also known as Dunkers, Tunkers and Dunkards) and the Pietist groups (especially the Unity of the Brethren, better known as Moravians). We have also ignored Jewish records and Latter-day Saint (Mormon) records. And on and on...

While we regret that further coverage cannot be given, we feel that our examples represent an appropriate cross-section of typical American church records and should give you a "feel" for almost any church records you might encounter. We think that it is more important for us to talk about how these records can be located than what they look like. If you find them, you can discover the nature of their contents quickly enough.

III. LOCATING CHURCH RECORDS

A. PROBLEMS AND SOLUTIONS

Church records are of no value if you cannot find the ones that fit your specific problems. In America, where church and state are separate and where people with ancestry from all over Europe live side by side and intermarry, there are two main problems:

1. Determining the church with which your ancestor had affiliation.
2. Locating the records of that church in the locality where your ancestor lived.

Clues to solve the first problem might come from many sources. Perhaps the family's present affiliation can help you, or the national origin of the family, or family tradition. You might find your answer in a will or a deed or on a tombstone. It may be in an obituary. Or there may be a clue in the locality where your ancestor resided—it may have been the settlement of a particular religious sect—but you must know the locality's history to determine this. [A person may have belonged to several churches during his lifetime. This was quite common on the frontier, because if a town had only one church, that was usually where the town's residents (especially the Protestants) went to worship, regardless of former affiliation.] In later years obituaries, death certificates, hospital records, etc., contain statements of religious preference.

The second problem may be the more difficult of the two. There are some helps and reference tools to assist us in locating church records, but even these are quite incomplete and may be misleading if we are not aware of their limitations. There is, in fact, no complete guide to American church records. This is an area which lies wide open to further study. The personnel of the Research Department at the LDS Genealogical Society are beginning some studies on the location of church records, but they have a long way to go before the true objective is attained. [3]

Some useful studies were made in the 1930's and early 1940's as part of the Historical Records Survey under the auspices of the Works Projects Administration (WPA) of the "New Deal." The "Inventories of Church Archives" which resulted from these studies were excellent for the geographic areas and the churches they covered and at the time they were made, but much of the information in them is now frightfully outdated. Many of the records have since been moved and many which were in private hands are now completely untraceable. [4]

We must not assume that church records do not exist just because we have been unable to find them; however, on the other hand, it would be foolish to say that no church records have ever been lost or destroyed, because

---

[3.] See Jimmy B. Parker and Wayne T. Morris, "A Definitive Study of Major U.S. Genealogical Records: Ecclesiastical and Secular" (Area I, no. 36), World Conference on Records and Genealogical Seminar (Salt Lake City: The Genealogical Society of The Church of Jesus Christ of Latter-day Saints, 1969).

[4.] See Chapter Nine for a complete list of the guides to the WPA inventories of church records in the several states.

many of these records are no longer in existence. The vestry minutes of the Immanuel Church in Hanover County, Virginia, of which we gave an example earlier, show this quite clearly. The biographical sketch (obituary) of George Washington Bassett tells some of the history of the Immanuel Church:

* * *

In the year 1843, soon after his removal, to his estate in Hanover, Mr. Bassett became much concerned at the prostrate condition of the Church in his neighborhood, and the adjoining counties of King William and New Kent. The parishes had died out and been without rectors or church services for more than half a century.... [Emphasis added.]

Was this common? What of records during this "more than half a century?" What about records of the earlier period before the church "died out?" All of these questions should be considered in a study of American church records. The same thing may have happened in hundreds of other churches. What does happen to the records when a church becomes defunct? It has been suggested by some that many records of the English Church met their doom during the Revolutionary War as part of an action of reprisal against the British, but we are not aware of any specific situations of this nature.

B. FINDING THE RECORDS

If you can find early American church records they are peerless as a genealogical source, so let's consider some steps you might take:

1. First consider that the records are still in the custody of the church where they were kept, if that church still exists.

2. An advertisement in a local newspaper will often lead to the whereabouts of available records, especially those in private hands.

3. Don't be afraid to ask questions—of ministers, chambers of commerce, old-timers; anyone who might know.

4. The records of many churches have been published, especially in genealogical and historical periodicals and are thus available. These are generally not too accessible either from the standpoint of finding the proper magazine or of knowing that an article of value is within it. One of the best approaches is to use the various periodical indexes listed in Chapter Five.

A few church records are also published in book form (both alone and in conjunction with other records) and you should be aware of this possibility. Look under the locality of interest in your library card catalog. We mentioned Hinshaw's works on the Quakers earlier in this chapter. [5] These seven volumes (in eight) contain abstracts of Monthly Meeting records, are indexed and are quite useful as far as they go; but they certainly do not cover all Quaker records. They are, however, a representative example of published American church records.

In using published church records, as all published sources, remember that they are secondary and frequently contain copying errors.

5. Many church records are now being microfilmed by the churches themselves and by other agencies. Historical societies often preserve microfilm copies as well as originals, and copies are frequently available for sale or for reading. The LDS Genealogical Society has microfilmed the records of many churches throughout the U.S. and you may find it worthwhile to check its holdings before you make a lot of other searches.

6. Libraries and historical societies have collected many church records (especially in their local areas) and these are readily available for searching. One of the big problems is to determine just who has the records.

C. SOME RECORD LOCATIONS

With no indication of specific congregations or the actual extent of the records, we offer the following as a <u>partial</u> list of church record depositories in states east of the Mississippi. Further information on the exact nature of the various collections and the addresses of these depositories must be determined from other sources.

ALABAMA:
    1. Samford University (formerly called Howard College)—Baptist (Georgia and Alabama).
    2. Department of Archives and History, Montgomery—Methodist, Baptist, P.E., Presbyterian, Roman Catholic.
ARKANSAS:
    1. Hendrix College, Conway—Methodist.
CONNECTICUT:
    1. Bristol Public Library, Bristol—Congregational (local).
    2. Farmington Museum, Farmington—Congregational (local).

[5.] William Wade Hinshaw, <u>Encyclopedia of American Quaker Genealogy</u>, 7 vols. (in 8), 1936——. (Vols. 1-3 have been reprinted by Genealogical Publishing Co., Baltimore, Md., 1969. Other volumes are out of print but all are available on microfilm from Frederic Luther Co., Indianapolis, Indiana.)

3. Archives of the Episcopal Diocese of Connecticut, Hartford—
   P. E.
4. Connecticut State Library, Hartford—various (more than 700 churches).
5. The Missionary Society of Connecticut, Hartford—Congregational.
6. Peck Memorial Library, Kensington—Congregational (local).
7. Wesleyan University Library, Middletown—Methodist.

DELAWARE:
1. Delaware Public Archives Commission, Dover—various.
2. University of Delaware Library, Newark—Presbyterian, Baptist.
3. Historical Society of Delaware, Wilmington—various.

GEORGIA:
1. Emory University Library, Atlanta—Methodist.

ILLINOIS:
1. McCormick Theological Seminary Library, Chicago—Presbyterian (including records formerly at Lane Theological Seminary in Cincinnati, Ohio).
2. Garrett Biblical Institute Library, Evanston—Methodist.
3. Knox College Library, Galesburg—Presbyterian, Congregational.

INDIANA:
1. Franklin College Library, Franklin—Baptist.
2. Archives of the Mennonite Church, Goshen—Mennonite and Amish Mennonite.
3. Archives of DePauw University and Indiana Methodism, Greencastle—Methodist.
4. Henry County Historical Society Museum, New Castle—Quaker (local).
5. New Harmony Workingmen's Institute Library, New Harmony —Methodist (local)
6. Earlham College Library, Richmond—Quaker.
7. Old Catholic Library, Vincennes—Roman Catholic.

KENTUCKY:
1. College of the Bible Library, Lexington—Disciples of Christ.
2. Margaret I. King Library, U. of Kentucky, Lexington—mainly Baptist and Presbyterian, but also Disciples of Christ and Shaker.
3. Filson Club, Louisville—Shaker (Mercer County).
4. Louisville Presbyterian Theological Seminary Library, Louisville—Presbyterian.

MAINE:
1. Parsons Memorial Library, Alfred—Baptist, Congregational, Methodist (all local).

2. Androscoggin Historical Society, Auburn—Baptist (Lewiston).
3. Bangor Public Library, Bangor—various (limited).
4. Hubbard Free Library, Hallowell—Congregational, Unitarian.
5. Louis T. Graves Memorial Library, Kennebunkport— ? (local).
6. University of Maine Library, Orono—Baptist (in Polermo).
7. Maine Historical Society, Portland—various (scattered).
8. Colby College Library, Waterville—local country churches.

MARYLAND:

1. Hall of Records, Annapolis—various (more than 400 volumes).
2. Archives of the Archdiocese of Baltimore, Baltimore—Roman Catholic.
3. Baltimore Yearly Meeting of Friends (Hicksite), Baltimore—Quaker.
4. Baltimore Yearly Meeting of Friends (Orthodox), Baltimore—Quaker (extensive).
5. Maryland Diocesan Library, Baltimore—P. E. (extensive).
6. Maryland Historical Society, Baltimore—P. E. (local).
7. Methodist Historical Society, Baltimore—Methodist.

MASSACHUSETTS:

1. Amesbury Public Library, Amesbury—Congregational (local).
2. Amherst College Library, Amherst— ? (local).
3. Barre Town Library, Barre— ? (local).
4. Beverly Historical Society, Beverly—Congregational (local).
5. Congregational Library, Boston—Congregational (extensive).
6. Massachusetts Diocesan Library, Boston—P. E.
7. New England Methodist Historical Library, Boston—Methodist (very few registers).
8. Dedham Historical Society, Dedham—Congregational, P. E. (local)
9. Haverhill Public Library, Haverhill—various (nearly 200 volumes).
10. Ipswich Town Hall, Ipswich— ? (local).
11. Marlborough Public Library, Marlborough— ? (local).
12. Universalist Historical Library, Crane Theological School, Tufts University, Medford—Universalist.
13. Nantucket Historical Association, Nantucket—Quaker (local).
14. Friends Meeting House, New Bedford—Quaker.
15. Andover Newton Theological School Library, Newton Center—Baptist. (Has collections formerly in New England Baptist Library.)
16. Forbes Library, Northampton—Congregational.
17. Northborough Historical Society, Northborough— ? (local).
18. Peabody Historical Society, Peabody—Congregational, Unitarian, Baptist (all local).

19. Petersham Historical Society, Petersham—Church of Christ (local).
20. Berkshire Athenaeum, Pittsfield—Shaker and (mainly) Quaker.
21. Essex Institute, Salem—various.
22. Shrewsbury Historical Society, Shrewsbury— ? (local).
23. Goodnow Public Library, South Sudbury— ? (local).
24. Historical Room, Stockbridge Library, Stockbridge—Congregational (local).
25. Old Colony Historical Society, Taunton—Congregational, Baptist.
26. Narragansett Historical Society of Templeton, Templeton— ? (local).
27. Westborough Historical Society, Westborough— ? (local).
28. J.V. Fletcher Library, Westford— ? (local).
29. Winthrop Public Library, Winthrop—Methodist (local).
30. Worcester Historical Society, Worcester—Congregational, Baptist, Universalist (local).
31. Woburn Public Library, Woburn—Congregational (Woburn and Burlington).

MICHIGAN:
1. Michigan Historical Collections, U. of Michigan, Ann Arbor—Presbyterian, Baptist, Congregational, Methodist, et al.
2. Archdiocese of Detroit Chancery, Detroit—Roman Catholic.
3. Burton Historical Collection, Detroit Public Library, Detroit—Roman Catholic and various Protestant (extensive).
4. Flushing Township Public Library, Flushing— ? (local).
5. Thompson Home Library, Ithaca—Congregational (local).
6. Jackson City Library, Jackson— ? (Jackson County).
7. Kalamazoo College Library, Kalamazoo—Baptist, et al.
8. Port Huron Public Library, Port Huron— ? (local).

MINNESOTA:
1. Pope County Historical Society, Glenwood— ? (local).
2. Blue Earth County Historical Society, Mankato— ? (local).
3. Hennepin County Historical Society, Minneapolis—various .
4. Historical Society of the Minnesota Conference of the Methodist Church, Minnesota Methodist Headquarters, Minneapolis—Methodist (extensive).
5. Evangelical Lutheran Church Archives. Luther Theological Seminary, St. Paul—Evangelical Lutheran.
6. Historical Committee of the Baptist General Conference, Bethel Theological Seminary, St. Paul—Baptist (extensive).
7. Minnesota Historical Society, St. Paul—P.E. (extensive for state).
8. Weyerhauser Library, Macalester College, St. Paul—Presbyterian.

    9. Gustavus Adolphus College Library, St. Peter—Evangelical Lutheran.

MISSISSIPPI:

    1. Mississippi Conference Methodist Historical Society, Millsaps College Library, Jackson—Methodist.

    2. Mississippi Department of Archives and History, Jackson—Southern Presbyterian.

NEW HAMPSHIRE:

    1. New Hampshire State Library, Concord—various.

    2. Dover Public Library, Dover—Baptist (local).

    3. University of New Hampshire Library, Durham— ? (local).

    4. Dartmouth College Library, Hanover—Congregational.

    5. New Hampshire Antiquarian Society, Hopkinton—various.

NEW JERSEY:

    1. Blair Academy Museum, Blairstown—Presbyterian, Methodist.

    2. Cape May County Historical Association, Cape May—Quaker.

    3. Monmouth County Historical Association, Freehold—various.

    4. Drew University Library, Madison—Methodist (including papers formerly held by the Methodist Historical Society of New Jersey).

    5. Morris County Historical Society, Morristown—various (local).

    6. New Brunswick Theological Seminary Library, New Brunswick —Reformed Church (extensive).

    7. Rutgers University Library, New Brunswick—various (on film).

    8. Sussex County Historical Society, Newton—various.

    9. Passaic County Historical Society, Paterson—various.

   10. Seventh Day Baptist Historical Society, Plainfield—Seventh Day Baptist.

   11. Princeton Theological Seminary, Princeton—Presbyterian (N. J. Synod).

   12. Salem County Historical Society, Salem—Quaker.

   13. Atlantic County Historical Society, Somers Point—Quaker, et al.

   14. Somerset County Historical Society, Somerville—various (local).

   15. State Library, Archives and History Bureau, Trenton—various.

NEW YORK:

    1. New York State Library, Albany—various (extensive).

    2. Cayuga County Historical Society, Auburn—Congregational.

    3. Buffalo Historical Society, Buffalo—Baptist, Presbyterian.

    4. Ontario County Historical Society, Canandaigua—various (local).

    5. Cobleskill Public Library, Cobleskill—various (local).

    6. New York State Historical Association and Farmers' Museum, Cooperstown—various (Otsego County).

7. Cortland County Historical Society, Cortland—various (local).
8. Green County Historical Society, Coxsackie—various (transcripts).
9. Department of History and Archives, Fonda—Dutch Reformed, et al.
10. Pember Library and Museum, Granville—Presbyterian (local).
11. Colgate University Archives, Hamilton—Baptist.
12. Hempstead Public Library, Hempstead—various (local)
13. Huntington Historical Society, Huntington—Presbyterian, P.E., et al.
14. Dewitt Historical Society of Tomkins County, Ithaca—Methodist, Presbyterian, et al.
15. Columbia County Historical Society, Kinderhook—various.
16. Senate House Museum, Kingston—Dutch Reformed, et al.
17. Daughters of the American Revolution Library, LeRoy—various.
18. Wayne County Division of Archives and History, Lyons—various (local).
19. Huguenot Historical Society, New Paltz—Huguenot.
20. Jean Hasbrouck Memorial House, New Paltz—Dutch Reformed, Methodist.
21. Holland Society of New York Library, New York City—Dutch Reformed, Lutheran, French Reformed, German Reformed.
22. New York Genealogical and Biographical Society, New York City—various (extensive).
23. New York Historical Society, New York City—P.E. and various.
24. Queens Borough Public Library, New York City—various.
25. Society of Friends Records Committee, New York City—Quaker.
26. Union Theological Seminary Library, New York City—Presbyterian (defunct parishes in Manhattan).
27. Yivo Institute of Jewish Research, New York City—Jewish.
28. Historical Society of Newburgh Bay and the Highland, Newburgh —various (local).
29. Shaker Museum Foundation, Inc., Old Chatham—Shaker.
30. Oswego County Historical Society, Oswego—Presbyterian (local).
31. Portville Free Public Library, Portville—Presbyterian (local).
32. Suffolk County Historical Society, Riverhead—various (local).
33. American Baptist Historical Society, Rochester—Baptist, (extensive, including Samuel Colgate Baptist Historical Collection formerly at Colgate University).
34. Colgate Rochester Divinity School Library, Rochester—Baptist plus some Dutch Reformed and German Evangelical.
35. Saratoga County Historian's Office, Saratoga Springs—various (local).

36. Schenectady County Historical Society, Schenectady—Presbyterian, Dutch Reformed
37. Schoharie County Historical Society, Schoharie—Dutch Reformed, Lutheran, Methodist, Presbyterian.
38. Staten Island Historical Society, Staten Island—Dutch Reformed, Methodist.
39. Onondago Historical Association, Syracuse—various (local).
40. Syracuse Public Library, Syracuse—various (transcripts).
41. Syracuse University Library, Syracuse—Methodist (central and western New York).
42. Hancock House, Ticonderoga—Quaker, Presbyterian, Methodist Episcopal, et al.
43. Troy Conference Historical Society, Ticonderoga—Methodist.
44. Utica Public Library, Utica—United Presbyterian, Congregational, et al. (of Paris, N. Y.).
45. Waterloo Library and Historical Society, Waterloo—various (local).
46. Westchester County Historical Society, White Plains—Baptist, Congregational, Methodist, Presbyterian.

NORTH CAROLINA:
1. Duke University, Durham—Methodist Episcopal (extensive).
2. Guilford College Library, Greensboro—Quaker (extensive).
3. High Point College Library, High Point—Methodist.
4. Historical Foundation of the Presbyterian and Reformed Churches, Montreat—Presbyterian, Reformed (very extensive).
5. Catawba College Library, Salisbury—German Reformed.
6. Moravian Archives, Winston-Salem—Moravian.
7. Smith Reynolds Library, Winston-Salem—Baptist.

OHIO:
1. Great Cleveland Methodist Historical Society, Berea—Methodist (especially German Methodist).
2. Mennonite Historical Library, Bluffton College, Bluffton—Mennonite, Anabaptist.
3. American Jewish Archives, Cincinnati—Jewish.
4. Historical and Philosophical Society of Ohio, Cincinnati—various.
5. Western Reserve Historical Society, Cleveland—Shakers, et al.
6. Ohio Historical Society, Columbus—Quaker, Freewill Baptist, Methodist, Presbyterian, Shaker.
7. Historical Society of the Evangelical United Brethren Church, Memorial Library, United Theological Seminary, Dayton—Evangelical United Brethren and predecessors.
8. Ohio Wesleyan University Library, Delaware—Methodist, Methodist Episcopal.

9. Rutherford B. Hayes Library, Fremont—P. E. (local).
10. Oberlin College Library, Oberlin—Congregational (formerly belonged to Ohio Church History Society).
11. Toledo Public Library, Toledo—Presbyterian (local).
12. Otterbein College Library, Westerville—Evangelical United Brethren.
13. Public Library of Youngstown and Mahoning County, Youngstown—various (typescript).

PENNSYLVANIA:

1. Lehigh County Historical Society, Allentown— ? (local).
2. Old Economy, Pennsylvania, Historical and Museum Commission, Ambridge—Harmony Society.
3. Tioga Point Museum and Historical Society, Athens— ? (local).
4. Archives of the Moravian Church, Bethlehem—Moravian.
5. Bethlehem Public Library, Bethlehem—various (typescript).
6. Delaware County Historical Society, Chester—various.
7. Presbyterian Historical Society of Coatesville—Presbyterian (local).
8. Bucks County Historical Society, Doylestown—various (extensive).
9. Easton Public Library, Easton—various.
10. Lutheran Historical Society, Gettysburg—Lutheran.
11. Lutheran Theological Seminary Library, Gettysburg—Lutheran.
12. Historical Society of the Evangelical and Reformed Church, Lancaster—Reformed.
13. Lancaster County Historical Society, Lancaster—various.
14. Vail Memorial Library, Lincoln University, Lincoln University —various.
15. Fulton County Historical Society, McConnellsburg—Presbyterian, Reformed (local).
16. Susquehanna County Historical Society, Montrose—various.
17. Moravian Historical Society, Nazareth—Moravian.
18. Historical Society of Montgomery County, Norristown—various.
19. Schwenkfelder Library, Fennsburg—Schwenkfelder.
20. American Swedish Historical Museum, Philadelphia—various (mostly Lutheran).
21. Christ Church Library, Philadelphia—P. E.
22. Department of Records, Society of Friends of Philadelphia— Quaker.
23. Genealogical Society of Philadelphia—various.
24. Historical Society of Pennsylvania, Philadelphia—Universalist, et al.
25. Historical Society of Philadelphia Annual Conference of Methodist Episcopal Church, Philadelphia—Methodist, Methodist Episcopal (extensive).

26. Lutheran Theological Seminary Library, Philadelphia—Lutheran (extensive).
27. Presbyterian Historical Society, Philadelphia—Presbyterian (extensive, including church records from Lyman C. Draper Collection in State Historical Society of Wisconsin).
28. Historical Society of Western Pennsylvania, Pittsburgh—Presbyterian, Reformed.
29. Pittsburgh Theological Seminary Library, Pittsburgh—Presbyterian, Reformed.
30. Historical Society of Berks County, Reading—various (local).
31. Lackawanna Historical Society, Scranton—various.
32. Scranton Public Library, Scranton—Baptist.
33. Monroe County Historical Society, Stroudsburg—various (local).
34. Northumberland County Historical Society, Sunbury—various (local).
35. Friends Historical Library, Swarthmore College, Swarthmore —Quaker.
36. Uniontown Public Library, Uniontown—various (local).
37. Washington and Jefferson College Historical Collections, Washington—various.
38. Greene County Historical Society, Waynesburg—various.
39. Wyoming Historical and Geological Society, Westtown—various.

RHODE ISLAND:
1. Newport Historical Society, Newport—Quaker, Congregational, Baptist.
2. Moses Brown School, Providence—Quaker.
3. Rhode Island Historical Society, Providence—Baptist, Unitarian, Congregational.

SOUTH CAROLINA:
1. South Carolina Historical Society, Charleston—Congregational, P. E.
2. South Carolina Department of Archives and History, Columbia —P. E.
3. South Caroliniana Library, U. of South Carolina, Columbia— various.
4. Wofford College Library, Spartanburg—Methodist.

TENNESSEE:
1. McClung Historical Collection, Lawson McGhee Library, Knoxville—Baptist, Methodist, Presbyterian.
2. Burrow Library, Memphis—Presbyterian.
3. Joint University Libraries, Nashville—various.
4. Methodist Publishing House Library, Nashville—Methodist.
5. Tennessee Historical Society, Nashville—various.
6. Tennessee State Library and Archives, Nashville—various.

VERMONT:
  1. Vermont Historical Society, Montpelier—Congregational, <u>et al.</u>
VIRGINIA:
  1. Randolph-Macon College Library, Ashland—Methodist.
  2. University of Virginia Library, Charlottesville—Baptist, Lutheran, Methodist, Presbyterian.
  3. Hampden-Sydney College Library, Hampden-Sydney—various (local).
  4. Union Theological Seminary Library, Richmond—Presbyterian (extensive).
  5. Valentine Museum, Richmond—Quaker (typescript).
  6. Virginia Baptist Historical Society, University of Richmond, Richmond—Baptist.
  7. Virginia Diocesan Library, Richmond—P. E.
  8. Virginia Historical Society, Richmond—various.
  9. Virginia State Library, Richmond—various, including Baptist, Methodist, Quaker, Lutheran, German Reformed, Presbyterian (extensive).
WEST VIRGINIA:
  1. West Virginia Department of Archives and History, Charleston —Baptist, Methodist.
  2. West Virginia Collection, West Virginia University Library, Morgantown—various.
WISCONSIN:
  1. State Historical Society of Wisconsin, Madison—various.
  2. Joyce Kilmer Memorial Library, Campion Jesuit High School, Prarie Du Chien—Roman Catholic (local).
  3. Racine County Historical Room, Racine—various (local).
  4. Waukesha County Historical Society, Waukesha—various (local).

These depositories are few but significant, and you should do all you can to locate the church records you need. After all, if they can be found, church records provide the best genealogical information available before the start of civil vital records. The examples in this chapter provide ample evidence of that fact. The effort you expend in search of church records is well used.

The researcher should become familiar with Peter G. Mode, <u>Source Book and Bibliographical Guide for American Church History</u>, 1921, (Boston: J. S. Canner & Co., 1964 reprint). This scholarly work is a peerless reference for the genealogist and historian who seek a better understanding of church history and religious development in America.

CHAPTER TWENTY

AMERICAN AIDS TO FINDING THE HOME OF
THE IMMIGRANT ANCESTOR

One of the most difficult problems which the American researcher must
face is tracing his ancestors across the ocean to a specific place in the Old
World. It does no good, generally, to know they came from England or
Germany or Denmark unless you know exactly where they lived in England
or Germany or Denmark. This is usually essential for continued research.
The purpose of this chapter is to help you solve this origin problem and to
provide assistance in solving other genealogical identification problems by
the use of American-generated records. We do not have all the answers
for either, but we think we can help.

We are primarily concerned here with immigration records or ships'
passenger lists—those lists which were made when our ancestors (none of
whom was native to this country unless he was an American Indian) came
here. The sad thing about this is that there is no complete collection of
passenger lists and some of the ones that are available are either quite difficult to use or have serious information gaps.

Fortunately passenger lists are not the only possible source of information about the ancestral home. Court records of various kinds, especially those relating to naturalization and citizenship, are very significant.
Land entry records in the public domain, certificates of vital events, obituaries, probate records, military records, church records, and others
(including old letters and family records) may contain the needed information.
If so, your problem is a much simpler one. Hence you should keep your
eyes open for this information right from the inception of your research.
We have already considered some of these possibilities in earlier chapters
so let's look now at the passenger lists and see just what they are and how
they can help us.

I. IMMIGRATION RECORDS: THEIR NATURE AND VALUE

There are three types of ships' passenger-arrival lists that are of
general interest to us:

A. Customs Passenger Lists.

      B. Immigration Passenger Lists.
      C. Customs Lists of Aliens.

The National Archives in Washington, D. C. , has most of the American passenger lists which are in existence. These date mostly from 1820 to 1902.

A. CUSTOMS PASSENGER LISTS

The catagory of Customs Passenger Lists can also be subdivided as there are (1) original lists, (2) copies and abstracts and (3) transcripts from the U. S. State Department.

1. Original lists. There are original lists available for only seven ports—Baltimore, Boston, Mobile (only a few), New Bedford, New Orleans, New York and Philadelphia—most of which do not cover the entire 1820-1902 period. The original lists for Baltimore, 1820-1891, have been filmed at the National Archives as have the Boston lists, 1883-1891; the New Orleans lists, 1820-1902; the New York lists, 1820-1897, and the Philadelphia lists, 1800- 1899. [1]

These records were prepared by the ships' masters and generally tell the. . .

> . . .name of the vessel, the quarter year in which it arrived, the name of its master, the name of the district or port of arrival, and, for each passenger, his name, age, sex, and occupation, name of the country to which he belonged, name of the country that he intended to inhabit, and if he died enroute, the date and circumstances of his death. [2]

2. Copies and abstracts. The copies and abstracts cover a period between 1820 and 1875. Some of these are just the same as the originals, and in many cases they can be used to fill gaps in the original lists. They were prepared by the customs collectors and were forwarded (usually every quarter) to the State Department in accordance with statute. Many collectors made abbreviated abstracts of the original lists to forward to Washington.

[1.] Some Cargo Manifests for 1800-1819—and a few later—with names of passengers not on Customs Passenger Lists have been filmed with the Philadelphia lists and comprise the pre-1820 portion.

[2.] Meredith B. Colket, Jr. , and Frank E. Bridgers, Guide to Genealogical Records in the National Archives (Washington, D. C. : The National Archives, 1964), p. 32.

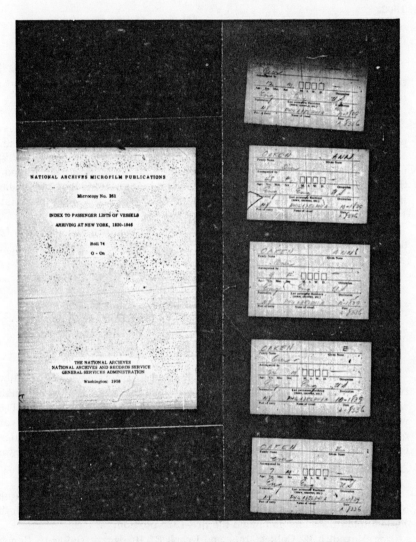

SOME CARDS FROM THE INDEX TO CUSTOMS
PASSENGER LISTS FOR THE PORT OF NEW YORK
(There is no additional information in the original manifests.
Their only advantage is that they are a primary source.)

The National Archives has some copies and abstracts of the Customs Passenger Lists for 71 Atlantic Coast and Gulf of Mexico ports.

3. Transcripts from the U.S. State Department. The transcripts of lists in the State Department typically give the...

...name of the vessel, the quarter year in which it arrived, the name of its master, the name of the district or port of arrival, and, for each passenger, his name, age, sex, and occupation, name of the country to which he belonged, the name of the country that he intended to inhabit. If his death occurred enroute, information about it is given. [3]

In the National Archives there are eight manuscript volumes of these transcripts covering only December 31, 1819, to December 31, 1832 (13 years), with one volume (No. 2) between September 30, 1820, and September, 1821, missing. The National Archives also has a printed manuscript volume entitled Letter from the Secretary of State with a Transcript of the List of Passengers Who Arrived in the United States from the 1st October, 1819, to the 30th September, 1820 (16th Cong., 2nd Sess., S. Doc. 118, Serial 45, Vol. 4). [4] You will note that this latter work begins the records three months earlier than the others. The National Archives has State Department transcripts for 47 ports. The records were apparently prepared by the State Department from the abstracts they received from the customs officials at the ports. [5]

One very useful tool is a book entitled Passengers Who Arrived in the United States, September, 1821 - December, 1823 (Baltimore: Magna Carta Book Co., 1969). This book was compiled from the State Department transcripts and contains more than 15,000 names of passengers on about 2,000 ships into 40 ports of entry. The book is indexed.

In addition to these Customs Passenger Lists, two ports—Alexandria, Virginia (1798-1819), and Philadelphia (1800-1819)—have Cargo Manifests available in the National Archives which extend their passenger lists to an earlier period than those of other ports.

You may be disappointed in the Customs Passenger Lists. Their contents, as you will have noted, do not include information on specific places of origin—only country. Though they may be useful for other purposes, they

---

3. Ibid., p. 35.

4. Reprinted in 1967 by Genealogical Publishing Company as Passenger Arrivals, 1819-1820, with an index.

5. For a table showing all ports with dates of all available passenger lists, see Colket and Bridgers, pp. 23-31.

do not solve the problem we set out to solve initially. And even though some of these lists are indexed—and they are the earliest official passenger lists available, and they are the easiest of the available passenger lists to use—they are not the most informational.

For the benefit of those who have access to the LDS Genealogical Society Library, we might also mention that it is these original Customs Passenger Lists (for New York, Philadelphia, Baltimore, New Orleans, Boston and "miscellaneous ports"—including Baltimore, Mobile, New Bedford, New Orleans and Philadelphia)—and their (Soundex) indexes which the Society has on microfilm.

B. IMMIGRATION PASSENGER LISTS

The earliest Immigration Passenger Lists are for the port of Philadelphia and begin in 1883. Most other ports have records beginning somewhat later than this, many starting in 1891. There is also, as you can probably guess, some restriction on the use of these records. Both the records and their indexes are considered confidential and are restricted for a 50-year period. The indexes are even more restricted because several years are indexed together and they cannot be used unless all entries on the roll of microfilm are over 50 years old. An additional problem is that the indexes are arranged chronologically and thus are only alphabetized (by initial letters of surnames only) day-by-day after first being arranged by shipping line. (You have to know quite a bit about the arrival of the person you seek to even use the indexes.) There are indexes available for the ports of Boston; New York; Philadelphia; Portland, Maine, and Providence, Rhode Island.

The 36 ports which have Immigration Passenger Lists in the National Archives are:

Mobile, Ala.------------Apr. 3, 1904 - Dec. 24, 1945
Hartford, Conn.-------------- Feb. 1929 - Dec. 1943
Apalachicola, Fla.--------------------Sept. 4, 1918
Boca Grande, Fla.------- Oct. 28, 1912 - Aug. 16, 1935
Clarabelle, Fla.---------------------Nov. 7, 1915
Fernandina, Fla.---------Aug. 29, 1904 - Oct. 7, 1932
Jacksonville, Fla.--------Jan. 18, 1904 - Dec. 17, 1945
Key West, Fla.----------------Nov. 1898 - Dec. 1945
Knights Key, Fla.---------Feb. 7, 1908 - Jan. 20, 1912
Mayport, Fla.----------- Nov. 16, 1907 - Apr. 13, 1916
Miami, Fla.------------------Oct. 1899 - Dec. 1945
Millville, Fla.--------------------------- July 4, 1916
Panama City, Fla.------- Nov. 10, 1927 - Dec. 12, 1939
Pensacola, Fla.----------May 12, 1900 - July 16, 1945
Port Everglades, Fla.-----Feb. 15, 1932 - Dec. 10, 1945

Port Inglis, Fla.----------Mar. 29, 1912 - Jan. 2, 1913
Port St. Joe, Fla.--------Jan. 12, 1923 - Oct. 13, 1939
St. Andrews, Fla.---------Jan. 2, 1916 - May 13, 1926
St. Petersburg, Fla.------Dec. 15, 1926 - Mar. 1, 1941
Tampa, Fla.-----------------Nov. 1898 - Dec. 1945
West Palm Beach, Fla.----- Sept. 8, 1920 - Nov. 21, 1945
Brunswick, Ga.---------- Nov. 22, 1901 - Nov. 27, 1939
Savannah, Ga.------------June 5, 1906 - Dec. 6, 1945
New Orleans, La.------------- Jan. 1903 - Dec. 1945
Portland and Falmouth, Me.------Nov. 1893 - Mar. 1943
Baltimore, Md.--------- Dec. 12, 1891 - Nov. 30, 1909
Boston and Charlestown, Mass.--Aug. 1, 1891 - Dec. 1943
Gloucester, Mass.---------Oct. 1906 - June 1923, Feb.
                                    1, 1930 - Dec. 1943
New Bedford, Mass.----------- July 1, 1902 - July 1942
Gulfport, Miss.-------------- Aug. 1904 - Sept. 1944
Pascagoula, Miss.-------- July 15, 1903 - May 21, 1935
New York, N.Y.--------------- June 16, 1897 - 1942
Philadelphia, Pa.-----------Jan. 1883 - Dec. 31, 1945
Providence, R.I.------------- June 1911 - June 1943
Charleston, S.C.---------- Apr. 9, 1906 - Dec. 3, 1945
Georgetown, S.C.-------- June 17, 1923 - Oct. 24, 1939[6]

The information in these Immigration Passenger Lists (or Manifests, as they are frequently called) varies somewhat with time period and with state statute. Those for Philadelphia (the earliest port to have them) contain the...

... name of the master, name of vessel, names of ports of arrival and embarkation, and date of arrival; and for each passenger, his name, place of birth, last legal residence, age, occupation, and sex, and remarks. [7]

Federal law began to prescribe the form in 1893 and, beginning that year, the form required the following information for each passenger:

His name in full, age, sex, marital status, occupation, nationality, last residence, port of arrival in the United States, and final destination in the United States; whether he had been in the United States before and, if so, when and where; and

---

6. Colket and Bridgers, pp. 23-30.
7. Ibid., p. 37.

whether he was going to join a relative and, if so, the relative's name, address, and relationship to the passenger. The format of the immigration passenger lists was revised... in 1906 to include a personal description and a birthplace; and in 1907 to include the name and address of the alien's nearest relative in the country from which he came. [8]

As you can see, under certain circumstances these can be very useful records.

C. CUSTOMS LISTS OF ALIENS

Customs Lists of Aliens are perhaps the least significant shipping or passenger lists in the National Archives, not because their information is lacking, but mainly because they relate to only Beverly and Salem, Massachusetts, 1798-1800. These records were made in compliance with an act of Congress, but the existence of any such records from other ports is currently unknown. There are no indexes because the records are so brief. Information in these records includes the...

... name of the vessel, name of the master, date of its arrival, and names of the ports of embarkation and arrival; and for each alien, his name, age, birthplace, name of the country from which he came, name of the nation to which he belonged and owed allegiance, occupation and personal description. [9]

These brief lists were published in the New England Historical and Genealogical Register in July 1952 (Vol. 106, pp. 203-209.)

D. OTHER IMMIGRATION RECORDS

In addition to the records described above, there are other records relating to immigration located in various depositories around the U.S. Some of these include:

Massachusetts Archives Division at the State House, Boston—has some immigration records, 1848-1891.
College of the Holy Cross Library at Worcester, Massachusetts—has a collection on Irish immigrants and their descendants in Worcester, 1840-1900.

---

8. Ibid., p. 37.
9. Ibid., pp. 35-36.

Burton Historical Collection, Detroit Public Library, Detroit, Michigan—has records of the Michigan immigration agency from 1848 to
1880 and papers relating to the Detroit and Mackinac customs offices, 1789-1876.

Museum of the Netherlands Pioneer and Historical Foundation, Holland,
Michigan—has extensive manuscripts relating to the settlement of
western Michigan by Dutch immigrants.

Hendrick Hudson Chapter Library, Hudson, New York—has Cargo Manifests, 1739-1744.

Yivo Institute for Jewish Research, New York City—has about 300 auto-
biographies of Jewish immigrants who came from eastern Europe
to the United States in the 1880's and 1890's, plus some 10,000
letters from European relatives to Jewish immigrants.

Federal Records Center, G.S.A., Philadelphia, Pennsylvania—has
official maritime records which include papers of the port of Philadelphia, 1716-1855, and ships' registers of the Province of Pennsylvania, 1722-1776.

Historical Society of Pennsylvania, Philadelphia—has the Gilbert Cope
Collection which includes some ships' registers among other historical and genealogical materials, 1682-1924.

University of Texas Library, Austin—has papers relating to German,
French and English immigration to Texas.

The Church of Jesus Christ of Latter-day Saints, Historical Dept.,
Salt Lake City, Utah—has records of LDS Church members im-
migrating to "Zion" from Europe between 1849 and 1932. There
are shipping lists from the British Mission (1849-1885, 1899-1925),
the Scandinavian Mission (1854-1896, 1901-1920), the Netherlands
Mission (1904-1914) and the Swedish Mission (1905-1932). There
is also a card index to these records, and both the records and the
index are on microfilm at the LDS Genealogical Society. [10]

Some of the records in the above lists you will find to be very good
sources while others will have little genealogical value. And you will, no
doubt, find other useful original immigration records in other depositories. *

E. BOOKS

There have been several books published which contain records and
lists of immigrations to America. Many of these are very early and though

---

[10.] For further details see "LDS Records and Research Aids" (Series
F, no. 1), Research Papers of The Genealogical Society of The Church of
Jesus Christ of Latter-day Saints.

  * See note at the end of this chapter.

they certainly do not cover all early immigrations, they can be quite useful. Following is a list of some of these books:

Banks, Charles Edward. English Ancestry and Homes of the Pilgrim Fathers. (1929). Baltimore: Genealogical Publishing Co. (1962 reprint).
_____. The Planters of the Commonwealth. (1930). Baltimore: Genealogical Publishing Co. (1961 reprint).
_____. Topographical Dictionary of 2,885 English Emigrants to New England, 1620-1650, Ed. by... Elijah E. Brownell. (1937). Baltimore: Genealogical Publishing Co. (1957 reprint).
_____. The Winthrop Fleet of 1630. (1930). Baltimore: Genealogical Publishing Co. (1961 reprint).
Bevier, Louis. Genealogy of the First Settlers of New Paltz. (1909). Baltimore: Genealogical Publishing Co. (1965 reprint).
Bolton, Ethel. Immigrants to New England, 1700-1775. (1931). Baltimore: Genealogical Publishing Co. (1966 reprint).
Bristol and America. A Record of the First Settlers in the Colonies of North America, 1654-1885... (1929 and 1931). Baltimore: Genealogical Publishing Co. (1967 reprint).
Brock, Robert A. Documents, Chiefly Unpublished, Relating to the Huguenot Emigration to Virginia and to the Settlement at Manakin-Town. (1886). Baltimore: Genealogical Publishing Co. (1962 reprint).
Browning, Charles H. Welsh Settlement of Pennsylvania. (1912). Baltimore: Genealogical Publishing Co. (1967 reprint).
Cameron, Viola Root. Emigrants from Scotland to America, 1774-1775. (1930). Baltimore: Genealogical Publishing Co. (1959 reprint).
De Ville, Winston. Louisiana Colonials: Soldiers and Vagabonds. Mobile, Ala. (1963). Distr. by Genealogical Publishing Co., Baltimore, Md.
Dickson, Robert J. Ulster Emigration to Colonial America, 1718-1775. London: Routledge and Kegan Paul (1966).
Drake, Samuel Gardiner. Result of Some Researches Among the British Archives for Information Relative to the Founders of New England. (1860). Baltimore: Genealogical Publishing Co. (1963 reprint).
Egle, William Henry. Names of Foreigners Who Took the Oath of Allegiance to the Province and State of Pennsylvania, 1727-1775, with the Foreign Arrivals, 1786-1808. (1892). Baltimore: Genealogical Publishing Co. (1967 reprint).
Faust, Albert Bernhardt and Gaius M. Brumbaugh. Lists of Swiss Emigrants in the Eighteenth Century to the American Colonies, 2 vols. (1920-25). Baltimore: Genealogical Publishing Co. (1968 reprint in 1 vol.).

Fothergill, Gerald. Emigrants from England, 1773-1776. (1898-1901).
    Baltimore: Genealogical Publishing Co. (1964 reprint).
_____. A List of Emigrant Ministers to America, 1690-
    1811. (1904). Baltimore: Genealogical Publishing Co. (1964 re-
    print).
French, Elizabeth. List of Emigrants to America from Liverpool, 1697-
    1707. (1913). Baltimore: Genealogical Publishing Co. (1962 re-
    print).
Giuseppi, Montague Spencer. Naturalizations of Foreign Protestants
    in the American and West Indian Colonies Pursuant to Statute 13,
    George II, C. 7. (1921). Baltimore: Genealogical Publishing Co.
    (1964 reprint).
Greer, George Cabell. Early Virginia Immigrants, 1623-1666. (1912).
    Baltimore: Genealogical Publishing Co. (1960 reprint).
Hackett, J. Dominick and Charles M. Early. Passenger Lists from
    Ireland (reprinted from the Journal of the American Irish Histori-
    cal Society, vols. 28, 29). (1929-1931). Baltimore: Genealogical
    Publishing Co. (1965).
Hartmann, Edward George. Americans from Wales. Boston: The
    Christopher Publishing House (1967).
Hinman, Royal R. A Catalogue of the Names of the First Puritan Set-
    tlers of the Colony of Connecticut; with the Time of Their Arrival
    in the Colony, and Their Standing in Society, Together with Their
    Place of Residence, as Far as Can be Discovered by the Records.
    (1846-   ). Baltimore: Genealogical Publishing Co. (1968 reprint).
Hotten, John Camden. The Original Lists of Persons of Quality: Emi-
    grants, etc., Who Went from Great Britain to the American Plan-
    tations, 1600-1700, 2nd ed. (1880). Baltimore: Genealogical
    Publishing Co. (1962 reprint).
Jewson, Charles Boardman. Transcript of Three Registers of Pas-
    sengers from Great Yarmouth to Holland and New England, 1637-
    1639. (1954). Baltimore: Genealogical Publishing Co. (1964
    reprint).
Joseph, Samuel. Jewish Immigration to the United States from 1881 to
    1910. New York: Arno Press (1969).
Kaminkow, Jack and Marion J. Kaminkow. A List of Emigrants from
    England to America, 1718-1759. Transcribed from... Original
    Records at the Guildhall, London. Baltimore: Magna Carta Book
    Co. (1964).
Kaminkow, Marion J. and Jack Kaminkow. Original Lists of Emigrants
    in Bondage from London to the American Colonies, 1719-1744.
    Baltimore: Magna Carta Book Co. (1967).
Knittle, Walter Allen. Early Eighteenth Century Palatine Emigration.
    (1937). Baltimore: Genealogical Publishing Co. (1965 reprint).

Krebbs, Fredrich. Emigrants from the Palatinate to the American Colonies in the Eighteenth Century. Norristown, Pa.: Pennsylvania German Society (1953).

Langguth, Otto. "Pennsylvania German Pioneers from the County of Wertheim." (Tr. and ed. by Donald H. Yoder in the Pennsylvania German Folklore Society Yearbook, Vol. XII). Allentown, Pa. (1947).

Munroe, J. B. A List of Alien Passengers Bonded from January 1, 1847, to January, 1851. (1851). Baltimore: Genealogical Publishing Co. (1971 reprint).

Myers, Albert Cook. Immigration of the Irish Quakers into Pennsylvania, 1682-1750. (1902). Baltimore: Genealogical Publishing Co. (1969 reprint).

Newsome, Albert R. Records of Emigrants from England and Scotland to North Carolina, 1774-1775. (1934). Raleigh, N. C.: Department of Archives and History (1962 reprint).

Persons Naturalized in the Province of Pennsylvania (1740-1773). (Reprinted from Pennsylvania Archives, Ser. 2, Vol. II). (1876). Baltimore: Genealogical Publishing Co. (1967).

Putnam, Eben. Two Early Passenger Lists, 1635-1637. Baltimore: Genealogical Publishing Co. (1964 reprint).

Revill, Janie. A Compilation of the Original Lists of Protestant Immigrants to South Carolina, 1763-1773. (1939). Baltimore: Genealogical Publishing Co. (1968 reprint).

Rupp, Israel Daniel. A Collection of Upwards of Thirty Thousand Names of German, Swiss, Dutch, French and Other Immigrants in Pennsylvania from 1727 to 1776, (2nd rev. and enl. ed., 1876). Baltimore: Genealogical Publishing Co. (1965 reprint).

_____. Index to the Names of Thirty Thousand Immigrants ... by M. V. Koger. n. p., 1935.

Sherwood, George. American Colonists in English Records, 2 vols. (1932-1933). Baltimore: Genealogical Publishing Co. (1961 reprint in 1 vol.).

Simmendinger, Ulrich. True and Authentic Register of Persons Who in the Year 1709 Journeyed from Germany to America. (Trans. by Herman F. Vesper.) (1934). Baltimore: Genealogical Publishing Co. (1963 reprint).

Skordas, Gust. The Early Settlers of Maryland. Baltimore: Genealogical Publishing Co. (1968).

Stanard, William G. Some Emigrants to Virginia. (2nd ed. enl., 1915). Baltimore: Genealogical Publishing Co. (1953 reprint).

Stapleton, Ammon. Memorials of the Huguenots in America, with Special Reference to Their Emigration to Pennsylvania. (1901). Baltimore: Genealogical Publishing Co. (1964 reprint).

Strassburger, Ralph Beaver and William J. Hinke. Pennsylvania German Pioneers, 3 vols. (1934). Baltimore: Genealogical Publishing Co. (1966 reprint of vols. 1 and 3).

Virkus, Frederick A. (ed.). Immigrant Ancestors. A List of 2,500 Immigrants to America Before 1750. (Excerpted from the Compendium of American Genealogy, Vol. VII). (1942). Baltimore: Genealogical Publishing Co. (1963).

Yoder, Donald H. (ed. and trans.). Emigrants from Wuerttemberg; the Adolf Gerber Lists. (Reprinted in the Pennsylvania German Folklore Society Yearbook, Vol. X). Allentown, Pa. (1945).

The above is only a partial list and should be considered as such; there are many more immigration sources. Of special note to the genealogist is A Bibliography of Ship Passenger Lists, 1538-1825, originally prepared by Harold Lancour and revised by R. J. Wolfe, 3rd ed. (New York: New York Public Library, 1966).

II. LOCATING AND USING IMMIGRATION RECORDS

With some genealogical problems there is untold value in immigration records. With this in mind let's review some of the information we have already given and provide more detailed information on locating and using these records.

If your ancestor was an early immigrant you would certainly not want to overlook the possibility of finding information about him and his origin in one of the available books. If he was a more recent immigrant the ships' passenger lists may be a worthwhile source for you to consider, especially the Immigration Passenger Lists where they apply, because of the information they contain about Old World origins. And though there are informational limitations in the Customs Passenger Lists, they too can be helpful.

Considering that the Customs Passenger Lists give name, age, sex and occupation of each immigrant and tell the date of his arrival in America, plus the port from which he sailed, they can be useful tools for identifying your ancestor and separating him from all other persons of the same name.

We have already mentioned that the main difficulty in locating people in the Immigration Passenger Lists is the chronological arrangement of the indexes. These indexes are arranged first by year; then under each year they are arranged by ship; under each ship or shipping line they are arranged, in part, by class of passenger, and then alphabetically by the first letter of the passenger's surname. There are slight variations from one port to another, but all are difficult to use.

There are alphabetical indexes to the Boston port from 1902 to June 30, 1906, and the New York port from June 16, 1897, to June 30, 1902; and the alphabetical card index to the Customs Passenger Lists in the Philadelphia port also serves as a partial index to its Immigration Passenger Lists until 1906. These indexes are located in the National Archives and make the lists a little easier to use.

The Immigration Passenger Lists are difficult to use. What it all boils down to is this: It is almost essential to have specific information about an immigration before you can find the record of it. You _must_ know the name of the port, and the moré specific the date you have the better off you are. The name of the ship is also very helpful. When you consider that several thousands of persons entered the U.S. through some of the larger ports each year you can appreciate the value of specific information. It is not impossible to make a general search of passenger lists for a given port, but we do not recommend it if there is some other way.

There are also records in the National Archives of the names and dates of arrival of the vessels in the several ports. These tell the ports from which each ship sailed and may help you find the name of the ship on which your ancestor arrived, if you know the approximate time—this information on ports of embarkation can save a lot of searching if it is properly used.

Other aids in finding passenger lists are naturalization records, land entry records (especially Homestead entries) and passport applications. Naturalization records tell the name of the port and date of arrival of the alien into the United States. [11] Homestead entry papers include a copy of naturalization proceedings and, of course, show the date and port of arrival also, plus the place of birth of the entryman. If a naturalized citizen applied for a passport to travel abroad, perhaps to return to his homeland for a visit, the application papers show the original date and port of his arrival into this country.

III. PASSPORT APPLICATIONS

All passport applications filed with the U.S. State Department from 1791 to 1905 are in the National Archives, but at no time during that period were passports required by law, except during part of the Civil War. Many persons, however, did secure passports for the protection which they afforded.

The applications from 1810 through 1905 are bound, and there are various card and book indexes covering the period from 1834 to 1905. The records, however, have a 75-year restriction on them.

[11.] See Chapter Eighteen for more information on naturalization records.

The earliest applications were merely letters of request, but other papers often accompanied them and were filed with them. Those other papers included expired passports, birth certificates, certificates of citizenship, etc. Regarding record content, Colket and Bridgers write:

> A passport application varies in content, the information being ordinarily less detailed before the Civil War period than afterward. It usually contains the name, signature, place of residence, age, and personal description of the applicant; the names or number of persons in his family intending to travel with him; the date; and, where appropriate, the date and court of naturalization. It sometimes contains the exact date and place of birth of the applicant and of his wife and minor children accompanying him, if any; and, if the applicant was a naturalized citizen, the date and port of his arrival in the United States and the name of the vessel on which he arrived. [12]

Passports, of course, are a source with limited value. They are of use only if your ancestor traveled abroad and happened to secure one. It was common for immigrants to secure passports when they traveled to their homelands to visit (even when not required to do so by law) because they were in danger of being drafted into military service if they went without them.

IV. CONCLUSION

Properly used, immigration records, passport records, etc., can lead to invaluable information about specific places of European origin which you may not find in other records. They may also lead you to information about your ancestor after his American arrival. In case his name is common, specific dates and places from these records can help you separate him from his contemporaries of the same name.

Be aware of the value of these records and, when the occasion calls for it, use them wisely. But don't expect them to solve all of your problems.

NOTE: Perhaps this is the proper place to note the possible existence of additional passenger lists for the port of New York beyond those kept under federal statutes and housed in the National Archives. In 1824 the New York Legislature adopted "An Act Concerning Passenger Vessels Arriving in the Port of New York." This act required the master of every vessel arriving in port to make a writing within 24 hours containing the name, place of birth, last legal settlement, age and occupation of every person who should have been on board. [13]

The location of these reports is unknown and the Municipal Archives and Records Center of New York reports knowing nothing of their existence. [14]

---

12. Colket and Bridgers, p. 137.
13. City of New York v. Miln [36 U.S. (Pet.) 102].
14. Letter from Elizabeth M. Eilerman, Assistant Director, dated January 10, 1973.

CHAPTER TWENTY-ONE

MILITARY RECORDS:
COLONIAL WARS AND THE AMERICAN REVOLUTION

Much of modern history can be told in wars. Nearly every generation of Americans has known war. Genealogically war is a two-sided coin—it is destructive on the one hand (to human lives and property as well as to records) and it is creative on the other hand (fostering great medical and technical advances, etc., to help people live longer and creating many useful records of its own). Thus, in retrospect, we look on past wars with mixed emotions; but as genealogists we must be familiar with various effects of war. Especially must we be familiar with military records; complete research depends upon it.

I. BACKGROUND AND HISTORY

Even the early colonists in America knew war's sting. From King Philip's War in 1675 down to the time of the Revolutionary War with Great Britain there were few periods of peace. The Indians and the French were the main adversaries of the British colonists.

The Revolutionary War, 1775-1783, pitted brother against brother and father against son as 13 of the 22 British-American colonies chose to declare their collective independence from Mother England.

Following the Revolution British opposition to the Embargo Act and a number of other factors, not excluding the greediness of the United States for more territory, led to another war with Britain, 1812-1814. This proved to be a very sad conflict for the Americans because their national capital, Washington, D.C., was seized by British troops and mostly burned.

Though the War of 1812 terminated major wars with Britain, the Indians still remained a threat on much of the American frontier and throughout the nineteenth century various and sundry Indian wars were waged.

In 1846, again mostly as a result of some greedy tendencies, the U.S. was drawn into war with Mexico. Texas had already been annexed and we had our collective eyes on a great deal more Mexican territory. This war ended in 1848.

In 1861, as a culmination of many pressures brought to bear by the slavery issue and the secession of certain southern states from the Union,

war was declared and the most costly war, in terms of human lives and suffering that our country has ever known, began. The war did not end until
1865 after 364,511 had died and 281,881 more had been wounded. This too
was a "family affair" as siblings fought under opposing flags.

The year 1898 brought war with Spain as a result of the Cuban insurrection of 1895, and then came the twentieth century with two great world
wars and other major military involvements in Korea and Vietnam. These
are the highlights in the story of American military activity and, for the
genealogist, each war has produced its own records, though most military
records arising in this century are not yet available for public searching.

II. THE RECORDS

As we use the term "military records" in the next two chapters we are
referring to any and all records of all branches of armed service—army,
navy, coast guard, marine, etc. These records can normally be divided
into two classes:

A. Service records.
B. Records of veterans' benefits.

We shall consider both types here as both are significant.

As you already know there is little conformity in American genealogical
sources. Many sources are undefinable in terms of specific content, and
though we have general ideas about what they contain (or at least ought to
contain), we are never really sure what any specific document is going to
say until we read it. This phenomenon is just as true of military records
as it is of any other records—especially those military records relating to
the early wars.

Our only advice is for you to seek out those which are pertinent and read
them—we think you will be pleasantly surprised. As far as service records
go, you are in a better position to locate information if your soldier ancestor had an officer's commission, but the enlisted man was, in his later
years, more often in a position to receive assistance through veterans' benefits. An excellent guide to those military records located in the National
Archives is Meredith B. Colket, Jr., and Frank E. Bridgers, Guide to Genealogical Records in the National Archives (1964), to which we have already
made frequent reference in other chapters and which we will lean upon
heavily in the next two chapters (even beyond what our footnotes might indicate).

III. COLONIAL WARS

There are no official national records of wars before the Revolution since the United States of America did not exist. The only records which have survived are a few colonial and local militia records—mainly rolls and rosters. These lists are not extensive (nor is the information they contain), but many of those located have been published. Most of these lists contain only the names of the soldiers and the military organizations in which they served. The chief value of these records is that they give names, dates and places allowing us to put the person thus found in a specific place at a specific time—often an important genealogical necessity. In most cases there were no particular benefits provided for veterans of colonial service though there were exceptions to this. For example, Governor Dinwiddie and the Council of Virginia offered 200,000 acres of bounty land in the Ohio River Valley to Virginia troops who served in the French and Indian War. Some other colonies did the same, but there are no general records. Those records which exist are in the individual states.

A short bibliography of a few published works arising out of the colonial wars follows:

Andrews, Frank DeWitte. Connecticut Soldiers in the French and Indian War. Vineland, N.J.: The compiler (1923).

Bodge, George M. Soldiers in King Philip's War, Being a Critical Account of that War, with a Concise History of the Indian Wars of New England from 1620-1677, Official Lists of the Soldiers of Massachusetts Colony Serving in Philip's War... (3rd ed., 1906). Baltimore: Genealogical Publishing Co. (1967 reprint).

Buckingham, Thomas. Roll and Journal of Connecticut Service in Queen Anne's War, 1710-1711. New Haven: Acorn Club of Connecticut (1916).

Chapin, Howard Millar. Rhode Island in the Colonial Wars. A List of Rhode Island Soldiers and Sailors in King George's War, 1740-1748. Providence: Rhode Island Historical Society (1920).

_____. Rhode Island in the Colonial Wars. A List of Rhode Island Soldiers and Sailors in the Old French and Indian Wars, 1755-1762. Providence: Rhode Island Historical Society (1918).

_____. Rhode Island Privateers in King George's War, 1739-1748. Providence: Rhode Island Historical Society (1926).

Connecticut Historical Society. Rolls of Connecticut Men in the French and Indian War, 1755-1762 (2 vols.). Hartford: The Society (1903-1905).

Lewis, Virgil A. Soldiery of West Virginia in the French and Indian War; Lord Dunmore's War; the Revolution; the Later Indian Wars ... (3rd Biennial Report of Department of Archives and History, 1911). Baltimore: Genealogical Publishing Co. (1967 reprint).

New York Historical Society. Muster Rolls of New York Provincial Troops, 1755-1764. New York: The Society (1892).

Pennsylvania Archives. "Officers and Soldiers in the Service of the Province of Pennsylvania, 1744-1764." Pennsylvania Archives, Series 5, Vol. 3, pp. 419-528. Harrisburg.

Pomeroy, Seth. Journals and Papers. Society of Colonial Wars (1926). (Published by the Society of Colonial Wars in the State of New York at the request of its Committee on Historical Documents; edited by Louis Effingham DeForest—Publ. No. 38).

Rhode Island. Society of Colonial Wars. Nine Muster Rolls of Rhode Island Troops Enlisted During the Old French War. Providence: The Society (1915).

Robinson, George Frederick and Albert Harrison Hall. Watertown Soldiers in the Colonial Wars and the American Revolution. Watertown, Mass.: Historical Society of Watertown (1939).

Taylor, Philip F. A Calendar of the Warrants for Land in Kentucky. Granted for Service in the French and Indian War. (Excerpted from the Year Book of the Society of Colonial Wars of Kentucky, 1917). Baltimore: Genealogical Publishing Co. (1967 reprint).

IV. THE REVOLUTIONARY WAR

A. SERVICE RECORDS

When the War for Independence began there was no official United States government and hence very few records were made of the troops who fought —rosters and rolls mainly, as in the colonial confrontations. However, this war was the beginning of the U. S. military records and machinery was set up to make a record of those who served. Though some of these already scant early records have been destroyed by fire, those that remain are still very important.

At the National Archives there are records which have been abstracted onto 3 1/2" x 8" cards by the Adjutant General's Office, containing all information from muster rolls (lists of men in a particular military unit), pay rolls, etc., for each individual soldier. Each soldier's cards have been placed in a separate jacket-envelope which is filed according to whether he served in the Continental Army, in a state organization or in another branch of the service. These compiled military service records are indexed in three indexes—a master name index, a name index for the Continental Army troops and an index for each state.

Though there is some variation, these records show such information as...

... the name, rank, and military organization of the soldier; if available, the name of the State from which he served; the date that his name appears on one or more of the rolls; sometimes the date or dates and period of his enlistment or the date of his appointment; and rarely the date of his separation from the service. [1]

There are also some other service-record documents at the National Archives which have been card-indexed by the names of the individual soldiers. These include many different kinds of records—orderly books, rosters, oaths of allegiance, receipts, enlistment papers, correspondence, etc.—and usually contain information on the soldier's military unit. However, the records are varied and there is no set information formula.

All of these records are in Record Group 93, War Department Collection of Revolutionary War Records at the National Archives.

B. VETERANS' BENEFITS

Records relating to veterans' benefits for Revolutionary service have more to offer the genealogist than do service records, mainly because most of the legislation bestowing or making possible such benefits was not passed until many years after the war's termination. There were basically two kinds of benefits available:

    1. Pensions.
    2. Bounty land.

1. Pensions. Pension benefits and their nature are ably described by Colket and Bridgers:

    Pensions were granted by Congress to invalid or disabled
    veterans; to widows and orphans of men who were killed or died
    in service; to veterans who served a minimum period of time if
    they were living at an advanced age; to widows of veterans who
    served a minimum period of time if the widows were living at an
    advanced age; and, in some instances, to other heirs. Pensions
    granted on the basis of death or disability incurred in service
    are known as death or disability pensions. Pensions granted on
    the basis of service for a minimum period of time are called
    service pensions. [2]

---

1. Meredith B. Colket, Jr. , and Frank E. Bridgers, Guide to Genealogical Records in the National Archives (Washington, D. C.: The National Archives, 1964), pp. 49-50.

2. Ibid. , p. 77.

There were some very early pensions granted by the individual states to those who were disabled in the Revolutionary War. Many of these were assumed by the federal government for payment beginning in September 1789. In 1792 it became possible for a disabled serviceman to apply directly to the federal government for a pension through the U.S. Circuit and District Courts, but the applications for these pensions were all destroyed by a fire in the War Department in November 1800. This is the reason that you find few Revolutionary pension applications dated prior to 1800. There was also a fire in August of 1814 (War of 1812), but it was not quite so thorough in its destruction.

About the only records from the old Invalid (death and disability) Series which seem to be extant are:

a. Reports submitted to Congress. There were eight reports of pensions during 1792, 1794 and 1795 submitted to Congress, all of which were published and indexed in "Class 9" of U.S. Congress, American State Papers on pages 58-67, 85-122, 125-128, 135-145, 150-172 (Washington, D.C.: Gales and Seaton, 1834). The originals have been transcribed and interfiled in separate envelopes with the Revolutionary service pension papers.

Each entry in the 1792 report contains the name of the invalid pensioner, his rank, his regiment, the nature of his disability, and the date of the commencement of the pension. Each entry in the 1794 and 1795 reports contains the name of the invalid applicant; his rank; his regiment, company, or ship; the date and place of his becoming disabled; the place of his residence at the date of the report; and, as a rule, evidence of action on the claim. [3]

b. Reports retained by the War Department. Some records, containing essentially the same types of information (with some duplication) as do the reports submitted to Congress, were retained by the War Department for the years 1794-1796 and are in the National Archives in a bound manuscript entitled "War Office Letter Book 1791-94" (pages 527-612). In 1958 the National Genealogical Society serialized the 1796 reports in their quarterly magazine. [4]

---

[3] Ibid., p. 79.

[4] "Recently Discovered Records Relating to Revolutionary War Veterans Who Applied for Pensions Under the Act of 1792," The National Genealogical Society Quarterly, XLVI, nos. 1, 2 (March and June 1958).

GENERAL SERVICES ADMINISTRATION NATIONAL ARCHIVES AND RECORDS SERVICE	RECEIPT NO.	DO NOT WRITE IN THIS SPACE
	62612	DATE 6-15-64
ORDER FOR PHOTOCOPIES **CONCERNING VETERAN**	SEARCHER	
	FILE DESIGNATION	David Hurlbut S 45401 R1114—
(See reverse for explanation)		

State of New York } On this 9th day of September 1820 person-
Broome County   } ally appeared before Jona Lewis one of the Judges of Broome
Common Pleas David Hurlbut aged 63 years resident in the
Town of Lisle in said County who being first duly sworn according
to law doth on his oath declare that he served in the revolutionary
War as follows— that he enlisted in the Company Commanded by
Captain Albert Chapman in Col. Herman Swofts Regiment in
the month of August in the year 1777 and served three years, —
Discharged at Peeks Kill. That he made a declaration to obtain
a pension on the 25th day of April in the year 1818 Number of Pension
Certificate   On I do solemnly swear that I was a
resident Citizen of the United States on the 18th day of March 1818
and that I have not since that time by gift sale or in any manner disposed of my property or any part thereof with intent there-
by so to diminish it as to bring my self within the provisions of an act
of Congress Entitled an act to provide for certain persons engaged
in the land and naval service in the Revolutionary War passed
on the 18th day of March 1818 And I have not nor has any person
in trust for me any property or Securities Contracts or debts due
to me nor have I any income other than what is contained in the
Schedule hereunto annexed and by me subscribed

Schedule

One Cow. Two Hogs—one pot. 2 old Kettles—Tea Kettle—old pair of Tongs
and Shovel— one Chain and Hooks— Two Spinning wheels— one Reel for flax
Chairs—old Chest with drawers— one Table— one old Chest—two wash tubs, 2
pails. three Tubs, 1 Keg— one Shider— four old meal bags— one old Churn
three wooden bowls — one brown Earthen pan. 6 earthen plates, four bowls—
one Sugar bowl —four Tea Cups and saucers— Tea Pots Cream pot two bottles, pair
Tea Sad Irons one Pitcher one pair old Steelyards— one old meat barrel. Eight
trays teeth one pair of a Plow Irons—one Chain two old axes two old Hoes; two
Shaves, 1 Crooked a do 1 Saw— one old Candlestick one Say the
Jona Lewis   David Hurlbut
This deponent further declares that he is by occupation a farmer
but is wholly unable to pursue it or any other business being only able to
walk the house and considered by Physicians to be in a consumption
has a wife and 5 Children—the name of his wife Lois, her health not very
good yet able the greatest part of the time to do her work in the house
aged 44 years. Henry oldest Child living at home aged 14 years
Albert aged 13 Years Maria aged 8 years Gideon aged 6 years
Louisa aged 3 years— The Children as may be presumed are not able
to do but very little towards their support

Jona Lewis   David Hurlbut

VETERAN'S DECLARATION AS PART OF A
REVOLUTIONARY WAR PENSION APPLICATION

c. A book entitled Revolutionary Pensioners of 1818, based on a report dated March 28, 1818, made by the Secretary of War listing all U.S. pensioners (including invalid veterans, widows and orphans) was published by Genealogical Publishing Co., Baltimore, Maryland, in 1959. Some 5,495 pensioners are listed.

Notwithstanding the loss of the early pension files, much of the information therein being forever lost, there are extensive records of pensions which were applied for after 1800 under the various acts of Congress. The first service pensions (remember Colket and Bridgers' distinction between invalid and service pensions) were granted under an act dated March 18, 1818, and the latest ones were granted by an act of February 3, 1853. There was much liberalization in the qualifications of a pensioner in those 35 years. Perhaps the most liberal act (as compared to its predecessors) was the one passed on June 7, 1832, which made pensions available to all who had served at least six months, regardless of their need. All acts after 1832 applied to widows of servicemen as well as to servicemen themselves.

At the National Archives the original pension application papers are in linen-lined envelopes arranged alphabetically by the names of the servicemen and are completely indexed. The index was published by the National Genealogical Society in their quarterly magazine during the period between 1946 and 1963 (volumes 20, 40, 44, 50). It is now available in book form [5] and has also been microfilmed. Many libraries have copies of it.

2. Bounty land   As an added inducement to get men to serve in the American forces, free land was promised. There was not money to pay the troops so this was the logical answer. Some soldiers or, if the soldiers were killed, their heirs, took up the land soon after the war (based on an act of 1788) on special reservations set aside for that purpose by Congress. Special warrants (bounty land warrants) were issued by the Secretary of War. Many others took up land under later acts. The last major bounty land act was passed in 1855. It provided a bounty of 160 acres to anyone who fought in a battle or served at least 14 days. It applied to all men who had served in any war up to that time and not just to those with Revolutionary service.

Beginning in 1830 it became possible for holders of warrants which had not been used to patent land in the designated reservations to surrender or

---

[5.] Index of Revolutionary War Pension Applications (rev.), comp. by Frank Johnson Metcalf, Max Ellsworth Hoyt, Agatha Bouson Hoyt, Sadye Giller, William H. Dumont and Louise Dumont (Washington, D.C.: National Genealogical Society, 1966).

or exchange them for scrip certificates (sometimes merely called scrip) which would allow the land to be taken up anywhere in the public domain. The warrants capable of surrender were of three types:

> a. Federal warrants to the U.S. Military District of Ohio.
> b. Virginia warrants (for service in the Virginia State Line) for land in Kentucky.
> c. Virginia warrants (for service in the Virginia Continental Line) for land in either Kentucky or the Virginia Military District of Ohio.

The records of these surrendered warrants generally provide (in addition to the warrantee's name) the names of any heirs filing the claim and their relationships to the warrantees, their places of residence, and the date the warrant was surrendered. They are in the National Archives and are all indexed.

You will note from the foregoing that Virginia, as a state, issued bounty land warrants to her veterans. The records of these Virginia warrants, as well as the federal warrants, are in the National Archives.

Many bounty land warrant applications filed prior to 1800 are also believed to have been destroyed by that same War Department fire which took the early pension applications, but records identifying the 14,757 applicants whose papers were destroyed (by name) still exist at the National Archives.

All remaining bounty land warrant applications for those who claimed land based on Revolutionary War service have been interfiled with the Revolutionary War pension application papers at the National Archives and are indexed with them in the National Genealogical Society's Index which we mentioned on the preceding page.

If both a veteran and his widow applied for a pension, or if one claimed bounty land in addition to a pension, all papers for all claims have been filed together in the same jacket-envelope.

C. INFORMATION IN THE FILES

It is difficult to tell exactly what kind of information you will find in a particular pension or bounty land application file, though we can give a general idea. You will usually find...

> ... the name, rank, military or naval unit, and period of service of the veteran. If he applied for a pension, it shows his age or date of birth, place of birth, and place of residence. If the widow applied, it shows the date and place of his death, her age and the place of her residence, the place and date of her marriage to the veteran, and her maiden name. [6]

---

6. Colket and Bridgers, pp. 80-81.

Though all of this information may not be found in every file, there might be other, additional information such as a page from a family Bible to establish proof of age or of a marriage. There may even be a marriage certificate. Often affidavits of relatives and in-laws are included in the file and relationships are stated. Frequently the veteran traces all his movements and tells of all the places he has lived between the time of his service and the filing of his application. And so on. There are many possibilities.

Sometimes the heirs of the veteran would file for benefits. The following is a declaration and power of attorney filed for that purpose.

State of New Hampshire
County of Coos
  On this Second Day of August A D 1851 Be it known that before me James Washburne Justice of the Peace in and for the County of Coos aforesaid Personally appeared Miles Hurlburt aged 51 years and Betsey Young aged 57 years and Maid oath in due form of Law that they are the Children of Daniel Hurlburt and that there is No widow Living of Daniel Hurlburt who was a Soldier in the revolutionary war and that the Said Daniel Hurlburt Died at Clarksville in the State of New Hampshire on or about the 14 Day of January A D 1829 and that their said Mother Died at Stewartstown New Hampshire on or about the 12 Day of october A D 1849 and that they make this Declaration for the Purpose of receive from the united States any and all money or moneys Back Pay or survey bounties or land or pension that May be Lawfully due them as Children afforesaid and onely Surviving heirs and That Furthermore they hereby Constitute and appoint F E Hassler Washington City D C their tru and Lawful attorney for and in their name to transact and receipt for any Money or Moneys they may be entitled to hereby rectifying and conforming whatsoever their Said attorney legally do in the Premises.

(signed)

Acknowledged Sworn to & Subscribed }   Miles Hubbert
before me the Day and Year afore Said.   Betsey Yonge
   (signed) James Washburn Justice of the Peace

A bounty land application file is much like a pension application file in its contents. The reason for this is that the same things had to be proven—that service was rendered and that the applicant was entitled to benefits. Generally a bounty land file contains...

  ... the name, age, residence, military or naval unit, and period of service of the veteran; and the name, age, and place

O'DONAGHY (or O DONAGHEY), Patrick, N. Y., Agness, W20997

O'DONOHY, Patrick, N. Y., BLWt. 7574. Issued 9/28/1790 to Alexander Robertson, assignee. No papers

O'DORNER (or O DORNEN), Murty, Pa., S40215

ODUM, Seybert, Ga. Agcy., Dis. No papers

O'FERRELL (or O'FARRELL), Dennis, Va., S25072

OFFICER, James, Pa., S31280

OFFUTT
Jessee, S. C., Obedience, R7769
Nathaniel, S. C., S31887

O'FLAHERTY, John, N. J., BLWt. 8618. Issued 4/20/1792. No papers

O'FLYING (or O FLING, FLING), Patrick, Cont., N. H., War of 1812, S35542, Rejected Bounty Land Claim of 1812. For family history, etc., consult Wid. Ctf. 16785 of Edmund O'Flying, Pvt. U. S. Inf. War of 1812. Also see Claim for bounty land allowed on account of services of Lt. Patrick O'Flying, War of 1812, 23 W. S. Inf. who died Nov. 1, 1815. Wt. 3 for 480 A., Act of 4/14/1816. (No original papers in this claim)

OGDEN
Aaron, N. J., S19013; BLWt. 1610-300-Capt. Issued 6/11/1789. No papers
Barne (or Barney), N. J., S38279, BLWt. 773-200
Benjamin, N. J., S31281
Daniel, N. Y., BLWt. 7563. Issued 7/30/1792. No papers
David, Conn., Sally, W17414
David, N. Y., BLWt. 7581. Issued 7/13/1792. No papers
David, N. Y., Susannah, W24364
Edmond, Conn., Navy, Sebal, R7777
Eliakim, N. J., BLWt. 8607. Issued 6/20/1789. No papers
Gilbert, N. Y., R7770
James, N. J., Ruth, R7772
Jedediah, N. J., S32419
John, Mass., Naomi Burnap, former wid., W15618
John, N. Y., BLWt. 7559. Issued 8/26/1790 to Elijah Rose, assignee. No papers
Jonathan, N. Y., S11154
Joseph, Conn., S38277
Joseph, N. J., S11155

OGDEN (continued)
Ludlow, N. J., Comfort, W187
Matthias, N. J., BLWt. 1609-500-Col. Issued 6/11/1789. No papers
Nathaniel, Cont., N. J., BLWt. 1281-100
Nathaniel, N. J., S34454
Noah, N. J., BLWt. 8610. Issued 6/11/1789 to Matthias Denman, assignee. No papers
Obadiah, N. Y., Martha, R7771, BLWt. 45715-160-55
Samuel, N. J., S38273
Stephen, N. Y., Va., S7775
Stephen D., N. J., R7776
Sturges (or Sturgess), Conn., S14049

OGEN, Thomas, Va., BLWt. 12444. Issued 3/1/1794. No papers

OGG, James, R. I., BLWt. 3369. Issued 5/16/1791 to Deborah May, Admx. No papers

OGILBY, George, Pa., BLWt. 10185. Issued 6/25/1794 to Gideon Merkle, assignee. No papers

OGILVIE, Kimbrough, N. C., S14050

OGLE, Benjamin, Va., R7778

OGLESBY
Elisha, Va., S1866
Jesse, Va., Celia, W1987; BLWt. 28525-160-55
Richard, Va. res. of wid. in 1812, Susan, R7779

O'GULLION (see GULLION), John B.

OHARA
(or O HARRO), Francis, Pa., Nancy, BLWt. 233-100
George, N. J., Elizabeth, W5442
John, Va., S25340
John, Md., Susan, W9215
(or OHARRA), Joseph, Pa., Mary, BLWt. 224-100
Patrick, Pa., BLWt. 10184. Issued 4/3/1794 to John Phillips, assignee. No papers

OHL
Henry, Pa., S2030
(or OHE), John, Pa., S22428

OHLEN
Henry G., N. Y., Cathrina, S43100, W19935
Henry G., N. Y., BLWt. 7570. Issued 8/26/1790 to William Carr, assignee. No papers

OHMET, John, Pa., S40218

O'KAIN (or CANE), James, Pa., BLWt. 319-100

A PAGE FROM <u>INDEX OF REVOLUTIONARY WAR PENSION APPLICATIONS</u>, PREPARED BY THE NATIONAL GENEALOGICAL SOCIETY.   (Courtesy of the Society.)

of residence of the widow or other claimant. If the application was approved, the file shows also the warrant number, the number of acres granted, the date issued, and, where appropriate, the name of the assignee.

If the file was destroyed, the card used as a substitute shows the name of the veteran, his grade, his military or naval unit, the warrant number, the number of acres granted, the date issued, and, where appropriate, the name of the assignee. [7]

D. THE INDEX

The Index of Revolutionary War Pensioners as prepared by the National Genealogical Society is very simple to use. It is arranged alphabetically (with cross-references for variant spellings of surnames). It gives the name of the serviceman, generally the state from which he served, the name of any other claimant (such as a widow) where appropriate, and the number of the pension or bounty land file. The file number may be prefixed with an "S" (indicating that the applicant was a Survivor and a pension was granted), an "R" (which means the application was Rejected), a "W" (indicating a Widow's pension), a "BLWt" (meaning it was a Bounty Land Warrant application) or a "BL Reg" (showing that the Bounty Land claim was Rejected).

There are asterisks (*) by some of the names in the index to indicate that the papers relating to those soldiers' applications have been published in the National Genealogical Society Quarterly. The date and page of publication are always given.

It is appropriate also to mention here that rejection of an application did not mean that the applicant was a liar fraudulently seeking a pension for service he did not render. Many applications were rejected because the veteran was unable to establish sufficient proof of his service—usually either a discharge or the affidavit of a fellow soldier was required. If you have served in the armed services yourself, think how difficult it might be for you to prove you served if no records of your service were kept. Other claims were rejected because of insufficient service, remarriage (in the case of a widow), service of a non-military nature, etc.

In several instances the words "no papers" appear after an applicant's name in the index. This means that the pension application papers of this veteran have been destroyed, probably by fire as indicated earlier.

E. OBTAINING THE RECORDS

It is not necessary for you to go personally to the National Archives to

---

[7.] Ibid., p. 92.

check these pension and bounty land files. A service has been established which allows you to request papers from these files through the mail. For $1 you can secure photocopies of ten pages from the file of any veteran you choose. There is a form—GSA-6751 (formerly NAR-288)—which you should use to request these records. Copies of the form can be obtained free from the General Services Administration, National Archives, Washington, D. C. 20408.

The ten pages you receive are supposed to be the most important pages of the file, based on the judgment of the archives worker who makes the search. Most of these employees seem to be quite careful in their selection, but a few who are less conscientious don't do quite so well. If those ten pages include the entire contents of the file, this is indicated in the reply.

If the ten pages sent do not include the entire file and you wish to have a copy of all papers (either a photocopy or microfilm), it will be necessary to submit a request for a cost quotation to the National Archives (Attn: Archivist, Early Wars Branch). You must remit the exact fee when requesting the copy. If you want a microfilm copy you will find it is less costly (and just as readable) if you request a negative copy.

It usually takes about one month to get an answer to most requests to the National Archives, so it will pay you to develop a little patience and perhaps work on another project while you wait.

Beginning in January 1969 a four-year program to microfilm the Revolutionary War pension and bounty land warrant applications was initiated by the General Services Administration. As the project progresses, various segments of the collection are temporarily removed from all use. (The time of closure is approximately six months.) The entire file is not being closed all at one time for the project.

The filming will result in two microfilm publications: (1) the complete contents of every file, and (2) selected documents from each file which will be of most interest and value to genealogists. Both publications will eventually be available for sale, and from the latter, print-outs will continue to be made of the file documents as they are now under present request procedures. Many genealogical libraries will no doubt procure copies of one or the other of these publications.

F. PENSION PAYMENT RECORDS

Other possible sources of information about a person who secured a pension for his service during the Revolution are in the records of the Pension Office and of the Treasury Department which are in the National Archives. There are several possibilities:

1. A printed manuscript entitled "Revolutionary War and Acts of Military Establishment, Invalid Pensioners' Payments, March 1801 through September 1815" is arranged alphabetically under the states in which the

GENERAL SERVICES ADMINISTRATION NATIONAL ARCHIVES AND RECORDS SERVICE **ORDER FOR PHOTOCOPIES CONCERNING VETERAN** *(See reverse for explanation)*	1. NAME OF VETERAN *(Last name, first, middle)*	

	2. DATE OF BIRTH	3. PLACE OF BIRTH

4. WAR IN WHICH OR DATES BETWEEN WHICH HE SERVED	5. STATE FROM WHICH HE SERVED	6. UNIT IN WHICH HE SERVED *(Name of regiment or number, company, etc., or name of ship)*

7. BRANCH IN WHICH HE SERVED

☐ INFANTRY   ☐ CAVALRY   ☐ ARTILLERY   ☐ NAVY

☐ OTHER *(Specify)*

8. KIND OF SERVICE

☐ VOLUNTEERS

☐ REGULARS

9. IF SERVICE WAS CIVIL WAR

☐ UNION

☐ CONFEDERATE

10. PLACE(S) WHERE VETERAN LIVED AFTER SERVICE	11. PENSION OR BOUNTY LAND FILE NO.	12. NAME OF WIDOW OR OTHER CLAIMANT

13. IF VETERAN LIVED IN A HOME FOR SOLDIERS, ENTER LOCATION *(City and State)*	14. DATE OF DEATH	15. PLACE OF DEATH

16. CHECK RECORD DESIRED *(Enclose $1 for each record requested)*

☐ PENSION   ☐ BOUNTY LAND *(Service before 1856 only)*   ☐ MILITARY

17. INDICATE HERE THE NUMBER OF ADDITIONAL COPIES OF THIS FORM (GSA FORM 6751) DESIRED

INSTRUCTIONS

Submit a separate form for each veteran. Enclose $1 for each record requested in item 16. Do not send cash. Make your check or money order payable to GSA (NNCS).
Mail to:

Cashier
National Archives (GSA)
Washington, D.C. 20408

DO NOT WRITE IN THIS AREA

REPLY

RECORD(S) ENCLOSED   ☐ PENSION   ☐ BOUNTY LAND   ☐ MILITARY

RECORD(S) NOT FOUND   ☐ PENSION   ☐ BOUNTY LAND   ☐ MILITARY

☐ SEE ATTACHED FORMS/LEAFLETS.

☐ ONLY ONE SET OF REPRODUCTIONS CAN BE SENT FOR $1. PLEASE SUBMIT THE ENCLOSED GSA FORM 6751 FOR THE VETERAN'S OTHER RECORDS.

☐ WILL BE SENT BY THE TREASURY DEPARTMENT

☐ A REFUND OF $_____

☐ IS ENCLOSED

REFUND AUTHORIZATION

RECEIPT NUMBER	SEARCHER	DATE
	FILE DESIGNATION	

Print or type your name and address (including Zip Code) within the dots below

GSA FORM AUG 70 **6751**

FORM GSA-6751 CAN BE USED TO ORDER PHOTOCOPIES
OF MILITARY RECORDS FROM THE NATIONAL ARCHIVES

GENERAL SERVICES ADMINISTRATION
NATIONAL ARCHIVES AND RECORDS SERVICE

EXPLANATION OF ORDER FOR PHOTOCOPIES

The August 1970 edition of this form supersedes all previous editions of GSA Form 6751 and NAR Form 288. Destroy all existing stocks of previous editions of GSA Form 6751 and all stock of NAR Form 288.

Use this form to order photocopies of records of veterans who served in the United States or Confederate armed forces. These records include:

Pension application files based on United States (not State) service before World War I.

Bounty-land warrant application files based on United States (not State) service before 1856.

Pension or bounty-land warrant application files usually include an official statement of the veteran's military or naval service, as well as information of a personal or genealogical nature. If we find such a file, we send copies of the documents we think will be most useful to you. If we do not find a file, we refund your money.

Military service records based on service in the United States Army (officers who served before June 30, 1917, enlisted men before October 31, 1912), Navy (officers and enlisted men who served before 1886), Marine Corps (officers and enlisted men who served before 1896), and Confederate armed forces (1861-65). If we do not find a file, we refund your money.

Military service records rarely contain family information. The record of a man's service in any one organization is entirely separate from the record of his service in any other organization. We are ordinarily unable to accurately establish the identity of men of the same name who served in different organizations. If you know that a man served in more than one organization and you desire copies of his military service record, submit a separate form and $1 fee for the service record in each organization.

More information about these records may be found in the following free General Information Leaflets:

No. 5. Genealogical Records in the National Archives.

No. 8. Pension and Bounty-Land Warrant Application Files in the National Archives.

No. 9. Compiled Military Service Records in the National Archives.

No. 10. Records in the National Archives Relating to Confederate Soldiers.

Send the completed form with your check or money order payable to GSA (NNCS) to the address on the front of the form. When sending more than one form at a time, you may submit a single check or money order covering all the requests. Each order will be handled separately; you may not receive all your replies at the same time.

GSA ᴬᵁᴳ⁷⁰ 6751 BACK

INSTRUCTIONS FOR COMPLETING FORM GSA 6751
ARE ON THE REVERSE SIDE

pensioners were living when they received their pensions. An entry in this manuscript...

        ... shows the name and rank of the pensioner, the name of the State in which payment was made, and amount paid in March and September of each year. If the pensioner died or moved to another State during the period of the records. the fact is indicated, and in some cases the date of death is shown. [8]

    2. There are 14 unnumbered manuscript volumes relating to the payment of Revolutionary pensioners in Alabama, Arkansas, California, Connecticut, Delaware, District of Columbia, Florida, Georgia, Illinois, Indiana, Iowa, Kentucky, Louisiana, Maine, Maryland, Massachusetts, Michigan, Minnesota, Mississippi, Missouri, Nebraska, New Hampshire, New Jersey, New York, North Carolina, Ohio, Oregon, Pennsylvania, Rhode Island, South Carolina, Tennessee, Texas, Vermont, Virginia and Wisconsin. These are for payments made under the various acts from 1818 to 1853, and under each state they are arranged in alphabetical groupings (first letter of surname) according to the act under which the pension was granted. There is not a lot of useful information in these volumes. An entry in them...

        ... shows the name of the agency through which payment was made, the name of the pensioner, and the amount of the allowance. Many entries also show the dates of death of the pensioners. [9]

    3. There are 23 pension-payment volumes (manuscript), from the records of the Treasury Department, which cover 1819 through 1871. The entries in these books are arranged according to the act of Congress under which they were obtained and the pension agency involved. The information necessary to locate an entry in these volumes can be found in the pension application file (i.e., the name of the veteran, the name of the pensioner, act of Congress under which latest payment was made, and the amount of payment only if there was more than one pensioner with the same name). There is a typed "Key to the Pension Payment Volumes Relating to Revolutionary War Pensioners" in the central search room of the National Archives which will guide you to the entry you seek.

The information in these pension-payment books includes...

---

[8]. Ibid., p. 86.
[9]. Ibid., p. 87.

... the name of the pensioner, the name of the veteran, the name of the pension agency through which payment was made, and the quarter and year of the final payment. In instances in which the heirs or legal representatives claimed an unpaid balance due the pensioner, the date of death of the pensioner is given. [10]

4. After you consult the pension-application file and the pension-payment volumes (#3) you will have sufficient information to enable you to locate a Final Payment Voucher. The vouchers cover 1819 through 1864 and are filed under the states of the pensioners' residences, by the pension agency, quarter year of final payment, the act under which the pension was granted, and then alphabetically by the first letter of the pensioner's surname. A few of these have been filed with the papers in the pension-application files. They contain...

... information concerning the date and place of death of the pensioner and the names of his heirs. These vouchers will show such information if the date of death of the pensioner appears in one of the pension-payment volumes described above. [11]

Items 1 and 2 above are in the National Archives in Record Group 15, Records of the Veterans' Administration (as are the pension and bounty land applications), and items 3 and 4 are in Record Group 217, Records of the U. S. General Accounting Office.

G. BOOKS ON REVOLUTIONARY WAR SOLDIERS

Another important source of information on persons who served in the War for Independence is books. Hundreds of books have been written (especially relating to the several states and even counties and towns) giving information about these servicemen. There are rosters, lists of soldiers buried in this or that place, histories, lineages, etc., any of which may prove helpful in determining if your ancestor served in the Revolutionary War.

Do not overlook these possibilities. Most libraries, especially genealogical libraries and libraries in the localities concerned, have many such books. And these books are essential when you consider that so many of the original records have been either lost or destroyed.

A number of books with lists of American (and allied) participants in

---

10. Ibid., p. 87.
11. Ibid., p. 88.

the Revolutionary War are listed here:

(Alabama) Mell, Annie R. W.   Revolutionary Soldiers Buried in Ala-
    bama. Montgomery (1904).
(Alabama) Owen, Thomas M. Revolutionary Soldiers in Alabama (Ala-
    bama State Archives Bulletin 5, 1911). Baltimore: Genealogical
    Publishing Co. (1967 reprint).
(Alabama) Thomas, Elizabeth W. Revolutionary Soldiers in Alabama
    (2 vols.). Tuscalloosa: Willo Publishing Co. (1960-61).
Callahan, Edward W. List of Officers of the Navy of the United States
    and of the Marine Corps, from 1775 to 1900... New York (1901).
(Connecticut) Lists and Returns of Connecticut Men in the Revolution,
    1775-1783. (Connecticut Historical Society Collections, Vol. 12).
    Hartford: The Society (1909).
(Connecticut) Middlebrook, Louis F. History of Maritime Connecticut
    During the American Revolution, 1775-1783 (2 vols.). Salem,
    Mass. (1925).
(Connecticut) Pension Records of the Revolutionary Soldiers from Con-
    necticut. (21st Report of the National Society, D. A. R.). Wash-
    ington, D. C. (1919).
(Connecticut) Record of Service of Connecticut Men in the I, War of
    the Revolution; II, War of 1812; III, Mexican War. Hartford: Ad-
    jutant General's Office (1889).
(Connecticut) Richards, J. E. Honor Roll of Litchfield County Revolu-
    tionary Soldiers. Litchfield, Conn.: D. A. R. (1912).
(Connecticut) Rolls and Lists of Connecticut Men in the Revolution,
    1775-1783. (Connecticut Historical Society Collections, Vol. 8).
    Hartford: The Society (1901).
Dandridge, Danske. American Prisoners of the Revolution. (Copied
    from the papers of the British War Dept., 1911). Baltimore: Gen-
    ealogical Publishing Co. (1967 reprint).
Delaware Archives (5 vols.). Public Archives Commission of Dela-
    ware (1911-19). Vols. 2 and 3 are in print (Dover: Public Archives
    Commission).
Dickore, Marie (trans.). Hessian Soldiers in the American Revolution:
    Records of Their Marriages and Baptisms of Their Children in
    America..., 1776-1783. Cincinnati: D. J. Krehbiel Co. (1959).
(District of Columbia) Ely, Selden M. The District of Columbia in the
    American Revolution, and Patriots of the Revolutionary Period
    Who are Interred in the District or in Arlington. (Records of the
    Columbia Historical Society, 21). Washington, D. C.: The Society
    (1918).
Eelking, Max von. The German Allied Troops in the North American
    War of Independence, 1776-1783. (Trans. and abridged from Ger-

man by J.G. Rosengarten, 1893). Baltimore: Genealogical Publishing Co. (1969 reprint).

Ellet, Elizabeth F.   The Women of the American Revolution (3 vols.). New York (1848-50).

France. Ministere des Affaires Etrangeres. Les Combattants Francais de la Guerre Americaine, 1778-1783 (Senate doc. 77, 58th Cong., 2d sess., 1905). Baltimore: Genealogical Publishing Co. (1969 reprint).

(Georgia) Blair, Ruth. Revolutionary Soldiers' Receipts for Georgia Bounty Grants. Atlanta: Department of Archives and History (1928).

(Georgia) Hitz, Alex M. Authentic List of All Land Lottery Grants Made to Veterans of the Revolutionary War by the State of Georgia (2nd ed.). Atlanta: Department of Archives and History (1966).

(Georgia) Houston, Martha L. Six Hundred Revolutionary Soldiers and Widows of Revolutionary Soldiers Living in Georgia, 1827-1828. Athens, Ga. (1965 reprint). Available from Heritage Press, Danielsville, Ga.

(Georgia) Knight, Lucian L. Georgia's Roster of the Revolution... (1920). Baltimore: Genealogical Publishing Co. (1967 reprint).

(Georgia) McCall, Mrs. Ettie S. Roster of Revolutionary Soldiers in Georgia and Other States (3 vols.). Vol. I (1941) is a reprint. Baltimore: Genealogical Publishing Co. (1968-69).

Hamersly, Thomas H.S.   Complete Army and Navy Register of the United States of America, from 1776 to 1887. New York (1888).

_____. Complete General Navy Register of the United States of America, from 1776-1887... New York (1888).

Hayward, Elizabeth McCoy. Soldiers and Patriots of the American Revolution. Ridgewood, N.J.: The Author (1947).

Heitman, Francis Bernard. Historical Register of Officers of the Continental Army During the War of the Revolution, April, 1775, to December, 1783. (new rev. enl. ed., 1914). Baltimore: Genealogical Publishing Co. (1967 reprint).

(Illinois) Clift, Garrett Glenn. List of Officers of the Illinois Regiment, and of Crockett's Regiment Who Have Received Land for Their Services. Frankfort, Ill.: S.A.R. (1962).

(Illinois) Meyer, Virginia M. Roster of Revolutionary War Soldiers and Widows Who Lived in Illinois Counties. Chicago: Illinois D.A.R. (1962).

(Illinois) Walker, Harriet J. Revolutionary Soldiers Buried in Illinois. (1917). Baltimore: Genealogical Publishing Co. (1967 reprint).

(Illinois) Walker, Homer A. Illinois Pensioners Lists of the Revolution, 1812, and Indian Wars. Washington, D.C. (c. 1955).

(Indiana) O'Byrne, Mrs. Estella. Roster of Soldiers and Patriots of the American Revolution Buried in Indiana (2 vols.). Brockville, Ind.: Indiana D.A.R. (1938, 1966). Volume I was reprinted by Genealogical Publishing Co., Baltimore, in 1968.

(Indiana) Waters, Margaret R. Revolutionary Soldiers Buried in Indiana. Three Hundred Names Not Listed in the Roster by Mrs. O'Byrne (2 vols.). (1949, 1954). Baltimore: Genealogical Publishing Co. (1970 reprint in 1 vol.).

Kaminkow, Marion J. and Jack Kaminkow. Mariners of the American Revolution. Baltimore: Magna Carta Book Co. (1967).

(Kentucky) Burns, Annie W. Abstracts of Pension Papers of Soldiers of the Revolutionary War, War of 1812, and Indian Wars, Who Settled... in Kentucky (at least 21 vols.). Washington, D.C. (1935——).

(Kentucky) Quisenberry, Anderson C. Revolutionary Soldiers in Kentucky. (Excerpted from Year Book, Kentucky Society, S.A.R., 1896). Baltimore: Genealogical Publishing Co. (1959 reprint).

(Kentucky) Wilson, Samuel M. Catalogue of Revolutionary Soldiers and Sailors of the Commonwealth of Virginia to Whom Land Bounty Warrants Were Granted by Virginia for Military Services in the War of Independence. (Excerpted from Year Book, Kentucky Society, S.A.R., 1913). Baltimore: Genealogical Publishing Co. (1953 reprint).

(Maine) Flagg, Charles Alcott. An Alphabetical Index of Revolutionary Pensioners Living in Maine. (1920). Baltimore: Genealogical Publishing Co. (1967 reprint).

(Maine) House, Charles J. Names of Soldiers of the American Revolution (from Maine), Who Applied for State Bounty Under Resolves of March 17, 1835, March 24, 1836, and March 20, 1836, as Appears of Record in Land Office. (1893). Baltimore: Genealogical Publishing Co. (1967 reprint).

(Maine) Houston, Ethel Rollins. Maine Revolutionary Soldiers' Graves. Maine D.A.R. (1940).

(Maine) Miller, Frank Burton. Soldiers and Sailors of the Plantation of Lower St. Georges Who Served in the War for American Independence. Rockland, Me.: A.J. Huston (1931).

(Maryland) Brumbaugh, Gaius Marcus and Margaret R. Hodges. Revolutionary Records of Maryland, Part I. (1924). Baltimore: Genealogical Publishing Co. (1967 reprint).

(Maryland) McGhee, Lucy K. Pension Abstracts of Maryland Soldiers of the Revolution, War of 1812, and Indian Wars Who Settled in Kentucky. Washington, D.C. (n.d.).

(Maryland) Muster Rolls and Other Records of Service of Maryland Troops in the American Revolution, 1775-1783. (Archives of Maryland, 18) Baltimore: Maryland Historical Society (1900). (Reprinted by Genealogical Publishing Co., 1972).

(Maryland) Newman, Harry Wright. Maryland Revolutionary Records. (1938). Baltimore: Genealogical Publishing Co. (1967 reprint).

Massachusetts Soldiers and Sailors of the Revolutionary War. (17 vols.). Boston: Massachusetts Secretary of State (1896-1908).

(Massachusetts) Smith, Elizur Yale. Vital Records of Saudisfield, Massachusetts...; Saudisfield Revolutionary Soldiers. Rutland, Vt.: Charles E. Tuttle Co. (1936).

(Massachusetts) Wolkins, George G. Beverly Men in the War of Independence. Beverly, Mass.: Beverly Historical Society (1932).

(Michigan) Silliman, Sue I. Michigan Military Records. (Michigan Historical Commission Bulletin 12, 1920). Baltimore: Genealogical Publishing Co. (1969 reprint).

(Mississippi) Welch, Alice T. Family Records, Mississippi Revolutionary Soldiers. Mississippi D.A.R. (1956). Distributor: Genealogical Publishing Co., Baltimore. (Now out of print.)

(Missouri) Burns, Annie W. Missouri Pension Records of Soldiers of the Revolutionary War, War of 1812, and Indian Wars. Washington, D.C. (1937).

(Missouri) Houts, Alice K. Revolutionary Soldiers Buried in Missouri. Kansas City: The Author (1966).

(Missouri) McGhee, Lucy K. Missouri Revolutionary Soldiers, War of 1812 and Indian Wars Pension List. Washington, D.C. (1955).

(Missouri) Pompey, Sherman L. A Partial Listing of Veterans of the American Revolution, the Civil War, and the Spanish War, That are Buried in Certain Missouri Cemeteries. Warrensburg, Mo.: Johnson County Historical Society (1962).

(New Hampshire) Miscellaneous Revolutionary Documents of New Hampshire, Including the Association Test, the Pension Rolls, and Other Important Papers. (New Hampshire State and Provincial Papers, 30). Manchester, N.H. (1910).

(New Hampshire) Rolls of the Soldiers of the Revolutionary War, 1775-1782. 4 vols. (New Hampshire State and Provincial Papers, 14-17). Concord and Manchester (1885-89).

(New Jersey) Stryker, William S. Official Register of the Officers and Men of New Jersey in the Revolutionary War. (1872). Baltimore: Genealogical Publishing Co. (1967 reprint). [12]

---

12. The index to this volume, Index of the Official Register of the Officers and Men of New Jersey in the Revolutionary War, as prepared by the

(New York) Beauchamp, William Martin. Revolutionary Soldiers Resident or Dying in Onondaga County, N.Y. Syracuse: Onondaga Historical Society (1913).

(New York) Daughters of the American Revolution. Chautauqua County Chapters. Soldiers of the American Revolution. Jamestown, N.Y.: Mrs. L. N. Shankland (1925).

(New York) Fernow, Berthold. New York in the Revolution. (Vol. 1 of New York State Archives and Vol. 15 of Documents Relating to the Colonial History of the State of New York). Albany (1887).

(New York) Mather, Frederic Gregory. The Refugees of 1776 from Long Island to Connecticut. (1913). Baltimore: Genealogical Publishing Co. (1972 reprint).

(New York) Muster and Pay Rolls of the War of the Revolution, 1775–1783. (2 vols.). New York: The New York Historical Society (1916).

New York [State]. Comptroller's Office. New York in the Revolution as Colony and State... (2nd ed.). Albany (1904).

_____. Supplement by Erastus C. Knight . . . Albany (1901).

(New York) Tallmadge, Samuel, et al. Orderly Books of the Fourth New York Regiment, 1778-1783. (2 vols.). New York: The New York Historical Society (1916).

(North Carolina) Daughters of the American Revolution, North Carolina. Roster of Soldiers from North Carolina in the American Revolution. (1932). Baltimore: Genealogical Publishing Co. (1967 reprint).

(Ohio) Daughters of the American Revolution, Ohio. Official Roster of the Soldiers of the American Revolution Buried in the State of Ohio. Columbus (1929).

(Ohio) _____. Soldiers of the American Revolution Who Lived in the State of Ohio. (Official Roster II and III). (1938, 1959).

(Pennsylvania) Cowan, Lucy Marie Davis. Revolutionary Soldiers of Warren County, Pennsylvania. New York: Frederick H. Hitchcock (1926),

(Pennsylvania) Egle, William H. Pennsylvania in the War of the Revolution: Associated Battalions and Militia, 1775-1783. (Pennsylvania Archives, Ser. 2, Vols. 13-14). Harrisburg (1890-92).

(Pennsylvania) Fendrick, Virginia Shannon. Revolutionary Soldiers of Franklin County, Pennsylvania. Waynesboro, Pa.: B. Rohrer (n.d.).

Historical Records Survey of the WPA in 1941, was reprinted by Genealogical Publishing Co., Baltimore, in 1965.

(Pennsylvania) "List of Officers and Men of the Pennsylvania Navy, 1775-1781." (Pennsylvania Archives, Ser. 2, Vol. 1, pp. 243-434). Harrisburg (1896).

Peterson, Clarence S. Known Military Dead During the American Revolutionary War, 1775-1783. (1959). Baltimore: Genealogical Publishing Co. (1967 reprint).

Pierce, John. "Register of the Certificates Issued by John Pierce, Esquire, Paymaster General and Commissioner of Army Accounts for the United States. To Officers and Soldiers of the Continental Army Under Act of July 4, 1783. First Published 1786 in Numerical Order." 17th Report of the National Society, Daughters of the American Revolution, pp. 147-712. Washington, D.C. (1915).

(Rhode Island) Cowell, Benjamin. Spirit of '76 in Rhode Island. Boston (1850).

Saffell, William T.R. Records of the Revolutionary War: Containing the Military and Financial Correspondence of Distinguished Officers, Names of the Officers and Privates of Regiments, Companies, and Corps, with Dates of Their Commissions and Enlistments... (3rd ed., 1894). Baltimore: Genealogical Publishing Co. (1968 reprint).

(South Carolina) Boddie, William Willis. Marion's Men; a List of Twenty-five Hundred. Charleston, S.C.: The Author (1938).

(South Carolina) Burns, Annie W. South Carolina Pension Abstracts of the Revolutionary War, War of 1812, and Indian Wars. (12 vols.). Washington, D.C. (c. 193?).

(South Carolina) Ervin, Sara Sullivan. South Carolinians in the Revolution. (1949). Baltimore: Genealogical Publishing Co. (1965 reprint).

(South Carolina) Pruitt, Jayne C.C. Revolutionary War Pension Applicants Who Served from South Carolina. Fairfax, Va.: Charlton Hall (1946).

(South Carolina) Revill, Janie. Copy of the Original Book Showing the Revolutionary Claims Filed in South Carolina Between August 20, 1783, and August 31, 1786. (1941). Baltimore: Genealogical Publishing Co. (1969 reprint).

(South Carolina) Salley, Alexander S. Accounts Audited of Revolutionary Claims Against South Carolina. (3 vols.). Columbia, S.C.: The State Co. (1935-43).

(South Carolina) Stub Entries of Indents Issued in Payment of Claims Against South Carolina Growing Out of the Revolution. (12 vols.). Columbia, S.C.: Department of Archives and History (1910-57).

(Tennessee) Allen, Penelope Johnson. Tennessee Soldiers in the Revolution. Bristol, Tenn.: King Printing Co. (1935).

(Tennessee) Armstrong, Zella. Some Tennessee Heroes of the Revolution. (5 vols.). Chattanooga: Lookout Publishing Co. (1935).

(Tennessee) _____. Twenty-four Hundred Tennessee Pensioners; Revolution, War of 1812. Chattanooga: Lookout Publishing Co. (1937).

United States. Bureau of the Census. A Census of Pensioners for Revolutionary or Military Services: With Their Names, Ages, and Places of Residence Taken in 1840. (1841). Baltimore: Genealogical Publishing Co. (1967 reprint).

_____. Census of Pensioners, A General Index for Revolutionary or Military Service (1840). (Prepared by The Genealogical Society of The Church of Jesus Christ of Latter-day Saints, Salt Lake City). Baltimore: Genealogical Publishing Co. (1965).

_____. House of Representatives. Digested Summary and Alphabetical List of Private Claims Which Have Been Presented to the House of Representatives from the First to the 31st Congress, Exhibiting the Action of Congress on Each Claim... (3 vols.). (1853). Baltimore: Genealogical Publishing Co. (1970 reprint).

_____. Secretary of War. Pension Roll of 1835. (Senate doc. 514, 23d Cong., 1st sess., ser. 249-51, 3 vols., 1835). Baltimore: Genealogical Publishing Co. (1968 reprint in 4 vols.).

_____. Secretary of War. Revolutionary Pensioners. A Transcript of the Pension List of the United States for 1813... (1813). Baltimore: Genealogical Publishing Co. (1959 reprint).

_____. Senate. Pension List of 1818. (Senate doc. 55, 16th Cong., 1st sess., ser. 34, vol. 4, 1820). Baltimore: Genealogical Publishing Co. (1955 reprint).

_____. Senate. Rejected or Suspended Applications for Revolutionary War Pensions, Report of the Secretary of the Interior, 1852. (1852). Baltimore: Genealogical Publishing Co. (1969 reprint).

_____. Revolutionary Pensioners of 1818. Message from the President of the United States, Transmitting a Report of the Secretary of War... (1818). Baltimore: Genealogical Publishing Co. (1959 reprint).

(Vermont) Crockett, Walter H. Revolutionary Soldiers Buried in Vermont. (1903-1907). Baltimore: Genealogical Publishing Co. (1973 reprint).

(Vermont) Goodrich, John E. Rolls of Soldiers in the Revolutionary War, 1775-1783. Rutland, Vt.: Charles E. Tuttle Co. (1904).

(Virginia) Brumbaugh, Gaius Marcus. Revolutionary War Records... Vol. I (all published). (1936). Baltimore: Genealogical Publishing Co. (1967 reprint).

(Virginia) Burgess, Louis Alexander. Virginia Soldiers of 1776. (3 vols.). Richmond: Richmond Press (1927-29).

(Virginia) Dorman, John F. Virginia Revolutionary Pension Applica-
  tions. (continuing series, vol. 1——). Washington, D.C.: The
  Author (1958——).
(Virginia) Eckenrode, Hamilton J. List of Revolutionary Soldiers of
  Virginia. (Special Report of Dept. of Archives and History, 1911).
  Richmond: Virginia State Library (1912).
(Virginia) _____ _____. Supplement. (Special
  Report..., 1912). Richmond: Virginia State Library (1913).
(Virginia) Gwathmey, John H. Historical Register of Virginians in the
  Revolution: Soldiers, Sailors, Marines, 1775-1783. Richmond:
  Dietz Press (1938).
(Virginia) McAllister, Joseph T. Virginia Militia in the Revolutionary
  War. Hot Springs, Va. (c. 1913).
(Virginia) Saffell, William. Records of the Revolutionary War. List
  of Virginia Soldiers... (3rd ed., 1894). Baltimore: Genealogical
  Publishing Co. (1969 reprint). The reprint edition includes an in-
  dex by Joseph T. McAllister originally published in 1913.
(Virginia) Stewart, Robert A. The History of Virginia's Navy of the
  Revolution. Richmond (1933).
(Virginia) Wilson, Samuel M. Catalogue of Revolutionary Soldiers and
  Sailors of the Commonwealth of Virginia to Whom Bounty Land
  Warrants Were Granted by Virginia for Military Service in the
  War for Independence. (1913). Baltimore: Genealogical Publish-
  ing Co. (1953 reprint).
(West Virginia) Johnston, Ross B. West Virginians in the American
  Revolution. Parkersburg: Augusta Historical and Genealogical
  Society (1959).
(West Virginia) Lewis, Virgil A. Soldiery of West Virginia in the
  French and Indian War; Lord Dunmore's War; the Revolution; the
  Later Indian Wars.... (1911). Baltimore: Genealogical Publishing
  Co. (1967 reprint).
(West Virginia) Reddy, Anne W. West Virginia Revolutionary Ances-
  tors Whose Services Were Non-military and Whose Names, There-
  fore, Do Not Appear in Revolutionary Indexes of Soldiers and Sail-
  ors. (1930). Baltimore: Genealogical Publishing Co. (1963 re-
  print).

V. USING REVOLUTIONARY RECORDS

Many beginning genealogists overlook Revolutionary War records as a
research source mainly because they do not recognize valid clues. Many
do not even think about the possibility that their ancestor may have served
unless they read somewhere that he actually did. However, there are several clues which might indicate the need for considering these records:

1. Any time the line on which you are working was in America prior to the time of the war you must consider these records. Even if a lineal ancestor did not serve, perhaps a relative (maybe a brother) of the same surname did, and records of his service or his pension application would also provide useful data about your ancestors of the same name—names, dates and places especially.

2. If a known male ancestor was in America at the time of the Revolution and was of age to serve, the possibility of service must certainly be considered.

3. If a known ancestor was born in America anytime within the period beginning just before the war and ending two decades after it, you must consider the possibility that his (or her) father served, even though you may not know the father's name. The index to pensioners provides a ready list of servicemen (at least those who applied for pensions) of the surname you seek who served from the state or the general region from which your ancestors came. Books about Revolutionary War veterans in the state(s) where your ancestors lived might also help suggest some possibilities to you.

If your ancestral line is not traced back to this period there is seldom good reason to spend time searching records of soldiers or of the war. You have too little to go on. There will be plenty of time to use these records when your research and analysis indicate the need for them.

VI. LOYALISTS AND THE REVOLUTIONARY WAR

Perhaps your people were in America before the Revolution but you can find no evidence of service by them. There may be a number of reasons for this, including the possibility that they belonged to a pacifist church such as the Quakers. But, on the other hand, there is also the possibility that they were sympathetic to the cause of the Crown rather than to that of the revolutionaries.

If you do not know where your ancestors were during the Revolution because you have not traced them that far, but you find them coming out of Canada (or even Florida or the West Indies) in later years, the same possibility exists. It is estimated that as many as one-third of the colonial population were Loyalists. Among the Loyalists were British government officials and their friends, English Church ministers and others whose positions or wealth depended upon British sovereignty. Technically speaking, however, all of these persons were not Loyalists though often called such— pro-British or Tories, yes—but not Loyalists. A true Loyalist was one who actively participated in the war to aid the cause of the Crown, usually in British uniform. The Tories did suffer, especially if they refused to take an oath of allegiance, but their property was not usually confiscated and they were not generally charged with treason as were their Loyalist cousins.

Many of these Tories have been called Loyalists—in fact all of those who went to Canada were so called—but many Tories went other directions too (and they were free to do so). However, there is generally no record of loyalism or of confiscation of property in the former American homes of the Tories who emigrated to Canada. Also, these Tories were not eligible for land grants there.

In addition to Canada and Florida, many Loyalists and Tories went to the West Indies (especially Jamaica) and some returned to Britain. Canada, however, seemed to be the favorite place; in Upper Canada (now Ontario) four-fifths of the settlers came from the American colonies.

A. PRINTED LOYALIST SOURCES

Some of the printed sources on Loyalists (and Tories) in the American Revolution are:

Bradley, Arthur Granville. Colonial Americans in Exile; Founders of British Canada. Toronto: E. B. Dutton and Co. (1932).

Brown, Wallace. The King's Friends. The Composition and Motives of the American Loyalist Claimants. Providence, R.I.: Brown University Press (1966).

_____. The Good Americans. The Loyalists in the American Revolution. New York: William Morrow and Co. (1969).

Bruce, R. M. Loyalist Trail. Kingston, Ont.: no publisher (no date).

Campbell, Wilfrid. Report on Manuscript Lists in the Archives Relating to the United Empire Loyalists, with Reference to Other Sources. Ottawa: printed for use of the Archives Branch (1909).

Canniff, William. The Settlement of Upper Canada. Toronto: Dudley and Burns, Printers (1869).

Craig, Gerald M. Upper Canada. The Formative Years, 1784-1841. Toronto: McClelland and Stewart, Ltd. (1966).

Cruikshank, Ernest Alexander (ed.). Settlement of the United Empire Loyalists on the Upper St. Lawrence and Bay of Quinte in 1784. Toronto: The Ontario Historical Society (1934).

DeMond, Robert O. Loyalists in North Carolina During the Revolution. (1940). Hampden, Conn.: Archer Books (1964 reprint).

Evans, G. N. D. Allegiance in America: The Case of the Loyalists. Reading, Mass.: Addison-Wesley Publishing Co. (1969).

Flick, Alexander Clarence. Loyalism in New York During the American Revolution. New York: Columbia University Press (1901).

Gilroy, Marion (comp.). Loyalists and Land Settlement in Nova Scotia. Halifax: Public Archives of Nova Scotia (1937).

Hancock, Harold Bell. Delaware Loyalists. Wilmington, Del.: Historical Society of Delaware (1940).

Harrell, Isaac Samuel. Loyalism in Virginia. Durham, N.C.: Duke University Press (1926).

Jones, Edward Alfred. Loyalists in Massachusetts, Their Memorials, Petitions and Claims. (1930). Baltimore: Genealogical Publishing Co. (1969 reprint).

_____. Loyalists of New Jersey. Newark, N.J.: New Jersey Historical Society (1927).

Kelby, William. Orderly Book of the Three Battalions of Loyalists Commanded by Brigadier-General Oliver de Lancey, 1776-1778. (1917). Baltimore: Genealogical Publishing Co. (1972 reprint).

New York [State]. Minutes of the Commissioners for Detecting and Defeating Conspiracies in the State of New York. Albany County Sessions, 1778-1781. (2 vols.). Albany: The State of New York (1909).

The Old United Empire Loyalist List. (Reprint of The Centennial of the Settlement of Upper Canada by the United Empire Loyalists, 1784-1884.). (1885). Baltimore: Genealogical Publishing Co. (1969 reprint).

Peck, Epaphroditus. Loyalists of Connecticut. New Haven, Conn: Yale University Press (1934).

Pringle, J.F. Lunenburgh or the Old Eastern District. Cornwall, Ont.: Standard Printing House (1890).

Raymond, W.O. Loyalist Transport Ships, 1783. Saint Johns: New Brunswick Historical Society (1904).

Ryerson, Adolphus E. The Loyalists of America and Their Times: 1620 to 1816. (2 vols.). Toronto (1880).

Sabine, Lorenzo. Biographical Sketches of Loyalists of the American Revolution. (2 vols.). (1864). Port Washington, N.Y.: Kennikat Press (1966 reprint).

Siebert, Wilbur Henry. The American Loyalists in the Eastern Seigniories and Townships of the Province of Quebec. (Transactions of the Royal Society of Canada). Ottawa: The Society (1913).

_____. The Colony of Massachusetts Loyalists at Bristol, England. Boston: Massachusetts Historical Society (1912).

_____. The Flight of American Loyalists to the British Isles. Columbus, Ohio: F.J. Heer Co. (1911).

_____. The Legacy of the American Revolution to the British West Indies and Bahamas. Columbus, Ohio: Ohio State University (1914).

_____. The Loyalists and Six Nation Indians in the Niagara Peninsula. (Transactions of the Royal Society of Canada). Ottawa: The Society (1916).

_____. Loyalists of East Florida, 1774 to 1785. (2 vols.). DeLand, Fla.: Florida State Historical Society (1929).

_____. The Refugee Loyalists of Connecticut. (Transactions of the Royal Society of Canada). Ottawa: The Society (1916).

_____. The Temporary Settlement of Loyalists at Machiche, P.Q. (Transactions of the Royal Society of Canada). Ottawa: The Society (1916).

Singer, Charles G. South Carolina in the Confederation. Philadelphia: University of Pennsylvania Press (1941).

Smith, Paul H. Loyalists and Redcoats. Chapel Hill, N.C.: University of North Carolina Press (1964).

Starke, James H. The Loyalists of Massachusetts, and the Other Side of the American Revolution. Boston: The Author (1910).

_____. The United Empire Loyalists. (United Empire Loyalist Transactions). Toronto: The United Empire Loyalists of Canada (1917).

Stewart, E. Rae. Jessup's Rangers as a Factor in Loyalist Settlement (three history theses). Toronto: The Ontario Archives (1961).

United Empire Loyalists: Enquiry into the Losses and Services in Consequence of Their Loyalty; Evidence in the Canadian Claim. (2 vols.). Toronto: Ontario Archives (1904-5).

Upton, L.F.S. The United Empire Loyalists: Men and Myths. Toronto: Copp Clark Publishing Co. (1967).

Van Tyne, Claude Halstead. Loyalists in the American Revolution. New York: Peter Smith (1929).

Wallace, W. Stewart. The United Empire Loyalists. A Chronicle of the Great Migration. (Vol. 13 of Chronicles of Canada). Toronto: Glasgow, Brook and Co. (1914).

Walton, Jesse M. Quaker Loyalist Settlement, Pennfield, New Brunswick, 1783. Aurora, Ont.: The Author (1940).

Waugh, John Thomas. United Empire Loyalists. Buffalo, N.Y.: University of Buffalo Press (1925).

Wright, Esther Clark. Loyalists of New Brunswick. Fredericton, N.B.: The Author (1955).

Yoshpe, Harry Beller. Disposition of Loyalist Estates in the Southern District of the State of New York. New York: Columbia University Press (1939).

The New York Public Library also has a collection of American Loyalist claims papers and the New Jersey State Library, Archives and History Department, has records of Loyalists in that state whose estates were confiscated. There is also information on Loyalists from Sussex County, New Jersey, in an article by Thomas B. Wilson entitled "Notes on Some Loyalists of Sussex County, New Jersey" in The Ontario Register, Vol. 2, No. 1 (1969), pages 31-47.

A useful periodical for the use of those interested in Loyalists and their records is the Loyalist Gazette, published by the United Empire Loyalists of Canada, 23 Prince Arthur Avenue, Toronto 180, Ontario. It is a semi-annual publication.

B. CANADIAN LOYALIST SOURCES

Concerning official Loyalist sources in Canada, let us quote from a genealogical booklet prepared by the Public Archives of Canada and published by the Queen's Printer and Controller of Stationery in Ottawa:

> * * * A list of Loyalists in Upper Canada, compiled in the Office of the Commissioner of Crown Lands, and presently kept in the Crown Lands Department in Toronto, records names, contemporary residence and descendants; we [the Public Archives of Canada in Ottawa] have a transcript of this list. A similar list also in our holdings was retained in the Executive Council Office. Comparable lists were not compiled in other colonies.
>
> The Audit Office Series (A.O. 12 and A.O. 13) is perhaps the most rewarding source for the genealogist. The first of these contains evidence in support of Loyalist claims for losses sustained during the American Revolution together with the proceedings of the investigating commission, and the second records the evidence of claimants only. It should be emphasized that by no means all of the Loyalists who suffered losses as a result of adherence to the Crown submitted claims, often because of the considerable expense entailed. These records give location of former residence in the various American colonies, size of families, often the dependants' names, details of military service and residence at the time of the claim... These records are on microfilm [at the Public Archives]. The originals are in the Public Record Office, London, England. The Series is completely indexed.
>
> A further source, though one generally listing heads of families with the number of dependants, are the nominal lists and returns of Loyalists in the Haldimand Papers [which list the settlers by township], the originals of which are in the British Museum, in London. We [the Public Archives] have transcript copies of these lists, completely indexed.... [13]

The LDS Genealogical Society in Salt Lake City also has a microfilm copy of these two Audit Office Series (A.O. 12 and A.O. 13) plus their indexes

---

13. The Public Archives of Canada, "Tracing Your Ancestors in Canada," (Ottawa: The Queen's Printer and Controller of Stationery, 1967), pp. 17-18.

CHAPTER TWENTY-TWO

MILITARY RECORDS: AFTER THE REVOLUTION

I. BETWEEN THE REVOLUTION AND FORT SUMTER

The records arising out of the American Revolution, though they contain
less information than some which followed, set a pattern for the records of
later wars. And as we look at these other wars we see that there are still
just two kinds of records:

    A. Service records.
    B. Records of veterans' benefits.

For our discussion of the records of wars between the Revolution and
the American Civil War let's again divide the records according to these
catagories rather than by war.

A. SERVICE RECORDS

1. There are compiled military service records (similar to those made
on 3 1/2" x 8" cards for Revolutionary soldiers) for those who served during
this period. They include the following:
    a. Records for the period between the Revolution and the War of
1812 (called the post-Revolutionary War period). These ordinarily
show the soldier's...

      ... name, rank, and military organization; the dates he
      was mustered in and out; and where available, the State from
      which he served. [1]

    b. Records for the War of 1812. These are dated 1812-1815 and
the information is basically the same as in the compiled service rec-

_____

[1] Meredith B. Colket, Jr., and Frank E. Bridgers, Guide to Genealogical Records in the National Archives (Washington, D.C.: The National
Archives, 1964), pp. 53-54.

ords of the post-Revolutionary War period.

c. Records of Indian and related wars. These are dated between 1817 and 1857 and, in addition to the Indian wars, include (among others) records of the troops who, under Colonel Albert Sidney Johnston, were sent to Utah in 1857 and 1858 to put down a chimerical rebellion—the so-called "Utah War" or the "Utah Expedition." The information is about the same as in the service records already mentioned except that the state from which the soldier served is not always indicated.

d. Records of the Mexican War, 1846-1848. The records contain all the information included in those of previously-mentioned wars, plus the soldier's age is sometimes given.

All of these compiled service records are indexed in their separate series. Each one has a master name index, and each set of records also has indexes to the various states and the non-state organizations from which the men served, except those of the Mexican War. This means that it is usually easier to locate a soldier's service record if you know the state from which he served or the organization with which he served. (This information is found in pension-application records if a pension was claimed.)

These compiled service records are all located in Record Group 94, Records of the Adjutant General's Office, in the National Archives.

2. Miscellaneous Military Records, 1784-1815, are also in this group. These records consist of:

a. Post-Revolutionary War manuscripts.
b. Miscellaneous records of the War of 1812.
c. Prisoner-of-war records of the War of 1812.

The first two groups of records here have master card indexes to all names therein, but the prisoner-of-war records are only partially indexed, and then in separate indexes. There are not a lot of genealogical data in any of these records, and most of the information of value can also be found in other service records. These miscellaneous military records are also in Records Group 94 along with the compiled service records.

3. Naval service records are varied, but are not unlike the army service records, though a little more complete during this early period. The records in the National Archives include:

a. Records relating to commissioned officers. There are several series of these, among which are:

1) Statements of the Place of Birth of Officers, 1816. This one manuscript volume includes name, age or date of birth, and place of birth for each officer and is almost exclusively for officers whose surnames begin with the letters "C" and "D."

2) Statements of the Place of Birth and Residence of Officers, 1826. Entries are alphabetical in two manuscript volumes (excluding chaplains and pursers) and show the name, state or territory of birth, state or territory from which appointed, and state or territory of which each officer was a citizen.

3) Records of Officers Serving in 1829. This is one indexed manuscript volume which outlines the service record of every officer then serving in the Navy.

4) Statements of Service Written by Officers, 1842-43. These are two bound manuscripts, largely filled out from memory in response to a questionnaire, outlining the service record of each officer then serving, to the end of 1842. There are two additional manuscript volumes with letters of transmittal and supplemental biographical statements of some officers.

5) Records of Officers in Lettered Volumes. These include all officers who served between 1798 and 1893 (including noncommissioned officers). There are 15 separate manuscript volumes, A-O, with two of the volumes being bound in two separate parts. Each bound manuscript covers a specific period of time. Some are indexed; others are alphabetical. They show for each officer the name, date of appointment, dates of changes in rank and nature of the termination of service.

6) Records of Officers in Numbered Volumes. These 38 manuscript volumes relate mainly to officers appointed between 1846 and 1902, though there are some later entries. There is a master index and an entry for an individual officer usually gives his name, birth date, birthplace, date of entering duty, ranks held, duty stations, place of residence, death date and place.

7) Register of Engineer Officers. This one manuscript volume relates to officers of the Engineer Corps of the Navy from 1843 to 1899. Each entry shows name, date of birth, place of birth, date of appointment, date of death or retirement, place of death, and a detailed service record.

b. Registers of Admissions of Midshipmen or Cadets. These registers relate to those admitted to the U.S. Naval Academy at Annapolis, 1849-1930, and are arranged chronologically by date of appointment. An entry for an appointee gives name, birth date (early registers give age instead), signature, name of parent or guardian, place of residence.

c. Records of Enlisted Men.

1) Muster Rolls and Pay Rolls of Vessels. These cover the period between 1798 and 1844 and are in bound manuscript volumes. They are not indexed, but one volume ordinarily relates to only one vessel for a specific period of time. Some vessels have several

volumes. They are arranged alphabetically by the names of the vessels, and each volume is arranged chronologically. Volumes relating to the Frigate Constitution, 1798-1815, are indexed. Once you find the person you seek these records often enable you to follow him throughout his naval career as some entries show the name of the vessel from which a man came or to which he went upon reassignment. If you find your ancestor on the Frigate Constitution, or find from other sources such as pension records that he served on a certain vessel, you might trace him through his entire naval service in these rolls.

2) Muster Rolls and Pay Rolls of Shore Establishments. These mainly cover 1800-1842 and are also in bound manuscript volumes. The arrangement is the same as for vessels in #1 above and the information and use are also basically the same.

3) Registers of Enlistments. These are three manuscript volumes covering 1845-1854, and the arrangement is alphabetical by the first letter of the surname. Volumes one and two are continuous for 1845 to 1853, and volume three is for 1854 only. These registers are indexed and the index, on microfilm, is incorporated into the master index to records of enlisted men. Each entry in the register shows name, date of enlistment, place of enlistment, birthplace and age. There is also a "remarks" column, often containing information on the names of ships and duty stations to which assigned and dates of discharge.

4) Weekly Returns of Enlistments at Naval Rendezvous. These returns cover the period 1855-1891 and are bound in volumes chronologically. The entry for each enlistee shows his name, date and term of enlistment, rating, birthplace, age, occupation, personal description and (sometimes) residence. Reference to any previous naval service is also included.

5) Jackets for Enlisted Men. The jackets are alphabetically arranged for the period 1842-1855 and normally show name, full service record and place of residence after service.

6) Certificates of Consent. This one manuscript volume covers 1838 to 1840 and contains certificates signed by parents or guardians allowing youths between 13 and 18 to become naval apprentices and to serve until they were 21. A certificate gives the boy's name, his birth date and the name of his parent or guardian. There is no index.

4. Marine Corps Service Records may also have some significance for you. They include:

    a. Records of Commissioned Officers.

        1) Letters of Acceptance. These consist of three manuscript

volumes dated 1808-1862. Volume one is alphabetical by surname and covers 1808-1816. The other two volumes cover 1812 to 1862 and are arranged chronologically. Each letter shows name, date commission was accepted, and (after 1830) state or territory of birth and state or territory from which appointed. Some give place of residence.

2) Card Records of the Names of Officers. These alphabetically-arranged cards, covering 1798 to 1941, show name, year of appointment and rank.

b. Records of Enlisted Men.
1) Service Records. These records, in individual jackets, cover 1798-1895. They are arranged by year of enlistment, then by first letter of the surname, and then by date of enlistment. There is a group of cards showing name and the date and place of enlistment which serve as an index to these records. The jackets themselves usually contain information relating to name, date of enlistment, place, term of enlistment, age, personal description, occupation and sometimes date and circumstances of separation from the Marine Corps.

2) Card Records of the Names of Enlisted Men. These records cover 1798 to 1941 and are the cards mentioned in #1 which serve as an index thereto. [2]

5. There are also books available which contain rolls and rosters and biographical information of servicemen during this period between the Revolution and the Civil War. Many libraries have good collections. We refer you to the bibliography at the end of this chapter. You should also refer to the bibliography in Chapter Twenty-one. Some of the books listed there relate to this period of military history as well as to the Revolution.

B. VETERANS' BENEFITS

1. There are four series of pension records which deal with those who served between the Revolution and the Civil War and, depending on the time or war of your ancestor's service, you may be interested in one or more of them.

a. The "Old Wars" (or "Old War") Series relates to death and disability claims for service during this entire period (excluding the War of 1812) under various Congressional acts (the first in 1790). The

_____

[2.] All preceding information on service records between the Revolution and the Civil War is from Colket and Bridgers, pp. 65-76.

three sub-series within the "Old Wars" Series include:

<u>1) Mexican War Death or Disability Files</u>.

<u>2) Civil War Death or Disability Files</u>. (These cover only naval pensions for a short period at the start of the war.)

<u>3) Miscellaneous Death and Disability Files</u>. (These claims are based on service in the Regular Establishment and the Indian wars.)

Each sub-series is arranged alphabetically at the National Archives and there is an index on microfilm to the entire series. The pension files contain information on...

> ... name, rank, military or naval unit, and period of service of the veteran. If he applied for a pension, it shows his age or date of birth, place of residence, and sometimes place of birth. If the widow applied, it shows her age and the place of her marriage to the veteran; and her maiden name. If the veteran left orphans, it shows their names, ages, and the places of their residence. [3]

b. The War of 1812 Series contains papers for claims based on service between 1812 and 1815, primarily granted under acts passed in 1871 and 1878. [4] The files are arranged alphabetically.

Interfiled with these pension papers at the National Archives is a sub-series relating to death and disability claims which was previously a part of the "Old Wars" Series, plus the War of 1812 bounty-land warrant applications. These additions increase the value of the files tremendously because the records of many additional soldiers are added and the added records originated soon after the war.

Regarding the information in these War of 1812 pension files, Colket and Bridgers tell us:

> A veteran's declaration shows the name, age, and place of residence of the veteran; if married, the maiden name of his wife; the place and date of their marriage; his rank; his military or naval unit; the date and place of his entering the service; and date and place of his discharge. A widow's declaration shows the name, age, and place of residence of

---

[3.] <u>Ibid.</u>, p. 82.

[4.] The fact that service pension acts were not passed until so long after the war is one of the chief shortcomings of these records. Relatively few servicemen, and even few widows, lived that long.

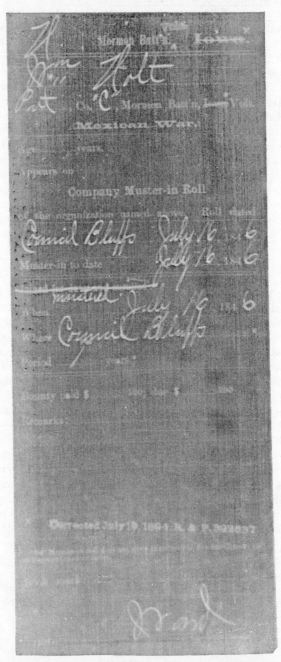

MUSTER ROLL NOTATION FROM THE COMPILED
SERVICE RECORDS OF THE MEXICAN WAR

the widow; the date and place of their marriage, with the name of the official who performed the ceremony, the date and place of the veteran's death; his rank; his military or naval unit; the date and place of his entering the service; and the date and place of his discharge. [5]

c. The Mexican War Series is the result of an act of Congress in 1887 and is based on service performed between 1846 and 1848. A few of the death and disability files from the "Old Wars" Series are now included among the files of this series. Several different documents are included in the files, though each pensioner's file will not contain all of them. The only way to locate pension files in this series is through its master index. Information in these files is as follows:

A veteran's declaration shows the name of the veteran; the dates and places of his birth, his enlistment, and his discharge; and the places of his residence since service. The declaration of a widow seeking a pension shows the same information about the service of the veteran; her name, age, and place of residence; the date and place of her marriage to the veteran, with the name of the person performing the ceremony; and the date and place of the death of the veteran. A filled-out questionnaire shows the maiden name of the wife; the date and place of the marriage of the couple and name of the person performing the ceremony; the name of a former wife, if any, and the date and place of her death or divorce; and the names and dates of birth of living children. [6]

d. The Indian Wars Series resulted from an act of Congress passed in 1892 and other, later acts. The first act provided service pensions to veterans of wars between 1832 and 1834 and their widows, if not remarried. Later acts extended the benefits to all who served in Indian wars between 1817 and 1898. There are also some files in this series which were formerly filed with the "Old Wars" Series. There is a microfilm index to this series at the National Archives.

The information in the files varies depending upon the act under which the pension was applied for, the number of years of the veteran's survival after the war, and whether or not he was survived by a widow. A file contains some or all

---

[5.] Colket and Bridgers, pp. 82-83.
[6.] Ibid., p. 83.

of the following information: the name, Army unit, and place
of residence of the veteran; a summary of his Army record;
his age or the date of his birth; the place of his birth; date
and place of his marriage; the date and place of his death;
and the names of their surviving children, with the date and
place of birth of each. [7]

Access to some files in all four of these pension series can be obtained
through the use of the first part of the Remarried Widows Index. This index is in two parts, one part relating to non-Revolutionary War claims prior
to the Civil War and the other part relating to the Civil War and all later
wars and military service up to World War I. The index is alphabetical by
the names of the remarried widows. The name of the former husband is
indicated plus his service unit and the file or certificate number.

2. Bounty-land warrant applications for service after the Revolutionary
War are all filed together in one series, except that the War of 1812 applications were interfiled with the pension claims relating to that same war as
we noted earlier. The files are much like the bounty-land application files
for the Revolutionary War—many in fact were granted as a result of the
same legislation. They are merely filed in separate series. All files in
this series are arranged alphabetically by the names of the veterans and
there is no index.

The information in a bounty-land application file usually includes...

... name, age, residence, rank, military or naval unit,
and period of service of the veteran, and sometimes his personal
description. If the applicant was an heir it shows such information as the date and place of death of the veteran, the name of the
heir or heirs, and the degree of relationship. If the application
was approved it also shows the number of the warrant, the number of acres granted, and the year of the act under which the
warrant was granted. [8]

Both the pension application files and the bounty-land application files
are in Record Group 15, Records of the Veteran's Administration, at the
National Archives. Copies of these records and the compiled service records can be secured by the process which we described earlier in connection
with records of Revolutionary service. You can use form GSA-6751 to acquire
a copy of ten pages from the file (see Chapter Twenty-one), or you can obtain a copy of the entire file, if you desire, after requesting a price quota-

---

7. Ibid., p. 85.
8. Ibid., p. 93.

tion. You should also note that much of the information given in pension and bounty-land applications is the very information you will need to locate a copy of a soldier's service record.

II. THE CIVIL WAR, 1861-1865

You have probably already noticed that military records are quite typical of most genealogical sources in that the later ones are better than the earlier ones. This fact holding true, records of the Civil War are better than those of any of the wars we have thus far discussed. Still, however, they are appropriately divided into the same two types:

> A. Service records.
> B. Records of veterans' benefits.

A. SERVICE RECORDS

Let Colket and Bridgers describe the Union Army service records for us:

> The compiled military service records of the Union forces of the Civil War... consist of card abstracts and documents relating to individual soldiers, such as voluntary enlistment papers, prisoner-of-war papers, hospital bed cards, and death reports. The cards and sometimes the documents relating to one soldier are filed in a jacket-envelope. The jacket-envelopes for men in State organizations are arranged by name of State; thereunder by arm of service such as cavalry, artillery, infantry; thereunder numerically by regiment; thereunder alphabetically by name of soldier. The jacket-envelopes for men in other organizations such as the U.S. Sharp Shooters are arranged similarly. Many of the documents relating to individual soldiers in State organizations are not filed in the jacket-envelopes with the related card abstracts but are filed separately in alphabetical order at the end of the file for the State. Some jacket-envelopes include cross-references to the names on the regimental papers that are filed with the muster rolls.
> In addition to these basic files there is a separate file of card abstracts pertaining to both volunteer and Regular Army staff officers, which is arranged alphabetically by name of officer. [9]

---

9. Ibid., p. 55.

There is no master index to these Civil War service records, but rather a separate name index for each state and for each organization not connected with a specific state This means that in order to locate the service record of your Union Army ancestor you must know the state or the organization with which he served.

These records contain the same information on each soldier as did the compiled service records of the earlier wars, plus...

... the date of a change in his rank, and the date, place, and nature of his discharge. For some soldiers there is a voluntary enlistment paper or an abstract that shows his age, the town or county of his birth, his occupation, and a personal description. If the soldier was hospitalized, a bed card shows his age, nativity, evidence of whether or not he was married, his place of residence, and the date and occasion of his being wounded. If he died in service, a casualty sheet shows the date and place of his death. [10]

Other records relating to Union Army service are as follows:
1. Civil War Draft Records.   There were three classes of CONSOLI-DATED LISTS made as a result of an act passed by Congress in March 1863. These three included:

a. Persons subject to military duty between the ages of 20 and 35 years and unmarried persons subject to military duty above the age of 35 years and under the age of 45.
b. Married men aged above 35 and under 45.
c. Volunteers.

Entries in each class are arranged in alphabetical order by the first letter of the surname within the various states and Congressional districts. Information relating to each man listed on these records includes...

... name, place of residence, age as of July 1, 1863, occupation, marital status, the State, territory, or country of his birth, and, if a volunteer, the designation of his military organization. [11]

There are also some DESCRIPTIVE ROLLS of varying formats and arrangements for each of the enrollment districts. They contain much good

---

10. Ibid., p. 56.
11. Ibid., p. 60.

information but, as with the consolidated lists, you must know the Congressional district in which a man lived in order to find him. If you know the county in which he lived, you can determine the Congressional district by checking the <u>Congressional Directory for the Second Session of the Thirty-Eighth Congress of the United States of America</u> (Washington, D. C. : 1865). A photocopy of this directory is in the National Archives central search room.

The descriptive rolls contain the same information as the consolidated lists, plus...

> ... the personal description of the man listed, the exact place of his birth, and evidence as to whether he was accepted or rejected for military service. The entries in many volumes, however, are not completely filled out. [12]

2. Burial Records of Soldiers. Most of the burials in these records (in fact almost all of them) relate to soldiers buried at U. S. military installations. There are four volumes relating to burials in the U. S. Soldiers' Home in Washington, D. C. , 1861-1868, and they are indexed. There is a checklist of installations included, and most of the registers are arranged alphabetically by the name of the installation.

> The arrangement, inclusive dates, and contents of the burial registers vary considerably. As a minimum they show for each soldier his name, his military organization, and the date and place of his burial. The registers for the U. S. Soldiers' Home also show the soldier's rank; the town, county, and State of residence before enlistment; the name and residence of his widow, relative, or friend; his age; his nativity; the cause, date, and place of death; the date of his burial; and, sometimes, the place of his burial. [13]

Some compiled lists of Union Soldiers buried at the U. S. Soldiers' Home, 1861-1918, give the name, military organization, date of death, and place of burial of each soldier. There is a separate set of lists for each state from which the soldiers originated.

There are also some lists of soldiers buried in national cemeteries, mainly between 1861 and 1865 (some as late as 1886). These lists give the same information as the lists of soldiers buried at the U. S. Soldiers' Home mentioned above.

---

12. <u>Ibid.</u>, pp. 60-61.
13. <u>Ibid.</u>, pp. 61-62.

Between the years 1879 and 1925 the federal government, by an act of Congress, erected headstones on the graves of Union servicemen, regardless of place of burial.   (Other acts provided for headstones on the graves of those who served in the Revolutionary and other wars.) The applications for these markers are arranged chronologically by state and county of burial, and there is a card index to applications filed between 1879 and 1903. Each application tells name, rank, military organization, date of death, cemetery of interment and its location, and name and address of applicant.

At the Federal Records Center in Alexandria, Virginia, there are some later applications, including those for headstones for Confederate soldiers, as per act of 1929.

3.   Naval Service Records.

a.   Age Certificates of Officers (both naval and marine).   These records were made as a result of an act approved by Congress in December 1861 relating to retirement.   They are for 1862 and 1863, are arranged alphabetically and are also indexed.   Each certificate shows name, rank and birth date, and is signed by the officer.

b.   Biographies of Officers.   There are three indexed manuscript volumes of these.   They were prepared about 1865 and contain much good, detailed information (though actual detail and content varies considerably).   Their chief shortcoming is that they are very incomplete in their coverage.

c.   Records of Appointees, 1862-1910, to the U.S. Naval Academy. These records are filed numerically in individual jacket-envelopes. They also include the applications of those who applied but were not accepted.   Though these records are in the National Archives, an index is located at the Bureau of Naval Personnel in Washington.   A jacket normally contains information on the applicant's. . .

. . . name, his place of residence, the name of his father and, where appropriate, the date of his appointment and the date of his commission as ensign. [14]

d.   Weekly Returns of Enlistments at Naval Rendezvous.   These are as we described them under naval service records of the pre-Civil War period.   However, you should be aware that there is a separate microfilm index relating to Civil War service.

In addition to the records we have listed here, there are also many records relating to service during the pre-Civil War period which overlap into the Civil War era and even later.   We discussed these earlier in the chapter.

[14.] Ibid., p. 70.

B. VETERANS' BENEFITS

When we discuss veterans' benefits for those who served in the Civil War, we are talking almost exclusively of pensions. As we mentioned in Chapter Fifteen in our discussion of land entry records in the public domain, there were no bounty land warrants issued for service in the Civil War. So far as land is concerned, Civil War veterans (both Union and Confederate) were given special consideration in Homestead legislation.

All pension applications relating to service between 1861 and 1934 are filed in one series, excluding World War I and certain Indian wars already discussed. [15] This series of pension applications is called the "Civil War and Later" Series and, in addition to Civil War pensioners, it includes pension applications relating to service in the Spanish American War, the Philippine Insurrection, the Boxer Rebellion and the Regular Army. Both death/disability pensions and service pensions are included in this one series. As mentioned earlier, a few naval death and disability pensions from the first part of the Civil War are also included in the "Old Wars" Series.

The information and the documents in the files vary tremendously, depending upon the act of Congress under which the applicant sought relief, as well as other factors. An applicant's file will contain some or all of the following information:

> [The applicant's]... name, military or naval unit, and place
> of residence...; a summary of his military or naval record; his
> age or the date of his birth; place of his birth; date and place of
> his marriage; date and place of his death; the maiden name of
> his wife; the date of her death; and the names of their surviving
> children with the date and place of birth of each. [16]

There are two indexes to these files—an alphabetical name index (name of veteran) and an organization index for use if you know the state and the organization in which the soldier served. There are definite advantages in the latter if you have the necessary information to use it. The "Veterans' Schedules" of the 1890 census can be of considerable assistance here. [17] Also remember that access to some of these files can be had through use of the second part of the Remarried Widows Index discussed earlier in this chapter.

[15.] Note that if the "Indian Wars" Series fails to disclose a pension application for a veteran of one of the later Indian wars, a search of the "Civil War and Later" Series is recommended.

[16.] Colket and Bridgers, p. 85.

[17.] See Chapter Ten.

Information from Union Army service and pension files can be obtained from the National Archives through your use of form GSA-6751 as we discussed in Chapter Twenty-one. Copies of complete files can also be procured. (For a price quotation write to the Archivist, Civil War Branch, General Services Administration, National Archives and Records Service.)

C. THE OTHER SIDE OF THE WAR: THE CONFEDERACY

Records for Confederate forces are not as good as the records of Union Army troops, but there are some records and you should be aware of them. There are three series in the National Archives of COMPILED SERVICE RECORDS of Confederate troops. (All of these have also been microfilmed.) These records were compiled on cards by the War Department from various records, including prison and parole records, muster rolls, returns, rosters, pay rolls, appointment books and hospital registers. All cards relating to the same individual soldier are generally in the same jacket-envelope. The three series are:

1. Those filed by state. (This is the largest series—by far.)
2. Those for troops who served in non-state organizations.
3. Those for officers and enlisted personnel doing staff jobs.

There is an alphabetical name index as well as an index for each of the states. All have been microfilmed. The information in these records is not extensive. Colket and Bridgers describe the records as follows:

A jacket-envelope shows the name of the soldier, the name of the State from which he served, the name of the company and regiment, and his rank. The cards and papers in the envelope show other information, such as the dates of changes in the soldier's rank, the date and place of his enlistment and discharge, his occupation, and his personal description. If the soldier was captured, they may show the date of his death, if it occurred in camp, or the date of his release and parole. References to the original records are included on the cards. [18]

There are also various minor records in the National Archives including some "Citizens Files" and some "Amnesty and Pardon Records," which mainly give information on places of residence.

These Confederate records in the National Archives are likewise available through the use of form GSA-6751, and you should also be aware that

---

[18.] Colket and Bridgers, p. 99.

the individual southern states provided pensions for veterans who served under the "Stars and Bars" and that records of these are available from those states. Inquiries regarding such pensions should be addressed to the appropriate state depositories and custodians. These include the following:

ALABAMA: The Alabama Department of Archives and History, Montgomery.

ARKANSAS: Arkansas History Commission, Old State House, Little Rock.

FLORIDA: State Board of Pensions Office, Tallahassee. (These are also on film at the LDS Genealogical Society.)

GEORGIA: Confederate Pension and Record Department, State Capitol, Atlanta.

LOUISIANA: Office of Supervisor of Confederate Pensions, State Department of Public Welfare, Baton Rouge.

MISSISSIPPI: The Mississippi Department of Archives and History, Jackson.

NORTH CAROLINA: The North Carolina Department of Archives and History, Raleigh.

SOUTH CAROLINA: The South Carolina Department of Archives and History, World War Memorial Building, Columbia.

TENNESSEE: Tennessee State Library and Archives, Nashville.

TEXAS   Comptroller Public Accounts, Austin.

VIRGINIA: Pension Clerk, Department of Accounts and Purchases, Richmond.

III. AFTER APPOMATTOX

The Civil War ended with Lee's surrender at Appomattox Courthouse in April 1865, but this did not end the United States' involvement in war. However, most of the wars have been in quite recent times so not too many records are readily available. In fact, there is a 75-year restriction on all service records. But let's take a quick peek at some of the records which are available (and a few which are not) that you ought to know about.

Not including the skirmishes with the Indians which we have already discussed, perhaps the major military and naval confrontations during the period prior to World War I had to do with America's encounters with Spain — the Spanish-American War (1898-99) and the Philippine Insurrection (1899-1901). The Puerto Rico Regiment of U.S. Volunteers (1899-1901) is included. There are compiled service records (separate) for those who served in these wars and in the Puerto Rico Regiment which contain...

... such information as the name, rank, and military organization of each soldier; the dates and places that he was mustered in and out; his place of residence; his occupation; and, if single, the name and address of a parent or guardian. [19]

There is a master name index to the service records of the Spanish-American War (and the Puerto Rico Regiment) as well as an index for each state's volunteer organizations and federal volunteer organizations. There is a master index, but no state or organizational index, to service records of the Philippine Insurrection.

As already mentioned, pension records for these wars are included in the "Civil War and Later" Series. All of these records are in the National Archives, Record Group 94, Records of the Adjutant General's Office.

The Boxer Rebellion in China in 1900 employed 5,000 American troops, but no special or separate service records have been compiled for these men. Records of service here are included among the records of the regular army discussed later in this chapter.

Many of the various records which relate to service in earlier periods overlap into this post-Civil War period, as you may have already noted; but there are a few other records in the National Archives coming exclusively out of this period which deserve mention:

A. Quarterly Returns of Naval Enlistments on Vessels, 1866-91, are bound in a chronological arrangement in the National Archives. Those between 1866 and 1884 are indexed with the Weekly Returns of Enlistments at Naval Rendezvous mentioned earlier. Concerning these returns, Colket and Bridgers tell us:

Each entry normally shows under the name of the vessel the name of the enlisted man, the date and term of his enlistment, his rating, a reference to his previous naval service if any, the place of his birth, his age, his occupation, and his personal description. Some entries show place of residence. [20]

B. Naval Apprenticeship Papers, 1864-1889, are alphabetically arranged as part of Record Group 24, Records of the Bureau of Naval Personnel, at the National Archives. These are forms filled out by the parents of 13 to 18 year-old youths being placed in naval apprenticeship. Each paper shows name, place of service, date entering service, name of parent or guardian, residence of parent or guardian, apprentice's birth date, birthplace, and relationship of apprentice to parent or guardian.

---

19. Ibid., p. 58.
20. Ibid., p. 72.

C. A Register of Naval Apprentices, 1864-1875, is indexed and has to do with apprentices who served on the training ships Sabine, Portsmouth and Saratoga. An entry in the register gives name, birth date, birthplace, date and place of enlistment, name of parent or guardian and date of leaving the service. This register is also a part of Record Group 24, Records of the Bureau of Naval Personnel.

D. A Register of Living and Retired Marine Corps Officers, 1899-1904, relates chiefly to those who served in the Spanish-American War. It is indexed and gives name, birth date and place, state from which appointed and service records from 1899 to 1904.

If a soldier happened to spend time in a home for soldiers there is another possibility of finding information about him. There are branches of the National Home for Disabled Volunteer Soldiers in Togus (near Augusta), Maine; Dayton, Ohio; Wood (near Milwaukee), Wisconsin; Kecoughtan (near Hampton), Virginia; Leavenworth, Kansas; Sawtelle (near Los Angeles), California; Marion, Indiana; Danville, Illinois; Mountain Home (near Johnson City), Tennessee; Hot Springs, South Dakota; and Bath, New York, with records at the National Archives for some of these beginning in the last half of the 1860's and going as late as 1934. There are historical registers for each branch, and all are indexed. One page in a register is devoted to each patient and includes his name, date admitted, service record, birthplace, age, personal description, religion, occupation, former occupation, former place of residence, marital status, next-of-kin (name and address) and date of death if he died while residing at the branch.

There are also records in the National Archives relating to inmates of the United States Soldiers' Home from 1851 with genealogical data about them and a record of their deaths.

IV. THE REGULAR ARMY OR REGULAR ESTABLISHMENT

The military records we have discussed thus far have dealt mainly with those who have been enlisted or drafted into service in the various wars. However, throughout U. S. history there have been men who have enlisted into the service without regard to whether there was a war. Many of these men were professional soldiers. Early records of the regular army are fragmentary but they do exist. There are muster rolls covering the period between 1784 and 1912 and registers of enlistments, 1793-1914, in addition to special records for those who had officers' commissions. Of all these papers, the enlistment papers and registers of enlistments contain the most genealogical data. The enlistment papers are in jacket-envelopes and are filed alphabetically, for the most part, in three separate series (1793-1820, 1821-1894, 1894-1912) at the National Archives.

These enlistment papers are similar to what the military now calls the soldier's "personnel file," and they usually give...

> ... the name of the enlisted man, his place of birth; age; occupation; the date and place of his enlistment or reenlistment; the period for which he enlisted; his personal description; and his military organization. [21]

Enlistment records made after July 15, 1894, give even more complete data. If the soldier died while in the service, a death report is included among his papers showing his name, rank, date of death, place of death, and sometimes place of burial.

Enlistment registers are also at the National Archives and are also arranged in three series (1793-1815, 1815-1821, 1821-1914); and they too are arranged more or less alphabetically. Each entry relates to a single enlistment, but the entries vary in their detail, some prior to 1815 being quite abbreviated.

> A full entry shows the name of the enlisted man; the date, place, and period of his enlistment or reenlistment; the name of the town, county, or State where he was born; his occupation and personal description; the designation of his regiment and company; and the date and nature of his separation from the service. [22]

Pension files for soldiers in the Regular Establishment are filed in the National Archives with the pensions of the other series.

V. WORLD WAR I

Service records and pension records for those who served in World War I and later wars are not available for public searching, though some information can be taken from them; and we are sure the time will come when they will be available. At present, however, you can have access to information in the World War I Selective Service (draft) records if you know the address at which your ancestor lived at the time he registered. This address is essential for the determining of the Selective Service board. This is mainly a problem in larger towns where there might have been more than one draft board, and city directories can frequently help you find the solution. These draft records are located in the Federal Records Center of the General Services Administration (Region 4), 221 St. Joseph Avenue, East

---

21. Ibid., p. 47.
22. Ibid., p. 48.

Point, Georgia 30044.

If you need additional information on men in the Armed Forces during periods later than the dates of the records in the National Archives, take note of the following addresses:

A. Army officers, separated from June 30, 1917-October 6, 1945, and Army enlisted personnel, separated from October 31, 1912-October 6, 1945 (including Army Air Corps and Air Force):

      Army Branch
      Military Personnel Record Center
      GSA
      9700 Page Blvd.
      St. Louis, Missouri

B. Army officers and enlisted personnel separated since October 6, 1945, and Air Force personnel separated from October 6, 1945-September 1947:

      Army Records Center
      Department of the Army
      9700 Page Blvd.
      St. Louis, Missouri

C. Naval officers who served after 1885:

      Bureau of Naval Personnel
      Department of the Navy
      Washington, D.C.

D. Naval enlisted personnel who served after 1885 and Marine officers and enlisted men who served since 1895:

      Navy Branch
      Military Personnel Record Center
      GSA
      9700 Page Blvd.
      St. Louis, Missouri

VI. MILITARY RECORDS IN THE STATES

In addition to the military records already discussed, many states have collections of records of soldiers who served from them. Very often state militia and other state-troop records are useful genealogical tools, and the state's Adjutant General or other record custodian can be a great benefactor to your genealogical cause. You should use these records as well as any books which might be published about the military men and military history of the states. Many of these records have been published in

genealogical periodicals and many others have been microfilmed.   If you
have access to the LDS Genealogical Society's collections, check its holdings very carefully for the states of your interest.

VII.   PRINTED MILITARY SOURCES

There are several books relating to those who have served in the armed
forces of this country since the Revolution. It would be impossible to name
all such sources here, especially since most of them relate to servicemen
from specific geographic areas. However, a brief bibliography follows:

Blakeney, Jane V. Heroes, U. S. Marine Corps, 1861-1955; Armed
    Forces Awards, Flags (1st ed.). Washington: Blakeney Publishers
    (1957).

Boatner, Mark Mayo. The Civil War Dictionary. New York: David
    McKay Co. (1959).

Cullum, George Washington. Biographical Register of the Officers and
    Graduates of the U. S. Military Academy at West Point, N. Y.,
    From Its Establishment, in 1802, to 1890; With the Early History
    of the United States Military Academy, 3 vols. (3rd ed.). Boston:
    Houghton, Mifflin Co. (1891).

Hamersly, Lewis Randolph. The Records of Living Officers of the U.S.
    Navy and Marine Corps. (7th ed. rev.). New York: L. R. Hamer-
    sly Co. (1902).

Moore, Frank (ed.). The Portrait Gallery of the War, Civil, Military,
    and Naval; A Biographical Record. New York: G. P. Putnam for
    Derby and Miller (1864).

Officers of the Army and Navy (Regular and Volunteer) Who Served in
    the Civil War. Philadelphia: L. R. Hamersly (1894).

Powell, William Henry. List of Officers of the Army of the United
    States from 1779-1900, Embracing a Register of All Appointments
    in the Volunteer Service During the Civil War and of Volunteer
    Officers in the Service of the United States, June 1, 1900. Com-
    piled from the Official Records. (1900). Detroit: Gale Research
    Co. (1967 reprint).

_____. Records of Living Officers of the United States Army.
    Philadelphia: L. R. Hamersly (1890).

_____ and Edward Shippin (ed.). Officers of the Army and
    Navy (Regular) Who Served in the Civil War. Philadelphia: L. R.
    Hamersly (1892, 1893).

Schuon, Karl. U. S. Marine Corps Biographical Dictionary; the Corps'
    Fighting Men, What They Did, Where They Served. New York:
    Franklin Watts, Inc. (1963).

_____. U.S. Navy Biographical Dictionary. New York:
     Franklin Watts, Inc. (1965).
Simmons, Henry Eugene. A Concise Encyclopedia of the Civil War.
     New York: A.S. Barnes and Co. (1965).
United States. Adjutant General's Office. Official Army Register.
     Washington, D.C.: U.S. Government Printing Office (1802——).
     The title varies somewhat over the years: Register of the Army
     of the United States; The Army Register of the United States; Army
     Register; Official Army and Air Force Register.
United States, Bureau of Naval Personnel. Register of Commissioned
     and Warrant Officers of the United States Navy and Marine Corps.
     Washington, D.C.: U.S. Government Printing Office (1814——).
United States Naval Academy, Annapolis. Alumni Association. Regis-
     ter of Alumni, Graduates and Former Naval Cadets and Midship-
     men. Annapolis: United States Naval Academy (1886——). The title
     varies somewhat over the years: Annual Reunion; Annual Reunion
     and Register of Graduates; Register of Graduates.

You might refer also to the bibliographies in Chapter Twenty-one.
Some of the works listed there relate to post-Revolutionary servicemen
and military history as well as to those of the earlier periods.

VIII..WHEN TO USE MILITARY RECORDS

We have already discussed some circumstances to which you need to
be sensitive in relation to the use of Revolutionary War records. The same
basic principles apply to the use of all American military records. If your
ancestor lived at a time when he could have served in a war or if any close
relatives of his (or hers) could have served in a war, then you must consider a search of military records as a simple research necessity. Do not
wait until you find a clue that your ancestor had military experience; just
go ahead and make your search in the records of the appropriate war.
     However, any clues you have can be helpful because they can help you
zero-in on your target with greater accuracy. We have mentioned many
times the increased usability of military records when you have specific
data on the organization to which your ancestor belonged, or at least the state
from which he served. Such clues can be found in various places—family
records, old letters, Bibles, tombstones, obituaries, local histories,
church records and vital records (especially death certificates), etc., are
all likely sources. You must know the state to use Civil War service records.
     There is no specific time during a search when military records should
be used—this varies with your problem, but usually they are one of the first
sources to consider once you begin research on an individual who may have

had military service or may have been closely related to someone else who did.   This is because the information found in military records is often of such a nature that it facilitates the use of other sources and suggests new possibilities.

IX. CONCLUSION

As we conclude our discussion of military records, let us re-state the basic fact which makes the use of these records so important: Wars have been an integral part of American history and, as such, have produced in-dispensible genealogical records of literally millions of persons. These are records which not only hold the key to extending successfully many pedi-grees, but also contain valuable historical and background information that makes your ancestors seem like real persons and not just names on a pedi-gree chart.

Study carefully Colket and Bridgers, Guide to Genealogical Records in the National Archives (Washington: 1964) in addition to what you have read in these two chapters.   Chapters III, IV, V and VI of that little book hold a vast store of knowledge about military records as a genealogical source.

CHAPTER TWENTY-THREE

CEMETERY AND BURIAL RECORDS

I. BACKGROUND

Many inexperienced genealogists get the idea that if they have found a death certificate or an obituary or a church register entry of a burial they have found all the important information arising out of a death. They are sometimes right, but there are occasions when it is a serious mistake to overlook the tombstone or other cemetery records.

This situation reminds us of a cartoon we saw recently showing a junior executive standing before his boss's desk receiving the following bit of wisdom: "We've never doubted your ambition and drive and self-discipline, Higgins. It's your lack of ability that concerns us."[1] Perhaps it would be appropriate to say that cemetery and burial records are to death certificates, obituaries and church burial registers what ability is to ambition, drive and self-discipline. Without them something significant is missing and you just might not get the job done. Also, you will frequently find that these other sources (i.e., death certificates, obituaries and burial registers) do not exist and hence cannot be used.

There are two kinds of cemetery records with which we are concerned:

A. Gravestone and monument inscriptions.
B. Records kept by cemetery management and caretakers (sextons' records).

There is a great deal of variation in both the completeness and the accuracy of these records as you will see from the examples we will show later, but because of the very nature of the information they deal with, they must be considered important and should be consulted early in your research.

There are five different kinds of cemeteries in America. They include:

1. The church yard, where members of a church are buried right on the church grounds. This custom was brought to America from the

---

Old World and was especially prevalent in the colonial states.

2. The church-owned cemetery, not connected with nor adjacent to the church building, but owned and operated by the church.

3. The government-owned cemetery—either town, county, state or national—owned collectively by the people and supported and maintained by tax monies.

4. The privately-owned, non-church, cemetery—usually owned by a corporation and operated as a business enterprise. The U.S. has many of these, and they are especially common in more-recent years.

5. The family cemetery. This is often just a small corner of the family farm or estate, perhaps in a grove of trees in an out-of-the-way location, set aside for the burial of family members and relatives.

All of these types of cemeteries are common in America and each presents its own problems for the genealogist. The cemetery may be difficult to locate, there may be no sextons' records, or it may be something else.

One of the most difficult problems is to determine the place of burial. If your ancestor lived in a large community there are usually several possible places of burial. Two of the best sources to help you solve this problem are obituaries and death certificates, but both have limitations if the death was early.

Once you find the name of the cemetery it is usually not too difficult to determine its location. Local government officials, church officials, funeral directors and old-timers can frequently provide the answers.

We will talk later about how to find the records, but let's look first at some typical tombstone inscriptions and see if we can determine how they might help us.

II. TOMBSTONE INSCRIPTIONS

A. From the Rexburg Cemetery, Madison County, Idaho:

> Charlotte Helena
> Dau. of
> Peter & Charlotte Flamm
> Died Apr. 5, 1891
> aged 3 Ys, 8 Ms, 7 Ds.

> Melissa Henry Smith
> Born July 11, 1827
> Wood Co., Virginia
> Died June 15, 1896

In memory of
Mary A. Roberts
& infant son
Wife of Alfred Ricks
Born Oct. 7, 1870
Died Jun. 30, 1892
We trust our loss will be their gain,
And that with Christ, they've gone to reign.

James Eckersell
Aug. 5, 1839 — Mar. 6, 1917

FARNSWORTH
Albert S.
1891 — 1895
Blanche
1906 — 1909
Ralph
1913 — 1914

Jacob Spori
Born Mar. 26, 1847
Died Sept. 27, 1903

Magdalena R. Spori
Born Feb. 6, 1851
Died Sept. 14, 1900

John Plain Smith
May 14, 1843
- - - - - - -
His Wife
Elizabeth Andrews
Feb. 6, 1846
Dec. 6, 1915
Sons
Mickle A.
Aug. 8, 1883
Jan 19, 1905
Joseph A.
Dec. 1, 1881
July 19, 1908

B. From the Long Cemetery, between Spencer and McMinnville, Tennessee.

Harriet Grissom
April 5, 1852 — October 27, 1883
Daughter of Elisha and Elizabeth Boulding
Wife of S. B. Grissom

S. B. Grissom
November 14, 1847 — November 1, 1908

William Grissom
March 7, 1797 — December 23, 1869

Evey Grissom
May 1, 1797 — Jan 25, 1816
Wife of William Grissom

C. From Spencer Cemetery #1, Spencer, Tennessee:

BURDIN WHEELER
TENNESSEE — 1 LT. ELLIOTT'S CO.
LAUDERDALE'S TENN. MTD. INF.
CHEROKEE WAR 1887

D. From Sycamore Cemetery at Gasaway (near Woodbury), Cannon County, Tennessee:

Mollie E. , Dau of
G. G. & Martha Melton
Wife of Geo. Hancock
Born May 22, 1862
Died February 11, 1894
"Blessed are they which do
hunger and thirst after
righteousness for they
shall be filled."

Selmar, Son of
G. E. and M. E. Hancock
Born May 10, 1883

Died February 6, 1900
Aged 16 y's, 8 m's, & 25 d's

Polly, Wife of Bartlet Marcum
Mother of Arch Marcum
Born January 24, 1807
Died May 7, 1855

Jacob K. King
Born March 5, 1844
Died August 2, 1897
Aged 53 Y's, 4 M's, 27 D's
"Think of me as you pass by.
As you are now, so once was I.
As I am now so you must be.
Prepare for death and follow me."

Mathie D. Keaton
June 15, 1897 — Dec. 11, 1918
Enlisted Oct. 29, 1918 at
Woodbury, Tennessee
Died at Camp Wadsworth, S. C.
Buried at Sycamore Church
December 15, 1918.
"Dearest brother thou hast left us.
Here thy loss we deeply feel
But tis God that has bereft us.
He can all our sorrows heal."

A. H. Markum
Born September 29, 1846
Died March 23, 1903
Aged 56 yrs. 5 m. 24 days
A. Markum & A. H. Owen
Married May 6, 1864
Joined the M. E. Church S. 1892

Pvt. John E. Hancock
Co. F. 57, Pis. Inf.
June 7, 1896
Died Oct. 10, 1918 in France.

E. From Highland Cemetery, Carter County, Tennessee:

Laura Etta Singleton
Feb. 4, 1853
Age 77 yrs. 1 mo. 2 days
Died March 6, 1930
"Member United Daughters of Confederacy"
She done all she could.

James Calvin Singleton
Nov. 12, 1843
Sept. 25, 1928
Served his country
In Co. A, 5th
Bat., N.C. Calvery [sic]
Southern Confederacy
Blessed are the dead which die in the Lord.

F. From the Dorsey graveyard, on a farm at Monongalia, West Virginia:

[All on one stone]

Mary E. Dorsey, born June 28, 1828, died Feb. 14, 1863
Emma L. Dorsey, born Sept 10, 1860, died Apr 10, 1863
Delia T. Dorsey, born Mar 10, 1831, died Aug 7, 1910
Warren C. Dorsey, born Oct 2, 1911, died Dec 16, 1911
Marion Hough Dorsey, born May 17, 1875, died Dec 16, 1900

It is plain, even from the few examples we have given, that the information found on tombstones is fairly unpredictable. You never know what might be on a gravestone until you see it. Usually you can count on finding at least a name and a death date (which do not help particularly unless you cannot obtain the information from other sources), but often, especially on those tombstones which are not too recent, you can find a wealth of genealogical data. Dates of birth, places of birth, places of marriage, names of parents, names of spouses, names of children, religious affiliation, military service (even specific organization and war)—these can all be found on gravestones. Our examples have illustrated this.

There is also an advantage when you go personally to a cemetery to view, as a whole, all of the graves on the same cemetery lot. People are usually related in some way or they would not be buried on the same lot. Perhaps herein lies another clue that will facilitate your research. It is best to go to the cemetery personally if you can because you will be aware of all aspects of the genealogical problem and will be in an excellent position to capitalize on clues that others might overlook. However, it is certainly permissible to send an agent, working in your behalf, to read tombstones. Also, if the tombstone inscriptions have been transcribed or published, you will find value in these. A publication is a poor substitute for a personal visit, but this is true of practically every source the genealogist uses.

There are two reasons why printed and transcribed tombstone inscriptions are inferior to the personal visit:

1. There is always the possibility of transcription errors.
2. The arrangement of these sources often causes confusion about who is buried in which lot, hence who is related to whom.

These shortcomings, however, may not be too serious and, in fact, may be outweighed by virtues. For example, the ravages of time and nature may have since rendered your ancestral tombstones unreadable, or "progress" may have destroyed or moved the cemetery, or vandals may have damaged or destroyed valuable monuments. Where these things have happened the transcripts are the only alternative.

Various local chapters of the Daughters of the American Revolution (DAR) have undertaken extensive projects of copying gravestone inscriptions and have copied inscriptions from many thousands of cemeteries. The Works Projects Administration (WPA) undertook similar projects during the great depression of the 1930's, but not so extensively. The Daughters of the Utah Pioneers (DUP) and the Idaho Genealogical Society have likewise engaged in these projects, as have many others. Also, genealogical and historical periodicals are replete with tombstone inscriptions.

When you venture to the cemetery on your own, be prepared and equipped to handle any contingency. We do not want to discourage you, but you will find that many cemeteries have been abandoned and thus have become overgrown with briars and brambles. So be prepared to deal with the problem. You may find that some tombstones have sunken into the ground or have tipped over. You will also find that many inscriptions have become eroded beyond the point of legibility. (Often those which have sunken and are overgrown with brush have withstood the erosive forces a little better because they have been protected.)

When you visit old cemeteries you should not wear your best clothing. You might also find it helpful to take along tools to cut through the thicket and to dig out buried gravestones. A good stiff-bristled (not wire) brush will also be useful for cleaning off the dirt.   An eroded inscription can often be made legible by rubbing chalk or soapstone over it.   (You use the side of the chalk stick for this.)   There are a number of techniques that different persons use, but we do not recommend anything that would mar or deface a gravestone in any way. Some persons clean the inscription sufficiently and then take a photograph. This way the copy is always accurate. Most tombstone hunters seem to favor this method, but you should not rely too much on the photographic processes unless you have high quality equipment and are proficient in its use.   If your pictures don't turn out you may have serious problems.

Be careful of the information on tombstones. Most of it is probably accurate, but remember that an engraver can make errors as easily as can a printer. Also, many a tombstone is not put on the grave until many years after the death, and the dates are usually supplied from someone's memory. Be especially watchful for errors in dates of one day, one month or one year —these are the most easily-made errors and are thus the most common.

III. SEXTONS' RECORDS

Sextons' records vary in content and nature even more than do tombstone inscriptions. For a family cemetery there will be no sextons' records at all.   In fact, you are fortunate if most graves have tombstones on them. Church cemeteries seldom have any record of burials aside from what is kept in the church's registers (and with some churches a book telling which church member owns which cemetery lot). Most other cemeteries— those owned by the government and those which are owned privately—usually maintain some type of record. Sometimes these are merely books or plats showing lot ownership, but even these can save you a lot of wandering and wondering when you are looking for the graves of your forebears in a large cemetery. Other cemeteries have extensive records on everyone buried therein—sometimes quite a bit more complete than the information engraved on the tombstones, but you never know this until the tombstones have been checked. (In more recent years the nature of these records has been the subject of legislation in most states.)

Let's look at two typical examples of sextons' records (of the not-too-recent variety).

A. From the town of Skowhegan, Somerset County, Maine:

Lot No. ___24___   ___Timothy Snow___

Date of decease	Name of person interred	Age
1867—Aug 7	Raymond Snow	Aged 22 years
	Child removed from Snow's tomb	
1880—Sept 23	Timothy Snow	Aged 77 years 6 mos
Sept 18, 1881	Lilliam M. Brageton	" 3 month 10 days
Aug 19, 1897	Lirluri [?] G. Tracy, Dau of	
	T. Snow	" 36 years

These records are indexed and are arranged numerically by lot number, which has nothing to do with the dates the lots were purchased. There are many relationships stated, though none are asked for, and if the ownership of the lot changed hands (after the death of the original purchaser) the old owner's name was crossed out and the new name entered. Both are readable and both are indexed. If a person's remains are moved to another lot or another cemetery the record usually gives the details. Also, the date of purchase for some of the lots is given.

B. From Spanish Fork City Cemetery, Utah County, Utah:

Name in full____ Johnson, William ____

Father ____ John Peterson ____

Mother ____ Vilborg Thordurson ____

Husb. or wife ____ single ____

When born ____ 27 April 1868 ____

Where born ____ Westmania Island, Iceland ____

When died ____ 7 March 1882 ____

Cemetery where buried ____ Spanish Fork, Utah ____

These cards are filed alphabetically, but here the married women are listed under their maiden surnames (quite unusual), so some of them may be difficult to find. Also, we find that the spouse's name is seldom given. The card usually just says "married" in the "Husb. or wife" blank and, in many other instances, the cards have blanks which have not been filled in. Few give the specific place of birth as does our sample card, but usually only the state or country.

As far as our experience goes, these are quite typical sextons' records and not unlike those you might find for your ancestors in numerous localities.   These records are generally in the custody of the present sexton or in the office of the county or town clerk.   If not, these people can tell you where they are kept.   The information found therein is basic genealogical data, and, unless you already have it, it is information you will need for your genealogical record.   Remember, however, that the information is mostly secondary (especially for older persons), and no more reliable than the informant who provided it (and you seldom know who that was).   Also, as with most other records, the more recent ones are better in many respects than those of older vintage.

IV. HELPS IN FINDING THE RECORDS

We have already discussed how difficult it might be to determine a place of burial, and we might add that even knowing the name of the cemetery doesn't solve all of your problems.   Large cemeteries are usually easy enough to find (they are probably listed in the telephone directory), but the smaller ones, especially family cemeteries (the ones you usually need), are more difficult.

It is not impossible to solve location problems, however.   One writer suggests three possible sources of help for you to consider:

1. Ask—chambers of commerce, city hall, anyone who might know or who would know whom to ask.

2. U.S. Government Geological Survey maps of the locality have sufficient detail that even the tiny grave yards are pinpointed.

3. Know the laws of the state which govern cemetery and burial policy. [2]

V. RECORDS OF FUNERAL DIRECTORS

Another record, closely related to those already discussed in this chapter, deserves mention.   This is the record kept by the funeral director (or undertaker) who performed the pre-burial duties for the dead ancestor. Today the funeral director is usually responsible for initiating and filing the death certificate, and frequently the obituary notice.   Most funeral directors also maintain private records equally as good as the official records

---

2. Richard H. Hale, "Cemetery Records as Aids to Genealogical Research" (Area I, no. 15), World Conference on Records and Genealogical Seminar (Salt Lake City: The Genealogical Society of The Church of Jesus Christ of Latter-day Saints, 1969).

which are kept. Some of these records contain useful information not included on the death certificate. (For example, they often give the name of the insurance companies with whom the deceased had his life covered, and, in case you are not aware, insurance companies also have extensive genealogical data in some of their records. However, insurance records are private and, like the funeral director's records, are available only at the discretion of company officials.)

It has been our experience that most funeral directors are very cooperative and more than willing to help you find information in their records. Remember, however, that their records are private, and when they open them to you it is as a favor and not as an obligation.

Since the beginning of vital records in America, death certificates have given the name and address (usually only the city) of the funeral director who took care of the body. Your local funeral director has a directory, the American Blue Book of Funeral Directors (New York: National Funeral Directors' Association, biennially), which can help you locate names and addresses, or you can find those names and addresses in local telephone directories.

When a person dies in a place where he did not reside, the body is often handled by a funeral director at the place of death. It is embalmed there and prepared for the return home. This is good to remember when you are looking for the funeral director's records and cannot locate them in the home town. When the problem is a recent one the obituary notice may provide a clue to this kind of situation, and the death certificate (filed in the state of death) would give specific information.

Some funeral directors' records go back more than 100 years, [3] but they certainly do not have to be that old to be valuable. As with death certificates, if they deal with persons who died in their old age, these records can bridge two or three generations of time. They can provide you with names, dates, places, etc., invaluable to continued research.

VI. CONCLUSION

In American genealogical research there are many sources to consider, and we often have no inkling of the contents of many of them. This uncertainty and the necessity of possessing a knowledge of myriad sources make American research the most difficult genealogical research in the world (and also the most interesting and challenging). And though this uncertainty is characteristic of records relating to burials, we take comfort

---

[3.] Norman E. Wright and David H. Pratt [Genealogical Research Essentials (Salt Lake City: Bookcraft, 1967), p. 282] report finding records as early as 1841.

in the knowledge that these records are a basic kind of source. You always
know that the information you discover will be solid genealogical data—
names, dates, places, relationships.

CHAPTER TWENTY-FOUR

CANADIAN RESEARCH

Since many American families have pre-U.S. roots somewhere north of the border, and since there is so little authoritative information published about Canadian ancestral research and records, we have added this chapter to our American text. We do not expect to cover all details of Canadian records in one chapter—this is not our purpose. Our purpose is rather to provide a guide (or a reference tool) to the principal Canadian depositories and to the sources which you will need in your research. We will not attempt to describe sources at length—only to make a few pertinent comments. Most sources have already been adequately described in the foregoing chapters.

There are two additional points that the Canadian researcher should understand:

1. In addition to the original sources which we discuss here, there is also a wealth of printed Canadian genealogical material available, especially for the Province of Quebec.

2. A study of history is just as important to Canadian research as it is to research in the U.S. (or any other country).

I. CANADIAN COUNTIES AND DISTRICTS

Because of record jurisdictions, the way the provinces are divided becomes quite important. Let's look first at the individual provinces, then we will examine jurisdictions as they relate to the various types of records.

A. ALBERTA

There are counties in Alberta but they do not form record-keeping jurisdictions. Thus they are not very significant for us. They include:

Athabaska	Forty Mile	Leduc
Barrhead	Grande Prairie	Lethbridge
Beaver	Lacombe	Minburn
Camrose	Lac Ste. Anne	Mountain View

Newell	Smokey Lake	Vermilion River
Paintearth	Stettler	Vulcan
Ponoka	Strathcona	Warner
Red Deer	Thorhild	Wetaskiwin
St Paul	Two Hills	Wheatland

For court and record-keeping purposes Alberta is divided into two large districts, one for the northern part of the province with its center in Edmonton, and one for the southern part of the province with its center in Lethbridge.

B. BRITISH COLUMBIA

The counties of British Columbia form important record jurisdictions. They are:

Cariboo	Prince Rupert	Westminster
Kootenay	Vancouver	Yale
Nanaimo	Victoria	

The province is also divided into Land Districts, but all of these do not have Land Registry Offices. The main districts are:

Barclay	New Westminster	Range 4, Coast
Cariboo	Nootka	Range 5, Coast
Cassiar	Osoyoos	Renfrew
Clayoquot	Peace River	Rupert
Comox	Queen Charlotte	Sayward
Kamloops	Range 1, Coast	Similkameen
Kootenay	Range 2, Coast	Yale
Lillcoet	Range 3, Coast	

In addition to the major land districts there are also many very small land districts on the south part of Vancouver Island and on other nearby islands south of the 49th Parallel. These include:

Alberni	Esquimalt	Nanoose
Cedar	Goldstream	Nelson
Chemainus	Helmcken	Newcastle
Comiaken	Highland	Nootka
Cowichan	Lake	North Saanich
Cowichan Lake	Malahat	Otter
Douglas	Metchosin	Quamichan
Dunsmuir	Nanaimo	Saltspring Island

| Shawnigan | South Saanich | Victoria |
| Sooke | Texada Island | et al. |

The British Columbia Land Registry Offices are located in Kamloops, Nelson, New Westminster, Prince George, Prince Rupert, Vancouver and Victoria.

C. MANITOBA

Manitoba is divided into judicial districts. They are:

Eastern Judicial District	(Winnipeg)
Central Judicial District	(Portage la Prairie)
Western Judicial District	(Brandon)
Dauphin Judicial District	(Dauphin)
Northern Judicial District	(The Pas)

The above districts are significant for probate records, bills of sale and chattel mortgages. For land records there are separate land registration districts with registrars in Boissevain, Brandon, Carman, Dauphin, Morden, Neepawa, Portage la Prairie and Winnipeg. The judicial districts are loosely (though not accurately) called counties and each has a County Court.

D. NEW BRUNSWICK

New Brunswick has 15 counties, and both land records and probate records are kept on a county basis. The counties and county seats are:

Albert County	seat at Hopewell Cape
Carleton County	seat at Woodstock
Charlotte County	seat at St. Andrews
Gloucester County	seat at Bathurst
Kent County	seat at Richibucto
Kings County	seat at Hampton
Madawaska County	seat at Edmundston
Northumberland County	seat at Newcastle
Queens County	seat at Gagetown
Restigouche County	seat at Dalhousie
Saint John County	seat at Saint John
Sunbury County	seat at Burton
Victoria County	seat at Andover
Westmorland County	seat at Dorchester
York County	seat at Fredericton

E. NEWFOUNDLAND

There are no county or district divisions with major record jurisdiction in Newfoundland. The provincial capital is St. John's, and most records are there.

F. NOVA SCOTIA

Nova Scotia has eighteen counties and, for the most part, the seats of those counties are the location of land, probate and civil action records. However, there are some land registry offices set up in towns other than the county seats. The following list of counties and county seats indicates these exceptions:

Annapolis County	seat at Annapolis Royal (Land Registry is at Bridgetown.)
Antigonish County	seat at Antigonish
Cape Breton County	seat at Sydney
Colchester County	seat at Truro (Land Registry is at Colchester.)
Cumberland County	seat at Amherst
Digby County	seat at Digby (Land Registry is at Weymouth.)
Guysborough County	seat at Guysborough
Halifax County	seat at Halifax
Hants County	seat at Windsor
Inverness County	seat at Port Hood
Kings County	seat at Kentville
Lunenburg County	seat at Lunenburg (Land Registry is at Bridgewater.)
Pictou County	seat at Pictou
Queens County	seat at Liverpool
Richmond County	seat at Arichat
Shelburne County	seat at Shelburne
Victoria County	seat at Baddeck
Yarmouth County	seat at Yarmouth

There are also three counties which have additional courthouses:

Guysborough County	There are both land and probate records at Sherbrooke (St. Mary's District).
Lunenburg County	There are land records at Chester (Chester District).

Shelburne County   There are both land and probate rec-
                          ords at Barrington (Barrington
                          District).

These records are in addition to those found at the county seats.

G. ONTARIO

Ontario has both counties (south) and districts (north), but the two are
functionally the same. All probate records and some civil action records
are in these jurisdictions. The land records are in special registration
divisions, each county having at least one such division. The counties and
districts (with county seats) and the land registration divisions within them
are as follow:

Algoma District	Sault Ste. Marie is seat
Brant County	Brantford is seat
Bruce County	Walkerton is seat
Carleton County	Ottawa is seat
Cochrane District	Cochrane is seat
Dufferin County	Orangeville is seat
Dundas County	Cornwall (Stormont County) is seat. (Land records are at Morrisburg.)
Durham County	Cobourg (Northumberland County) is seat. (East Durham land records are at Port Hope and West Durham land records are at Bowmanville.)
Elgin County	St. Thomas is seat
Essex County	Windsor is seat
Frontenac County	Kingston is seat
Glengary County	Cornwall (Stormont County) is seat. (Land records are at Alexandria.)
Grenville County	Brockville (Leeds County) is seat. (Land records are at Prescott.)
Grey County	Owen Sound is seat. (In addition to the North Grey Land Registry Office at Owen Sound, there is also a South Grey Land Registry Office at Durham.)
Haldimand County	Cayuga is seat
Haliburton County	Minden is seat
Halton County	Milton is seat
Hastings County	Belleville is seat
Huron County	Goderich is seat

Kenora County	Kenora is seat
Kent County	Chatham is seat
Lambton County	Sarnia is seat
Lanark County	Perth is seat. (In addition to the South Lanark Land Registry Office at Perth, there is also a North Lanark Land Registry Office at Almonte.)
Leeds County	Brockville is seat. (Brockville is also the seat of Grenville County.)
Lennox and Addington County	Napanee is seat
Lincoln County	St. Catharines is seat
Manitoulin District	Gore Bay is seat
Middlesex County	London is seat. (In addition to the two land registry offices in London, there is also a West Middlesex Land Registry Office at Glencoe.)
Muskoka County	Bracebridge is seat
Nipissing District	North Bay is seat
Norfolk County	Simcoe is seat
Northumberland County	Cobourg is seat. (In addition to the West Northumberland Land Registry Office at Cobourg, there is also an East Northumberland Land Registry at Colborne.) (Cobourg is also the seat of Durham County.)
Ontario County	Whitby is seat
Oxford County	Woodstock is seat
Parry Sound District	Parry Sound is seat
Peel County	Brampton is seat
Perth County	Stratford is seat
Peterborough County	Peterborough is seat
Prescott County	L'Original is seat. (L'Original is also the seat of Russell County.)
Prince Edward County	Picton is seat
Rainy River District	Fort Frances is seat
Renfrew County	Pembroke is seat
Russell County	L'Original (Prescott County) is seat. (Land records are at Russell.)
Simcoe County	Barrie is seat
Stormont County	Cornwall is seat. (Cornwall is also the seat of Dundas and Glengary Counties.)
Sudbury District	Sudbury is seat
Temiskaming District	Haileybury is seat

Thunder Bay District	Port Arthur is seat. (In addition to the Port Arthur Land Registry Office at Port Arthur, there is also a Fort William Land Registry Office at Fort William.)
Victoria County	Lindsay is seat
Waterloo County	Kitchener is seat
Welland County	Welland is seat
Wellington County	Guelph is seat. (In addition to the South and Central Wellington Land Registry Office at Guelph, there is also a North Wellington Land Registry Office at Arthur.)
Wentworth County	Hamilton is seat
York County	Toronto is seat. (In addition to the three land registry offices in Toronto, there is also a North York Land Registry Office at Newmarket.

Three of the above-named county seats have more than one land registration division. The three are:

-Ottawa (Carleton County) has (1) the Carleton Division and (2) the Ottawa Division.
- London (Middlesex County) has (1) the East and North Middlesex Division and (2) the London Division.
-Toronto (York County) has (1) the East and West York Division, (2) the York Division and (3) the Toronto Division.

H. PRINCE EDWARD ISLAND

There are three counties on Prince Edward Island and they are important to us because land records are kept in county jurisdictions. The counties are:

Prince County	Summerside is seat
Queens County	Charlottetown is seat
Kings County	Georgetown is seat, but the Registrar of Deeds is in Charlottetown.

I. QUEBEC

For Superior Court purposes (probate), Quebec is divided into eight districts. They are:

District of Quebec (Judges at Quebec City, Rimouski, Beauce Thetford Mines).
District of Montreal, at Montreal.
District of Sherbrooke (St-Francois), at Sherbrooke.
District of Trois-Rivieres, at Trois-Rivieres.
District of Hull, at Hull.
District of Abitibi and Rouyn, at Amos and Rouyn.
District of Chicoutimi, at Chicoutimi.
District of St-Maurice, at Shawinigan.

For the purposes of filing vital (parish) records prior to 1926 and for notarial records (consisting of numerous wills, marriage contracts, orphan records, deeds, etc.), thirty-two District Court judicial districts (under the direction of the Superior Courts) were set up. The districts include:

Abitibi District, at Amos.
Arthabaska District, at Arthabaska.
Beauce District, at St-Joseph de Beauce.
Beauharnois District, at Valleyfield.
Bedford District, at Sweetsburg.
Bonaventure District, at New Carlisle.
Chicoutimi District, at Chicoutimi.
Drummond District, at Drummondville.
Gaspe District, at Perce.
Hauterive District, Baie Comeau.
Hull District, at Hull.
Iberville District, at St-Jean.
Joliette District, at Joliette.
Kamouraska District, at Riviere-du-Loup.
Labelle District, at Mont-Laurier.
Megantic District, at Thetford Mines.
Montmagny District, at Montmagny.
Montreal District, at Montreal.
Nicolet District, at Nicolet.
Pontiac District, at Campbell's Bay.
Quebec District, at Quebec City.
Richelieu District, at Sorel.
Rimouski District, at Rimouski.
Roberval District, at Roberval.
Rouyn-Noranda District, at Rouyn.
Saguenay District, at La Malbaie.
St-Francois District, at Sherbrooke.
St-Hyacinthe District, at St-Hyacinthe.
St-Maurice District, at Shawinigan.

Temiscamingue District, at Ville-Marie.
Terrebone District, at St-Jerome.
Trois-Rivieres District, at Trois-Rivieres. [1]

Prior to 1760 there were only three districts—Quebec, Montreal and Trois-Rivieres—but many of the earliest records have become victims of time and nature and are no longer in existence. The best guide to research in these judicial districts is the 1966 Municipal Guide for the Province of Quebec, which tells the judicial district in which each town is situated.

Land registration divisions and offices in the Province of Quebec are also important. Following is a list of registration divisions, including the judicial district within which each is situated and the location of the registry office:

DIVISION	SUPERIOR COURT JUDICIAL DISTRICT	SITE OF REGISTRY OFFICE
Abitibi	Abitibi	Amos (court house)
Argenteuil	Terrebonne	Lachute
Arthabaska	Arthabaska	Arthabaska (court house)
Bagot	St-Hyacinthe	St-Liboire
Beauce	Beauce	Beauceville (court house)
Beauharnois	Beauharnois	Beauharnois
Bellechasse	Montmagny	St-Raphael
Berthier	Joliette	Berthierville
Bonaventure (Div. no. 1)	Bonaventure	New Carlisle (court house)
Bonaventure (Div. no. 2)	Eonaventure	Carlston
Brome	Bedford	Knowlton
Chambly	Montreal	Longueuil
Champlain	Trois-Rivieres	Ste-Genevieve de Batiscan
Charlevoix (Div. no. 1)	Saguenay	La Malbaie (court house)
Charlevoix (Div. no. 2)	Saguenay	Baie St-Paul
Chateauguay	Beauharnois	Ste-Martine
Chicoutimi	Chicoutimi	Chicoutimi (court house)
Coaticook	St-Francois	Coaticook
Compton	St-Francois	Cookshire
Deaux-Montagnes	Terrebone	Ste-Scholastique
Dorchester	Beauce	Ste-Henedine
Drummond	Drummond	Drummondville (ct house)
Frontenac	Beauce and St-Francois	Village Megantic
Gaspe	Gaspe	Perce (court house)

[1]. McGraw-Hill Directory and Alamanac of Canada (Toronto: McGraw-Hill of Canada, 1968), pp. 713-714.

488   THE RESEARCHER'S GUIDE TO AMERICAN GENEALOGY

Gatineau	Labelle	Maniwaki
Hull	Hull	Hull (court house)
Huntingdon	Beauharnois	Huntingdon
Iberville	Iberville	Iberville
Ile D'Orleans	Quebec	St-Laurent L.O.
Iles de la Madeleine	Gaspe	Havre-Aubert
Joliette	Joliette	Joliette (court house)
Kamouraska	Kamouraska	St-Pascal
Labelle	Labelle	Mont-Laurier (court house)
Lac St-Jean est	Roberval	Hebertville
Lac St-Jean ouest	Roberval	Roberval (court house)
Laprairie	Montreal	Laprairie
L'Assomption	Joliette	L'Assomption
La Tuque	St-Maurice	La Tuque
Laval	Montreal	Ste-Rose
Levis	Quebec	Levis
L'Islet	Montmagny	St-Jean Port-Joli
Lotbiniere	Quebec	Ste-Croix
Maskinonge	St-Maurice	Louiseville
Matane	Rimouski	Matane
Matapedia	Rimouski	Amqui
Megantic	Megantic	Inverness
Missisquoi	Bedford	Bedford
Montcalm	Joliette and Labelle	Ste-Julienne
Montmagny	Montmagny	Montmagny (court house)
Montmorency	Quebec	Chateau-Richer
Montreal	Montreal	Montreal (court house)
		450, rue St-Vincent
Napierville	Iberville	Napierville
Nicolet (Div. no. 1)	Nicolet	Becancour
Nicolet (Div. no. 2)	Nicolet	Nicolet (court house)
Papineau	Hull	Papineauville
Pontiac	Pontiac	Campbell's Bay (ct house)
Portneuf	Quebec	Cap-Sante
Quebec	Quebec	Quebec
		20, ave Chaveau
Richelieu	Richelieu	Sorel (court house)
Richmond	St-Francois	Richmond
Rimouski	Rimouski	Rimouski (court house)
Rouville	St-Hyacinthe	Marieville
Rouyn-Noranda	Rouyn-Noranda	Rouyn (court house)
Saguenay	Hauterive	Baie-Comeau (court house)
Ste-Anne des Monts	Gaspe	Ste-Anne des Monts
St-Hyacinthe	St-Hyacinthe	St-Hyacinthe (court house)

St-Jean	Iberville	St-Jean (court house)
Sept-Iles	Hauterive	Sept-Iles (court house)
Shawinigan	St-Maurice	Shawinigan (court house)
Shefford	Bedford	Waterloo
Sherbrooke	St-Francois	Sherbrooke
		174, Palais St.
Soulanges	Montreal	Coteau Landing
Stanstead	St-Francois	Stanstead Plain
Temiscamingue	Temiscamingue	Ville-Marie (court house)
Temiscouata	Kamouraska	Riviere-du-Loup (ct house)
Terrebonne	Terrebonne	St-Jerome
		190, Parent St.
Thetford	Megantic	Thetford Mines (ct house)
Trois-Rivieres	Trois-Rivieres	Trois-Rivieres (ct house)
Vaudreuil	Montreal	Vaudreuil
Vercheres	Richelieu	Vercheres
Wolfe	St-Francois	Ham-sud
Yamaska	Richelieu	St-Francois du Lac [2]

There are also counties in the Province of Quebec, but they are of little significance in the keeping of records though the land registry offices are mostly in the counties, often in the county courts. The counties and their seats are as follows:

Abitibi County	seat at Amos
Argenteuil County	seat at Lachute
Arthabaska County	seat at Arthabaska
Bagot County	seat at St-Liboire
Beauce County	seat at Beauceville-Est
Beauharnois County	seat at Beauharnois
Bellechasse County	seat at St-Raphael
Berthier County	seat at Berthierville
Bonaventure County	seat at New Carlisle
Brome County	seat at Knowlton
Chambly County	seat at Longueuil
Champlain County	seat at Ste-Genevieve de Batiscan
Charlevoix-Est County	seat at La Malbaie
Charlevoix-Ouest County	seat at Baie-St-Paul
Chateauguay County	seat at Ste-Martine
Chicoutimi County	seat at Chicoutimi

---

2. List of registration divisions in a letter from Raymond Roy, Director of Registry Offices of the Province of Quebec, August 11, 1969.

Compton County	seat at Cookshire
Deaux-Montagnes County	seat at Ste-Scholastique
Dorchester County	seat at Ste-Henedine
Drummond County	seat at Drummondville
Frontenac County	seat at Lac-Megantic
Gaspe-Est County	seat at Perce
Gaspe-Ouest County	seat at Ste-Anne-des-Monts
Gatineau County	seat at Maniwaki
Hochelaga County	seat at Montreal
Hull County	seat at Hull
Huntingdon County	seat at Huntingdon
Iberville County	seat at Iberville
Ile-Anticosti County	seat at Port-Menier
Jacques Cartier County	seat at Pte-Claire
Joliette County	seat at Joliette
Kamouraska County˙	seat at St-Pascal
Labelle County	seat at Mont-Laurier
Lac-St-Jean-Est County	seat at Alma
Lac-St-Jean-Ouest County	seat at Roberval
Laprairie County	seat at Laprairie
L'Assomption County	seat at L'Assomption
Laval County	seat at Ste-Rose
Levis County	seat at St-Romaule-d'Etchemin
L'Islet County	seat at St-Jean-Port-Joli
Lotbiniere County	seat at Ste-Croix
Maskinonge County	seat at Louiseville
Matane County	seat at Matane
Matapedia County	seat at Amqui
Megantic County	seat at Inverness
Missisquoi County	seat at Bedford
Montcalm County	seat at Ste-Julienne
Montmagny County	seat at Montmagny
Montmorency No. 1 County	seat at Chateau-Richer
Montmorency No. 2 County	seat at Ste-Famille
Napierville County	seat at Napierville
Nicolet County	seat at Becancour
Nouveau Quebec District	
Papineau County	seat at Papineauville
Portneuf County	seat at Cap-Sante
Quebec County	seat at Loretteville
Richelieu County	seat at Sorel
Richmond County	seat at Richmond
Rimouski County	seat at Rimouski
Riviere-du-Loup County	seat at Riviere-du-Loup

Rouville County	seat at Marieville
Saguenay County	seat at Tadoussac
St-Hyacinthe County	seat at St-Hyacinthe
St-Jean County	seat at St-Jean
St-Maurice County	seat at Trois-Rivieres
Shefford County	seat at Waterloo
Sherbrooke County	seat at Sherbrooke
Soulanges County	seat at Coteau Landing
Stanstead County	seat at Ayers Cliff
Temiscamingue County	seat at Ville-Marie
Temiscouata County	seat at Notre-Dame-du-Lac
Terrebone County	seat at St-Jerome
Vaudreuil County	seat at Vaudreuil
Vercheres County	seat at Vercheres
Wolfe County	seat at Hum-sud
Yamaska County	seat at St-Francois-du-Lac

J. SASKATCHEWAN

The Province of Saskatchewan is divided into districts for different purposes. See the discussion under the various record types later in this chapter.

II. CIVIL VITAL RECORDS

A. ALBERTA

In Alberta complete vital records (births, marriages, deaths) date from 1898, though there are some births recorded as early as 1853 and deaths as early as 1893. The Director of Vital Statistics, Edmonton, has custody of these for the entire province.

B. BRITISH COLUMBIA

In British Columbia vital records (early ones incomplete) date from 1872. They include births, marriages, deaths and adoptions. The Director of Vital Statistics, Parliament Building, Victoria, has custody of the records.

C. MANITOBA

Births, marriages, deaths, adoptions and divorces in Manitoba are at the Department of Health, Vital Statistics Branch, Winnipeg. These are mostly complete from 1882.

D. NEW BRUNSWICK

New Brunswick birth, marriage and death records are complete from 1888, with a few earlier records. The custodian of these is the Registrar General, Department of Health, Fredericton.

E. NEWFOUNDLAND

In Newfoundland vital records date from 1892. They are in the custody of the Registrar of Vital Statistics, Department of Health, St. John's.

F. NOVA SCOTIA

Birth, marriage and death records in Nova Scotia date 1864-1876 and then from 1909 on. Between 1876 and 1909 there are only marriage records. The records custodian is the Registrar General, Department of Public Health, Halifax.

G. ONTARIO

In Ontario vital records include births, marriages, deaths, divorces, adoptions and changes of name. Births, marriages and deaths from July 1, 1869, are in the custody of the Deputy Registrar General, Bay and Wellesley Streets, Toronto.

H. PRINCE EDWARD ISLAND

Births, marriages and deaths on the island are complete from 1888, with a few earlier. The Director of Vital Statistics, Department of Health, Charlottetown, is records custodian.

I. QUEBEC

In Quebec, ministers (both Catholic and Protestant) were required to keep registers of births, marriages and deaths in duplicate, to be bound and deposited in the office of the prothonotary of the Superior Court in the judicial district where the church was located. Some of these records go back to 1621. Records of births, marriages and deaths since 1926 are in the custody of the Department of Health, Demography Branch, Quebec City.

J. SASKATCHEWAN

In Saskatchewan birth, marriage, death and divorce records from 1878 are at the Division of Vital Statistics, Health and Welfare Building, Regina.

The records are complete from 1920.

The Public Archives in Ottawa, Ontario, also has extensive collections of Ontario (Upper Canada) and Quebec (Lower Canada) marriage bonds. The Ontario bonds date from 1803 to 1845 and the Quebec bonds are for 1779, 1818-1867

III. CENSUS RETURNS

To help us better understand Canadian censuses let's look at a little recent Canadian history for a moment. In 1841 an Act of Union brought to-gether Upper Canada (Ontario) and Lower Canada (Quebec) and renamed them Canada West and Canada East, respectively. The maritime provinces existed independently until July 1, 1867, when the colonies of New Bruns-wick and Nova Scotia united with the two Canadas (renamed Ontario and Quebec) to form the Dominion of Canada. Manitoba joined the Dominion in 1870, British Columbia in 1871, Prince Edward Island in 1873, Alberta and Saskatchewan in 1905 and Newfoundland (including Labrador) in 1950.

From the above dates you can see that there were no early censuses for the entire country, and though there were censuses for some of the provinces individually, there are differences between them. The censuses available for general use (1972) are as follow:

A. ACADIA (former French province comprised mostly of what is now Nova Scotia)

There are censuses which were taken in 1703, 1707 and 1739 which show the names of heads of families and some taken in 1671, 1686, 1693, 1698, 1701 and 1714 which enumerated every person. There are also some early censuses of both types for some of the individual cities.

B. MANITOBA

Censuses showing heads of families were taken in 1832, 1834, 1835, 1840, 1843, 1846 and 1849. A census in 1870 enumerated every person.

C. NEW BRUNSWICK

The only available censuses were taken in 1851, 1861 and 1871; all three enumerated every person.

D. NEWFOUNDLAND (as a French possession)

Two censuses enumerating all persons were taken in 1691 and 1693.

A census showing only heads of families was taken in 1704. There are also several enumerations for Plaisance only.

E. NOVA SCOTIA

Nova Scotia has heads-of-family censuses for 1770, 1773, 1775, 1787 and 1861, plus a complete enumeration (of all persons) in 1871. (See Acadia.)

F. ONTARIO

There are four available censuses: 1842 (heads of families only) and 1851 (52), 1861 and 1871. The latter three were enumerations of complete families.

G. PRINCE EDWARD ISLAND

There are two available censuses—1841 and 1861—and both enumerate only heads of families.

H. QUEBEC

Heads-of-family censuses in the Province of Quebec were taken in 1825, 1831 and 1842. Enumerations of all persons were made in the censuses of 1666, 1667, 1681, 1851, 1861 and 1871.[3]

All of the above census schedules are on microfilm at the Canadian Public Archives in Ottawa except the 1770, 1773, 1775 and 1787 censuses of Nova Scotia. [4] The LDS Genealogical Society in Salt Lake City has microfilm copies of all the available New Brunswick censuses, all the available Ontario censuses, the 1871 census of Nova Scotia and the 1851, 1861 and 1871 censuses of Quebec. There are no censuses for Alberta, British Columbia or Saskatchewan early enough to be available since no censuses later than 1871 are available for public use or research. The Public Archives has published four check lists—one each for Ontario, Quebec, New Brunswick and Nova Scotia—showing which censuses are available for each town and the number of the microfilm on which each census is located. The Public Archives sells these check lists for $1 each.

---

[3]. The Public Archives of Canada, "Tracing Your Ancestors in Canada," (Ottawa: Queen's Printer and Controller of Stationery, 1967), pp. 5-7.
[4]. These Nova Scotia censuses are available at the Provincial Archives in Halifax.

Since 1851 a census has been taken every ten years which enumerates each person as an individual within the household where he lived. Generally these censuses give name, age, sex, country or province of birth, religion, racial origin, occupation, marital status, education and, where appropriate, physical disabilities.

IV. PROBATE RECORDS

A. ALBERTA

Probate matters in Alberta are handled by the District Courts. There are only two such courts but these are divided into judicial districts for administrative purposes. All wills and probate records are in the courts of the judicial districts where they were probated. In the District of Northern Alberta all probate records are at the court house in Edmonton. In the District of Southern Alberta there are records on file with the judges at the judicial district court houses in Lethbridge and Calgary.

It is also worth noting here that in Alberta a child gets only what he is given by his parent's will (when the parent dies testate). He may be completely disowned by merely leaving him out of the will.

B. BRITISH COLUMBIA

In British Columbia the County Courts have probate jurisdiction in cases where the personal estate is under $5,000 and the Supreme Court has jurisdiction in estates of greater value. However, in the latter situation the County Court judges act as "local judges of the Supreme Court." There is a provision in the provincial law which allows for optional probate registration at the local land registry office. When such registration takes place, the Director of Vital Statistics must be notified of the place of registration.

A will in British Columbia must provide adequately for the surviving spouse and children, or it can be altered following application to the Supreme Court.

C. MANITOBA

Manitoba probate records are filed originally with the Surrogate Court of the proper district (County Court judges are ex officio Surrogate Court judges) and a copy is recorded with the Provincial Surrogate Clerk at Winnipeg. There are five districts.

As in Alberta, a child can be disinherited by not naming him in the will.

D. NEW BRUNSWICK

All wills and probate matters in New Brunswick are within the jurisdiction of the Probate Court in the county where the decedent **was** a resident at the time of his death.

As in Alberta and Manitoba, children can be disinherited without any statement in the will of intent to do so.

E. NEWFOUNDLAND

The Supreme Court of Newfoundland at St. John's has exclusive probate jurisdiction and is custodian of all records.

F. NOVA SCOTIA

Probate matters in Nova Scotia are under the jurisdiction of the Probate Court of the district where the decedent resided or owned property at the time of his death. There are twenty such districts (eighteen of them are counties). See the information on "Canadian Counties and Districts" at the beginning of this chapter.

Much like British Columbia, Nova Scotia law stipulates that heirs not adequately provided for in a will can make application to the court for proper support. Posthumous children are provided for as if there had been no will, as is typical of most states in the U. S.

G. ONTARIO

All probate matters in Ontario are in the hands of the County Surrogate Courts (District Surrogate Courts in areas where there are no counties). Venue is in the county where the decedent resided at the time of death. There are only forty-eight such courts because in some instances more than one county uses the same Surrogate Court. (See the information on Ontario counties and districts at the beginning of this chapter.)

H. PRINCE EDWARD ISLAND

The Supreme Court at Charlottetown is the court of original probate jurisdiction and the records are filed there. A child not named in the will of his parents has no legal recourse, and the executor must prove and file the will in the court within thirty days after the testator's death.

I. QUEBEC

Quebec probate law is unique in that there are three kinds of wills requiring two different probate procedures. A "will in authentic form" (i.e., one made before two notaries or one notary and two witnesses) does not require probate. It becomes effective upon the death of the testator without further court action.

A "holographic will" (in the testator's own handwriting and requiring no witnesses) and a "will in form of English law" (i.e., made before two witnesses in the presence of the testator and of each other) must be probated in the Superior Court of the district where the decedent had residence at the time of his death. There are eight districts.

All probate records of the latter two forms are in these district Superior Courts at the various Palaces of Justice. Records of wills in authentic form are in the custody of the notaries.

Children can be disinherited by merely not mentioning them in the will.

J. SASKATCHEWAN

In Saskatchewan the Surrogate Court in any judicial center in the province can have jurisdiction in any probate case. These district Surrogate Courts are located in Battleford, Humboldt, Melville, Moose Jaw, Prince Albert, Regina, Saskatoon, Swift Current, Weyburn and Yorkton. The court in the most convenient location is ordinarily used.

V. LAND RECORDS

The Public Archives in Ottawa has custody o˙ the original petitions for grants from the British Crown in Upper and Lower Canada. These often contain information about military service, country of origin, and the petitioner's family. These grants cover 1764 to 1829 (Lower Canada) and 1791 to 1867 (Upper Canada) and are card indexed. Many of the grantees were Loyalists or descendants of Loyalists from the American Revolution. The petitions seldom tell the location of the grant but usually contain notations as to whether the grant was given as a result of the petition.

Most land grants, as well as deeds and other local land records, are in the custody of the local land registries, and it is necessary to know the district in which the land was located in order to locate the records.

Local land registry offices are as follow:

A. ALBERTA

1. North Alberta Land Registration District
   Land Titles Building
   101 A Street & 102 A Avenue
   Edmonton, Alberta

2. South Alberta Land Registration District
   Land Titles Building
   7 Ave. W., bet. 4 & 5 Streets
   Calgary, Alberta

B. BRITISH COLUMBIA

    1. Land Registrar
       Court House
       Kamloops, B. C.   (Yale County)

    2. Land Registrar
       Court House
       320 Ward Street
       Nelson, B. C.   (Kootenay County)

    3. Land Registrar
       Court House
       653 Clarkson Street
       New Westminster, B. C.   (Westminster County)

    4. Land Registrar
       Court House
       1600 Third Avenue
       Prince George, B. C.   (Cariboo County)

    5. Land Registrar
       Court House
       Market Street
       Prince Rupert, B. C.   (Prince Rupert County)

    6. Land Registrar
       Court House
       800 W. Georgia Street
       Vancouver, B. C.   (Vancouver County)

    7. Land Registrar
       Law Courts
       850 Burdett Avenue
       Victoria, B. C.   (Victoria County)

C. MANITOBA

Land registry offices are located in Boissevain, Brandon, Carman, Dauphin, Morden, Neepawa, Portage la Prairie and Winnipeg.

D. NEW BRUNSWICK

In New Brunswick there is a land registry office in every one of the fifteen county seats.

E. NEWFOUNDLAND

There are three separate offices for registering different types of titles. All are in St. John's:

    1. Registry of Companies (records of companies).
    2. Registry of Deeds (deeds and related conveyances—including Crown grants).
    3. Department of Natural Resources (Crown lands).

F. NOVA SCOTIA

There is a land registry office (or registry of deeds) in each one of the eighteen counties, and three counties have two land registry offices. Most land registry offices are at the county seat, but there are a few exceptions to this also. (See the information on Nova Scotia counties at the beginning of this chapter.)

G. ONTARIO

There are sixty-six separate land registration divisions in Ontario, each with a registrar's office. There is at least one in every county or district, and several counties have more than one.

H. PRINCE EDWARD ISLAND

There is a separate registrar of deeds for each of the three counties.

I. QUEBEC

The province is divided into eighty-two registration divisions and there is a land registration office in each division. There is at least one registration division in each county. Quebec is a community property jurisdiction.

Certain types of deeds must be notarized and copies of these are part of the records of the Notary Courts. Any deed may be received before a notary if the parties so desire, but it is not required of most.

J. SASKATCHEWAN

There are district land registration offices at North Battleford, Humboldt, Moose Jaw, Prince Albert, Regina, Saskatoon, Swift Current and Yorkton, each one having a registrar.

Another matter which is important to your understanding and use of

Canadian land records is that the law, in most provinces, requires some type of probate document to be filed in the land registry office in order for title to pass in a probate case. The exact situation as it prevails in each province is as follows:

In ALBERTA a certified copy of the probate grant must be recorded in the land registry office and a title thereto is then issued to the administrator or executor. He in turn deeds the property to the proper heir. (This is in accordance with the terms of the Torrens Act adopted by Alberta in 1906. The Torrens Act provides for a system of registering titles to real property much like one would register the title to an automobile. The Torrens Act—which originated in Australia—has also been adopted in some states of the U.S., but registration is not compulsory.)

In BRITISH COLUMBIA wills are registered in the land registry offices.

MANITOBA has no provision for recording any probate document in the land registry office.

In NEW BRUNSWICK a deed from the executor or administrator to the beneficiary must be recorded in the land registry office.

In NEWFOUNDLAND a deed from the executor or administrator to the beneficiary is usually filed in the land registry office.

In NOVA SCOTIA a certified copy of the will must be registered in the registry of deeds.

In ONTARIO a deed from the administrator or executor to the beneficiary should be made and recorded in the proper land registrar's office (if made within three years of the decedent's death).

In PRINCE EDWARD ISLAND a deed from the administrator or executor to the beneficiary should be made and recorded with the registrar of deeds.

In QUEBEC a deed (before a notary) must be made from the administrator or executor to the beneficiary and must be appropriately recorded in the land registration office. The notary before whom a deed is executed will also have a record of it.

In SASKATCHEWAN an application for transfer of title into his name is made by the administrator or executor to the proper land title office. This application must be accompanied by letters of administration or letters testamentary and a copy of the certificate of title (Torrens registration). After approval of the application he can then deed the land to the proper beneficiaries and these deeds and land titles will likewise be recorded.

VI. CIVIL COURT ACTIONS

Actions at law and in equity (or chancery) in the several provinces are under the following jurisdictions:

A. ALBERTA

In Alberta there is a distinction maintained between law and equity actions, but both are within the jurisdiction of the Supreme Court of the province (for actions over $2,000) and in the District Courts (Northern District at Edmonton and Southern District at Lethbridge) for actions under $2,000.

B. BRITISH COLUMBIA

There is also a distinction maintained between law and equity actions in British Columbia. The Supreme Court of the province at Vancouver has jurisdiction in both. However, County Courts have concurrent jurisdiction in actions under $3,000.

C. MANITOBA

Since 1895 original jurisdiction of all law and equity matters in Manitoba over $2,000 has been in the Court of the Queen's Bench at Winnipeg. Before 1895 there was a separate Court of Common Law and a Court of Chancery in the province. In matters under $2,000 the County Courts have jurisdiction.

D. NEW BRUNSWICK

The Supreme Court, Moncton, has original jurisdiction in both law and equity cases (distinction maintained). Actions under $2,000 can be brought in County Courts unless titles of land are involved.

E. NEWFOUNDLAND

In Newfoundland there is no distinction observed between actions at law and actions in equity. The Supreme Court at St. John's has original jurisdiction, though District Courts have some jurisdiction in matters under $1,000.

F. NOVA SCOTIA

In Nova Scotia the Supreme Court and the County Courts have concurrent jurisdiction in cases of both law and equity, though the County Courts have jurisdiction only in matters under $10,000. There is no distinction maintained between the two types of action.

G. ONTARIO

Law and equity matters, combined into one form of civil action, are handled in the same courts in Ontario. The Supreme Court in Toronto has original jurisdiction in all matters, but its jurisdiction is concurrent with the County and District Courts in matters under $3,000.

H. PRINCE EDWARD ISLAND

On Prince Edward Island there is a separate Court of Chancery at Charlottetown for the entire province. Law actions are under the original jurisdiction of the Supreme Court, except that County Courts have some concurrent jurisdiction in matters under $1,000. Equity claims may be appealed to the Supreme Court.

I. QUEBEC

There has never been a distinction between legal and equitable actions in Quebec. They are both handled as civil actions and are under the original jurisdiction of the Superior Courts in the various districts.

J. SASKATCHEWAN

In Saskatchewan formal distinction between law and equity actions do not exist; there is only one form of civil action. The Court of the Queen's Bench at Regina has original jurisdiction in all cases, with some concurrent jurisdiction in actions under $5,000 lying in the District Courts.

VII. DIVORCES

Matters of divorce in Canada are quite different from most states of the U.S., and, generally speaking, the power of the provinces and their courts in divorce matters are as they existed in 1867 at the time of Confederation. This means that Alberta, British Columbia, Manitoba, New Brunswick, Nova Scotia, Prince Edward Island and Saskatchewan have power to grant divorces, but divorces in Quebec and Newfoundland are granted only by special act of the Canadian Parliament. Ontario did not originally have divorce jurisdiction but was granted such in 1930. The Yukon and Northwest Territories have no divorce jurisdiction.

In all provinces divorces are granted only infrequently, and then for only the most serious reasons (adultery, sodomy, bestiality, etc.). Most provinces allow only adultery as a cause, and then only upon adequate proof. This, of course, tends to make Canadian divorce records quite a rare genealogical source.

Jurisdictions in the several provinces are as follow:

ALBERTA: The Provincial Supreme Court, Edmonton.
BRITISH COLUMBIA: The Provincial Supreme Court, Vancouver.
MANITOBA: The Court of the Queen's Bench, Winnipeg. (Divorce

records are also kept at the Department of Health, Vital Statistics Branch, Winnipeg.)

NEW BRUNSWICK: The Court of Divorce and Matrimonial Causes in the county.

NEWFOUNDLAND: Divorces are not granted in the province but only by act of the Canadian Parliament.

NOVA SCOTIA: The Court of Divorce and Matrimonial Causes in the county.

ONTARIO: The Provincial Supreme Court, Toronto. Divorce records are also kept in the custody of the Deputy Registrar General, Toronto.

PRINCE EDWARD ISLAND: The Provincial Court of Judicature, with concurrent jurisdiction in the Supreme Court of Judicature since 1949.

QUEBEC: Divorces are not granted in the province but only by act of the Canadian Parliament.

SASKATCHEWAN: The Court of the Queen's Bench, Regina.

One of the biggest problems which has arisen out of the difficulty involved in getting a Canadian divorce is that couples who have not had successful marriages often merely separate, without the benefit of a divorce, and then begin domestic cohabitation with someone else, without the benefit of a marriage. Many children have been born of these "common-law" unions and many very difficult genealogical problems have resulted.

VIII. CHURCH RECORDS

Canadian church records pose some of the same kinds of problems as American church records. You must know the denomination and the church in order to locate the records, and you must be able to determine the location of the records. But regardless of these factors, church registers are one of the most important genealogical sources available because of the time period they cover and the nature of the data contained therein.

The Public Archives in Ottawa has a few records, mostly microfilm and transcript, but most church records are still in the churches where they were originated. The Province of Quebec, where the ministers were required to keep church registers as vital records, is the only bright spot.

Cemetery records are also an excellent source if you can determine the place of burial.

IX. MILITARY RECORDS

Military records are not extensive in Canada, but they can be significant if your ancestor was in military service. Most records are available only if you know the regiment in which the soldier served. Records at the Public Archives include muster rolls, pay lists, medal registers and some bounty claims. Some are microfilmed, but others are not. Note also that Loyalist sources are discussed in Chapter Twenty-one.

X. AIDS TO RESEARCH

As we stated earlier, most of the information published about Canadian research is incomplete and inaccurate, so our list of aids will not be long. However, there are a few basic tools with which you should be familiar so that you can refer to them as required. They include:

Atherton, James J. "Records of Genealogical Interest in the Public Archives of Canada" (Area I, no. 43). Seminar paper from World Conference on Records and Genealogical Seminar. Salt Lake City: The Genealogical Society of The Church of Jesus Christ of Latter-day Saints (1969).

Auger, Roland-J. "Tracing Ancestors Through the Province of Quebec and Acadia to France" (Area F, no. 6). Seminar paper from World Conference on Records and Genealogical Seminar. Salt Lake City: The Genealogical Society of The Church of Jesus Christ of Latter-day Saints (1969).

Bullinger's Postal and Shippers Guide for the United States and Canada. Westwood, N.J.: Bullinger's Guides, Inc. (annual). This is a good source for helping to locate places.

Canadian Permanent Committee on Geographical Names. Gazetteer of Canada (for each individual province). Ottawa: Queen's Printer and Controller of Stationery (various dates). These have good maps, good historical data, and are excellent for locating places.

Directory—Historical Societies and Agencies in the United States and Canada. Nashville, Tenn.: American Association of State and Local History (bi-annual).

Fergusson, C. Bruce. "Pre-Revolutionary Settlements in Nova Scotia" (Area I, no. 45). Seminar paper from World Conference on Records and Genealogical Seminar. Salt Lake City: The Genealogical Society of The Church of Jesus Christ of Latter-day Saints (1969).

Guillaume, Sandra. "Sources for Genealogical Research in Ontario" (Area I, no. 44). Seminar paper from World Conference on Records and Genealogical Seminar. Salt Lake City: The Genealogical Society of The Church of Jesus Christ of Latter-day Saints (1969).

Kirk, Robert F. and Audrey Kirk. "The Exodus of British Loyalists (Royalists) from the U.S. to Canada, England, the Caribbean, and Spanish Territories" (Area I, no. 46). Seminar paper from World Conference on Records and Genealogical Seminar. Salt Lake City: The Genealogical Society of The Church of Jesus Christ of Latter-day Saints (1969).

"Major Genealogical Sources for Canada, Quebec and Acadia" (Series B, no. 3, of Research Papers). Salt Lake City: The Genealogical Society of The Church of Jesus Christ of Latter-day Saints (1969).

Martindale-Hubbell Law Directory. Vol. V. Summit, N.J.: Martindale-Hubbell, Inc. (annual). This is an excellent guide to courts, laws and legal procedures.

McGraw-Hill Directory and Almanac of Canada. Toronto: McGraw-Hill Company of Canada, Ltd. (various dates). This book gives good information on court jurisdictions and land divisions in the provinces.

Meikleham, Marget and Glenn Lucas, T.R. Millman, Francois Beaudin, Erich Schultz. "Church Records of Canada" (Area I, nos. 48 and 49). Seminar papers from World Conference on Records and Genealogical Seminar. Salt Lake City: The Genealogical Society of The Church of Jesus Christ of Latter-day Saints (1969).

Municipal Guide for the Province of Quebec. Quebec City: Quebec Bureau of Statistics (1966). This useful guide is available for fifty cents from the Quebec Bureau of Statistics, Hotel du Gouvernment, Quebec City, Quebec. It tells in which judicial district of the Superior Court each town in the province is located.

Public Archives of Canada. "Tracing Your Ancestors in Canada." Ottawa: Queen's Printer and Controller of Stationery (1967). This is a good basic guide to research sources in various depositories.

Rubincam, Milton. "Basic Bibliography." The Ontario Genealogical Society Bulletin, Vol. III, No. 3 (September 1964). Unpaged.

_____, et al. "Canada." Genealogical Research: Methods and Sources. Ed. by Milton Rubincam. Washington, D.C.: The American Society of Genealogists (1960). Pp. 261-288.

Wilson, Donald. "Post 1815 Settlement in Canada" (Area I, no. 47). Seminar paper from World Conference on Records and Genealogical Seminar. Salt Lake City: The Genealogical Society of The Church of Jesus Christ of Latter-day Saints (1969).

You will also need a good map showing the locality of your problem in some detail.

There are a few Canadian genealogical periodicals that can help you, too. These include:

French Canadian and Acadian Genealogical Review, Case Postale 845, Haute-Ville, Quebec 4, Quebec.

Loyalist Gazette, 23 Prince Arthur Ave., Toronto 180, Ontario.

The Ontario Genealogical Society Bulletin, Box 66, Station Q, Toronto 7, Ontario.

Societe Genealogique Canadienne-Francaise, Memoirs, Case Postale 335, Place d'Armes, Montreal 1, Quebec.

ADDENDUM

Of interest to the genealogist or historian seeking a record of American land grants is a special computerized index to the nine volumes in classes eight and nine of the American State Papers. The index was published in 1972 by the Gendex Corporation of Salt Lake City and is entitled Grassroots of America. It was edited by Phillip W. McMullin and covers land grants and claims between 1789 and 1837. The entries are primarily from the territory included in the Louisiana Purchase, but all land grants in the public domain during this period are covered, plus Georgia land grants.

The American State Papers themselves (all 38 volumes) are indexed in the back of each volume, but those indexes are totally unreliable. The Papers were published in a limited edition (750 original sets), and it may be hard to locate a set. Many large libraries, however, have microfilm or microcard copies.

Faust, Albert Bernhardt, 408
Fee simple title, 210, 284
Fendrick, Virginia Shannon, 435
Fergusson, C. Bruce, 504
Fernow, Berthold, 435
Feudal system, 211, 284
Field, Thomas P., 60
Filby, P. William, 62, 68
Fisher, Carleton E., 64
Flagg, Charles Alcott, 433
Flick, Alexander Clarence, 440
Florida,
  Census schedules, 144, 175, 177,
    178, 179
  Church records, 125
  Civil court actions, 338, 340
  Divorce records, 345
  Guardianship records, 259
  Immigration records, 404-405
  Land records, 274, 275, 277, 278,
    281, 309
  Loyalists, 440, 441
  Military records, 429, 459
  Mortality schedules,
    See Census schedules
  Probate records, 235
  Vital records, 125
Fothergill, Gerald, 409
Four-S formula for correspondence,
  90-91
Fox, Dixon Ryan, 59
France,
  Emigration from, 410
  Ministere des Affaires Etrangeres,
    432
Franklin, Neil W., 165
Free Magyar Reformed Church, 387
French, Elizabeth, 409
  John H., 47, 59
French and Indian War,
  See Military records
French Canadian and Acadian Genea-
  logical Review, 505
French Reformed Church,
  See Reformed churches

Friends,
  See Society of Friends
Funeral directors' records,
  See Cemetery and burial records
GSA-6751, 426, 452, 458
Gannett, Henry, 60
Gardner, David E. and Frank Smith,
  15
Gazetteer of Canada by the Canadian
  Permanent Comm. on Geographical
  Names, 504
Gazetteers, 46-47, 59-60, 504
Gendex Corp., 187, 507
Genealogical and historical periodi-
  cals,
  Bibliographies, 62
  Canadian, 505
  Directories, 105
  Indexes, 63-64, 105
  List, 104-105, 505
  Value and use, 103-106
Genealogical compendia,
  See Compendium genealogies
Genealogical Forum of Portland,
  Oregon, 278
Genealogical Periodical Annual In-
  dex, 63, 105
Genealogical periodicals,
  See Genealogical and historical
    periodicals
Genealogical Society of New Jersey,
  53
Genealogical Society of Pennsylvania,
  53
Genealogical Society of The Church
  of Jesus Christ of Latter-day Saints,
  Accreditation of genealogists, 10-
    11
  Address, 39, 53, 104
  Census records at, 165
  Church Records Archives, 38
  Church records at, 390
  Church records study project, 388
  Court records at, 336
  English probate records at, 241

Gwathmey, John H., 438

Hackett, J. Dominick and Charles M.
 Early, 409

Haldimand papers, 443

Hale, Richard H., 476

Hale collection (Conn. vital records),
 130

Hall, Albert Harrison,
 See Robinson, George Frederick
 Henry, 102

Hamer, Philip May, 62

Hamersly, Lewis Randolph, 464
 Thomas H.S., 432

Hancock, Harold Bell, 440

Handwriting, 15-29

Handy Book for Genealogists by
 Everton and Rasmuson, 50,60

Hardy, Stella Pickett, 106

Harland, Derek, 78

Harmony Society, 397

Harper's Atlas of American History
 by Fox, 59

Harrell, Isaac Samuel, 441

Hartmann, Edward George, 409

Hawaii,
 Census schedules, 144
 Civil court actions, 340
 Divorce records, 345,348
 Guardianship records, 259
 Land records, 309
 Probate records, 235

Hayward, Elizabeth McCoy, 432

Headright grants, 269

Heitman, Francis Bernard, 99,432

Hendrick Hudson Chapter Library,
 407

Herringshaw, Thomas W., 102

Hicks, Frederick R., 357

Hinke, William J.,
 See Strassburger, Ralph Beaver

Hinman, Royal R., 99,409

Hinshaw, William Wade, 378-381,
 390

Historical periodicals,
 See Genealogical and historical
 periodicals

Historical Records Survey,
 See "Inventory of Church Archives"
 See "Inventory of County Archives"
 See "WPA List of Vital Statistical
 Records"

Historical societies, 52-54
 Directories, 61,504

Historical Society of Pennsylvania,
 53,407

Histories, local, 61,63,98-99

History and genealogy,
 See Genealogy

Hitz, Alex M., 432

Hodges, Margaret R., 433

Holland,
 See Netherlands

Holland Society of New York, 53

Holmes, Frank R., 100

Holy Cross College (Massachusetts),
 406

Homestead grants, 275,277,280-281,
 352,412

Hornbook of Virginia History by Va.
 State Library, 356

Hotten, John Camden, 409

House, Charles J., 433

Houston, Ethel Rollins, 433
 Martha Lou, 67,432

Houts, Alice K., 434

Huddleston, George, 165

Huguenots, 387,395

Hummel, Ray O., Jr., 60

Hutterites, 387

Idaho,
 Census schedules, 144,179
 Civil court actions, 335,340
 Divorce records, 345,348
 Guardianship records, 259
 Land records, 309,315
 Mortality schedules,
 See Census schedules
 Periodicals, 104
 Probate records, 235
 Vital Records, 126

Idaho Genealogical Society, 473

Idem sonans, rule of, 27

New York—Cont'd
Loyalists, 440,441,442
Military records, 416,417,429,435,
461
Mortality schedules,
See Census schedules
Periodicals, 104
Probate records, 236-237
Vital records, 127,130
New York City, 115, 127, 129, 342,
401,404,405,407
New York Genealogical and Bio-
graphical Record, 104
New York Genealogical and Bio-
graphical Society, 54
New York Historical Society, 416,435
New York Public Library, 54,103,442
New York State Library, 54
New Yorker, 467
Newberry Library, 54,63
Newfoundland,
Census schedules, 493-494
Civil court actions, 501
Counties and districts, 482
Divorces, 502,503
Land records, 499,500
Probate records, 496
Vital records, 492
Newman, Harry Wright, 434
Newsholme, Sir Arthur, 115
Newsome, Albert R., 410
Newspapers, 107-109
Directories, 61,62,109
Value and use, 108-109
Niles, J.M.,
See Pease, John C.
North Carolina,
Census schedules, 149,167,168,
181,189
Church records, 396
Civil court actions, 336,342
County origins, 50
Divorce records, 346,348
Guardianship records, 260

North Carolina—Cont'd
Immigration records, 410
Land records, 269,311
Libraries and historical societies,
396
Loyalists, 440
Military records, 429,435,459
Mortality schedules,
See Census schedules
Newspapers, 108
Periodicals, 104
Probate records, 237,238,240
Reference sources, 60,65
Vital records, 127
North Dakota,
Census schedules, 149,177,178,182
Church records, 127
Civil court actions, 342
Divorce records, 346,349
Guardianship records, 260
Land records, 311
Mortality schedules,
See Census schedules
Probate records, 237
Vital records, 127
Northwest Ordinance,
See Land Ordinance of 1785
Northwest Territory, 270,281
Notes,
See Research notes
Nova Scotia,
Census schedules, 494
Civil court actions, 501
Counties, 482-483
Divorces, 502,503
Land records, 499,500
Loyalists, 440
Probate records, 496
Research aids, 494,504
Vital records, 492
Noyes, Sybil, Charles T. Libby and
Walter G. Davis, 100
Nugent, Nell M., 269
Numbers,

Pennsylvania—Cont'd
  Naturalization records, 350
  Periodicals, 105
  Probate records, 237
  Reference sources, 60
Pennsylvania Archives, 410,417,436
Pennsylvania German Folklore So-
  ciety, 410,411
Pennsylvania Magazine of History
  and Biography, 105
Periodicals,
  See Genealogical and historical
    periodicals
Personal Census Service Branch,
  Pittsburg, Kansas, 167,171
Peterson, Clarence S., 63,99,436
Petition, 255,266,292-293
Petition for probate, 243,255
Philadelphia, 115,130,401,403,404,
  405,407
Philippine Insurrection,
  See Military records
Pierce, John, 436
Pittman, Hannah D., 106
Pittsburgh, Pa., 130
Places,
  Analysis of, 45-51
  Genealogy of, 48-51
  How to find, 46-48
  Understanding, 42
Plat, 267
Plymouth (or New Plymouth) Colony,
  See Old Colony
Pomeroy, Seth, 417
Pompey, Sherman L., 434
Pope, Charles Henry, 100
Postage, 89
Postal directories, 46,50,60
Powell, William Henry, 464
Power of attorney, 293-294
Pratt, David H.,
  See Wright, Norman E.
Preemption land claims, 274,275
Preliminary survey, 2,38-39

Prerogative Court of Canterbury, 241
Presbyterian Church, 359,386,387
Pretermitted child, 233
Primary sources,
  Definition, 58
  Guides to, 65-68
  Value of, 2-3
Prince Edward Island,
  Census schedules, 494
  Civil court actions, 502
  Counties, 485
  Divorces, 502,503
  Land records, 499,500
  Probate records, 496
  Vital records, 492
Pringle, J. F., 441
Printed secondary sources,
  See Compiled sources
Private land claims, 276,281
Probate decree,
  See Decree of distribution
Probate process, 216-220
  Intestate, 242-246
  Testate, 225-228
  See, also, Administration
Probate records,
  Availability, 231,234-238,296
  Canadian, 495-497
  Contests, 228-231
  Definition and background, 202-203,
    216-220
  Indexes, 227,240-241
  Jurisdictions, 234-238
  Limitations, 203-205,232-234
  Published and abstracted, 239-240
  Record types, 222-224, 246-258
  Terms, 205-216
  Value and use, 202-203,231-232,242
Professional genealogists,
  See Genealogists
Protestant Episcopal Church, 359,
  363-373
Pruitt, Jayne C. C., 436
Public Archives of Canada, 443,493,
  503,504,505

Notes

Notes

Notes

Notes

Notes

Notes

Notes

Notes

Notes